Stradivarius

TOBY FABER

STRADIVARIUS

One cello, five violins and a genius

MACMILLAN

First published 2004 by Macmillan
an imprint of Pan Macmillan Ltd
Pan Macmillan, 20 New Wharf Road, London N1 9RR
Basingstoke and Oxford
Associated companies throughout the world
www.panmacmillan.com

ISBN 0 333 98976 7

Typeset by SetSystems Ltd, Saffron Walden, Essex
Printed and bound in Great Britain by
Mackays of Chatham plc, Chatham, Kent

To

my mother Penny,

my wife Amanda

and

my daughter Lucy

Violins are the lively, forward, importunate wits, that distinguish themselves by the Flourishes of Imagination, Sharpness of Repartee, Glances of Satyr, and bear away the upper Part in every Consort. I cannot however but observe, that when a Man is not dispos'd to hear Musick, there is not a more disagreeable Sound in Harmony than that of a Violin.

The Tatler, 1 April 1710

I have a violin that was born in 1713. It was alive long before me, and I hope it lives long after me. I don't consider it as my violin. Rather, I am perhaps its violinist; I am passing through its life.

Ivry Gitlis, *The Art of Violin*, 2000

A great violin is alive; its very shape embodies its maker's intentions, and its wood stores the history, or the soul, of its successive owners. I never play without feeling that I have released or, alas, violated spirits.

Yehudi Menuhin, *Unfinished Journey*, 1996

Contents

Introduction

WHEN I WAS about ten my parents bought me a violin. Comparing instruments was a way for those of us at the back of the second violins to fill the inevitable longueurs of school orchestra rehearsals. One had an elaborately carved fish at the end of its neck instead of the usual snail-shell scroll. Another was a striking, if rather nauseating, olive-green. But we had three more standard criteria to use in comparisons: the violin's age, where it was made, and the name of its maker. On most of our violins we could establish all three from the labels visible through their left-hand soundholes.

My own violin did reasonably well on our first criterion: the 1809 on its label meant it was pretty old, although, I knew even then, too young to date back to the true golden era of violin-making. Age added more to violins than just antiquity; they needed to be old to sound good. It was this that caused my second-hand damaged instrument by a nondescript maker to cost more than a brand-new one. It had a good tone, despite the small crack in its belly.

On our other two criteria, however, my violin scored rather poorly. It was made in Mittenwald, in Germany. The name meant nothing to us, although a lot of our school violins seemed to come from there. As far as we were concerned, good violins came from Italy. If we had known enough, I am sure we would have graded towns within Italy into a pyramid with Cremona at its apex, but I don't think we had even heard of the place. We were most definitely familiar, however, with its most famous citizen. Stradivarius was the only violin-maker whose name carried any weight with us at all. That was the third criterion: your violin either carried the meaningless name of a long-dead maker or it was a Stradivarius.

One of those orchestral instruments met all our requirements gloriously: 'Antonius Stradivarius Cremonensis Faciebat Anno 1716' (or some similar date), its label proclaimed with splendid confidence. It was a fake, of course. We knew that much. But despite this the violin retained some sort of fascination; it achieved distinction just through bearing the name.

I GAVE UP the violin when I left school. In the twenty years since, I have come to understand as a listener what I never did as a mediocre player – that the members of the violin family (principally the violin itself, the viola and the cello) are indisputably the kings of all the instruments. The violin, so deceptively simple, can both portray and inspire every emotion imaginable, imitating the braying of a donkey or delivering a tune of heartrending beauty. Lyrical and expressive, or harsh and violent, it is the master of adaptability; only the human voice can match it. By comparison, the piano's eighty-odd notes a semitone apart may make it a mechanical marvel of polyphony, but where is the ability to thrill with almost imperceptible changes in pitch or volume? As for the other members of the orchestra – woodwind, brass, percussion – the very names hint at the paucity of their tonal range.

Not only do the violin and its sister instruments dominate the orchestra, there remains no question of who is their most famous maker – perhaps the most celebrated craftsman in history. From Melbourne to Milwaukee, the bus driver will ask you, as you struggle with your violin case, 'Is that a Stradivarius?' His reputation for excellence is ubiquitous.

This reputation springs from the players themselves. To anyone, but most of all those lucky enough to perform on them, Strads are far more than just instruments. They are works of art, bringing together utility and aesthetics in a way that no other object can quite match. The British cellist, Steven Isserlis, borrows his Stradivarius from the Nippon Music Foundation: 'My heart leaps every day when I take it out of the case. Its beautiful colour glows.' In 1986 one of the most successful performers of our era, Itzhak Perlman, acquired the favourite Strad of an even more celebrated predecessor – Yehudi Menuhin: 'When it became available, I was the happiest violinist in the world . . . It has Stradivari's most beautiful varnish and its shape is perfection. I feel very lucky and privileged to own the *Soil*.'*

The connection the *Soil* makes between Perlman and Menuhin is typical; all the great Strads have histories that can hardly fail to inspire. Any one may have been admired by Beethoven, heard by Mozart. One of Isserlis's predecessors on his cello was Emanuel Feuermann, possibly the

---

* All Strads have names, often, as in this case, derived from a previous owner.

most talented cellist of the twentieth century. On a practical level, this meant Isserlis pursued adjustments to his Strad until its clarity matched what he heard on a Feuermann recording. More intriguingly, he describes teaching a masterclass in the 'Schelomo', a piece by Ernest Bloch that is now a standard part of the repertoire: 'Before I remembered what cello I was playing, I thought, hang on, my cello knows this.' It could have known it by heart: Feuermann was asked to perform the *Schelomo* so often that he grew to hate it. In a similar vein, when the Russian violinist Louis Krasner bought the *Dancla* Strad from Nathan Milstein, one of the twentieth century's greatest virtuosi, he found that his predecessor's 'playing and sonorities were, I would sense, still in the violin'. He could only rationalize it with the view that 'A Strad violin, like a sensitive animal, knows its master and, like the living being that it is, has memory and loyalty.'

Milstein explained the sale of his Strad to Krasner – he moved on to another – in explicitly anthropomorphic terms: 'My love for this violin did not diminish. It was just that after years with a sparkling, eager blonde, I came to feel that I should turn to a more sombre and perhaps quieter and more composed, sedate brunette.' The quote exemplifies a third way in which Strads transcend their status as mere objects: the devotion they both inspire and require in their players. I once naively asked a successful musician if he'd ever thought of getting a new violin. His reply came with a mixture of shock and the very faintest longing: 'That's like asking a man if he'd considered changing his wife.' Maxim Vengerov, a Russian who is probably the most admired of the younger generation of performers, is even more direct about his relationship with his Strad: 'It is a marriage.' The violin is such a feminine instrument that the metaphor seems almost inescapable, at least for men. Women are more likely to regard their violins as an extension of themselves. One friend told me this is why she does not use a shoulder-rest. The German virtuosa, Anne-Sophie Mutter, rests her Stradivarius on her bare shoulder: even clothes are too great a barrier. The exception only seems to prove the rule. When the young Soviet violinist Viktoria Mullova took a taxi across the border from Finland into Sweden in 1983, she left her government-owned Strad on the hotel-room bed. As a result her KGB minders wasted valuable hours on the assumption that she could not possibly be defecting.

Finally, there is the most obvious and concrete way in which violinists put a value on their instruments. Vengerov's Strad – the *Kreutzer* – set an auction record of £947,500 when it was bought for him in 1998. Even that figure is put in the shade by private deals. Scarcity and the need for age have combined to drive a seemingly unstoppable rise in the prices of string instruments. What other profession faces a situation where the tools of its trade have become so expensive as to be almost unobtainable? Every maker has his price – the violin says something about its player's status, even before bow is put to string – but none commands more respect than Antonio Stradivari.

FAME, BEAUTY, history, value, the peculiar devotion that Strads inspire: it is a heady mix. And it all results from their most remarkable characteristic. More than 250 years after his death, Stradivari's violins and cellos remain the best in the world. On song and in the right hands they are magnificent, projecting a glorious tone to the back of the largest concert hall. A violinist who is attuned to his Strad, and knows that it will do everything required of it, can relax into playing, confident that he will not have to force to be heard. Of five soloists in a recent season at London's Royal Festival Hall, four played Strads. They are the ultimate rebuke to the arrogance of the modern age: science does not have all the answers; Renaissance technology still cannot be bettered.

How can that be? The continuing supremacy of Stradivari is one of the great mysteries of our era. What made him so special? Why were his techniques not maintained by his successors? Is there any likelihood that one day he will be displaced? If the answers to these questions lie anywhere, it must be in Stradivari's instruments themselves. He made over 1,000 of them; around 600 are known to survive. Their continuing appeal is at the core of the Stradivarius legend. It is commonplace to speak of artists achieving immortality through their work, but there can be few better examples than this.

So six Strads will be the central characters of this book. They are not their maker's six most celebrated instruments; nor do all currently boast a famous player. But over the last three centuries they have been heard and admired by millions. Their lives, and those of the people they have touched, both illustrate and frame the enigma of Stradivari's inimitability. This book tells the story of five violins, one cello and a genius.

Chapter One

FIVE VIOLINS AND ONE CELLO

The *Messiah,* the *Viotti,* the *Khevenhüller,*
the *Paganini,* the *Lipiński* and the *Davidov*

THE *MESSIAH*

Oxford's Ashmolean Museum, founded in 1683, is the
oldest institution of its kind in Britain. From Elias Ash-
mole's original bequest, it has gone on to establish an
enviable reputation for excellence in research and teaching, with an appearance impressive enough to match.
Wide stone steps lead up to a grand, if slightly austere,
classical façade. The Ashmolean may be smaller than
London's British Museum, or New York's Metropolitan
Museum of Art, but the overall effect is similar. You
feel a proper sense of awe even before stepping over the
threshold. Once you do, and if you're lucky, the guard
on duty at the front door will tell you the short cut: don't
go up the main stairs but turn left, go to the end of
the gallery, take the stairs you see on your right, and the
Hill Music Room is immediately at the top on the first
floor. On your arrival, as likely as not, the room will be
shut, with a sign on the door blaming staff shortages and
suggesting that, if you particularly wish to see the room's
contents, you should try the invigilator next door.

It is an unpropitious beginning. When you manage to

get in, you will find a room only perhaps 15 by 30 feet. On hot days there will be a fan in the corner to compensate for the lack of air-conditioning. The cork tiles on the floor are scuffed about; protruding nails catch the unwary foot. Curious Old Masters with little obvious connection to music line the walls above the harpsichords and virginals that comprise the less interesting part of the Hill Collection. Elsewhere, one case contains bows, another includes a guitar made by Stradivari himself. It is plain but superbly constructed – testimony to its maker's range, but far from being the main attraction. In the middle of the room a further case is crowded with eight violins, a viola and a bass viol. One of the violins was made by Andrea Amati in 1564, part of a commission for Charles IX of France. It is the oldest surviving violin in the world, an exquisite piece of workmanship. The Civic Museum in Cremona has one from the same set, but dated 1566, that was recently valued at $10 million. The Ashmolean's example has been laid on its back to fit into the case, obscuring what remains of the gilded painting with which the violin was decorated.

Almost every exhibit in this display would be the highlight of another museum's collection, but here they are no more than also-rans to the star, the only instrument to get its own cabinet, the one that greets you as you walk through the door: the *Messiah*. There it hangs, suspended in its case, visible from every angle, pristine, its varnish as flawless as when Stradivari applied the last few drops in 1716. It is in mint condition because this, the most famous violin in the world, template for countless copies, has hardly ever been played.

Figure 1. The *Messiah* – a 'matchless new violin amidst its time-worn, rubbed and fractured brethren'.

THE *VIOTTI*

On 6 May 1990 Thomas Bowes gave a recital at the Purcell Room, a small concert hall in London. He was playing a violin he called the *Viotti-Marie Hall*, after two previous owners. Its looks alone were striking: the immaculate maple back had natural horizontal stripes whose effect Bowes describes as almost psychedelic. But it is the sound that he most remembers now: 'That violin was absolutely deafening to play, when you played a sort of high harmonic in G or something on the E string you would actually be slightly in pain; it was so focused; it was like a sort of laser beam ... It gave an incredible feeling of power just to know that the smallest touch would just ping out to the back of the biggest hall ... There was a kind of awesome perfection about it.'

Bowes's recital was billed as revisiting the 'Golden Age of the violin': the Edwardian era when musicians faced no competition from modern technology for the ears of their prosperous audience. One of the Strad's eponymous owners, Marie Hall, had been a leading English violinist in the early twentieth century. The recital consisted mainly of music that she would have played, exhibition pieces by some of the great nineteenth-century violinist-composers: Paganini, Spohr, Vieuxtemps, Ernst and Wieniawski. As for the violin's connection with Viotti, Europe's most influential violinist at the beginning of the nineteenth century, the programme had this to say: 'The *Viotti* Stradivarius of 1709 was used by Viotti until his death, when it was sold in Paris with other instruments in his possession. Viotti was perhaps one of the first great players to fully appreciate the merits of Stradivarius. The "Marie Hall" ex Viotti Stradivarius is said to have been Viotti's favourite instrument and is reputed to be the instrument he used when he first visited Paris. It is a magnificent violin, with superb tone; a perfect Stradivarius in every respect.' It is our second violin.

THE *KHEVENHÜLLER*

Urbane and charming, with a penchant for expensive cigars and a fund of amusing stories, Peter Biddulph is everything one expects a violin expert to be. His dealership has a fine address in London's West End and its safe has played host to violins that most players can only covet. He is one of the few dealers in the world who can identify the real thing with confidence and who have the reputation to match their skill. Biddulph's habit of conducting transactions at either end of a trip on Concorde earned him, in happier times, the nickname 'the Flying Fiddle'. Nowadays he probably regrets the double entendre. A case brought by the heirs of Gerald Segelman, whose violin collection Biddulph helped to disperse after its owner's death, ended in an out-of-court settlement of £3 million. Biddulph had to sell the building that houses his London shop, although he still operates from the basement and a ground-floor reception. Nevertheless he protests his innocence of anything more serious than bad record-keeping; it was, he says, only his inability to afford a protracted case that led to the settlement.

The Segelman affair has turned an unwelcome spot-

light on violin dealers and their role as the final arbiters
of authenticity and value. Biddulph could be forgiven
for avoiding questions. Nevertheless he is happy to talk,
over a mint tea, about the *Khevenhüller*, the third of
our violins, which he sold in 2000 on behalf of one of the
oldest violin shops in Japan.

The *Khevenhüller* Stradivarius was made in 1733,
a late masterpiece. One previous owner describes it as
'ample and round, varnished a deep glowing red, its
grand proportions . . . matched by a sound at once powerful, mellow and sweet'. In the last twenty years it has
changed hands many times; this was the second time
that Biddulph acted as intermediary. On this occasion it
was valued at $4 million. Another dealer had shown it to
Maxim Vengerov. He 'loved it', but not enough, apparently, to make him give up the *Kreutzer*; we should
admire him for refusing to abandon his 'marriage' for
a new paramour. Jaime Laredo, the Bolivian-American
violinist, also tried the *Khevenhüller*. He too 'would have
loved it' as a partner to his other great Strad, the *Gariel*,
made in 1717. But he could not raise the funds. Who
could afford an asking price like that?

THE *PAGANINI*

'If the Tokyo String Quartet isn't the world's greatest
chamber music ensemble, it's hard to imagine which
group is.' Unsurprisingly, the Quartet's publicity likes to
repeat that quote from the *Washington Post*. Less definitive but almost as flattering reviews remark on both the
group's succulent tone and a cohesiveness that persists

despite the numerous changes of personnel since the ensemble's formation in 1969. It would be pleasing to think that both these attributes may partly result from another fact, also repeated in every press release: since 1995 the Tokyo Quartet has played the same set of instruments, all made by Stradivari, the Paganini Quartet.

Named after the nineteenth-century Italian virtuoso who once owned all four instruments, the Paganini Quartet has a legendary status that is almost matched by the quality of its constituent pieces. Stradivari only made two or three great violas and the Quartet's, made in 1731, is one of them. The first violin, four years older, was described by Paganini as having a tone as big as a double bass; it too is recognized as a masterpiece. The cello's label dates it to 1736, the year before its maker's death, although many place it earlier. It has the reputation of being among the best works of Stradivari's last years, with perfect proportions that hark back to an earlier era of the Master's life.

In such exalted company the second violin, made around 1680, is an oddity. Stradivari's early works are generally thought to be in a lower league than his more mature output, and this violin – the 1680 *Paganini* – is fifty years older than its counterparts in the Quartet. A string quartet is a partnership of equals. The second violin should never be of poorer quality than the instruments with which it must balance. The answer to why the 1680 *Paganini* became part of the Quartet lies in its history. It is our fourth violin.

THE *LIPIŃSKI*

For 200 years the 1715 *Lipiński* boasted a succession of famous players. One of the biggest violins Stradivari produced, made when he was at his peak, its construction speaks of its maker's confidence, and the longevity of its fame is surely evidence of his genius. But for over fifty years it has figured in no performances. Since its last recorded sale in 1962, the *Lipiński* – our final violin – has dropped from sight.

THE *DAVIDOV*

No such fate is likely to befall the *Davidov* cello, made in 1712. Yo-Yo Ma, who has played it for the last twenty years, is probably the world's most celebrated cellist and he is eloquent when he describes getting to know his great Stradivarius: 'The pianissimos float effortlessly. The instrument's response is instantaneous. The sound can be rich, sensuous or throbbing at every range, yet can also be clear, cultured and pure. Each sound stimulates the player's imagination. However, there is no room for error as one cannot push the sound, rather it needs to be released. I had to learn not to be seduced by the sheer beauty of the sound in my mind before trying to coax it from the cello.'

Makers have a similar response to the quality of the *Davidov*'s workmanship. In a recent article one says: 'Antonio Stradivari made this cello to give us all a lesson in humility.' Every aspect of the instrument is remark-

Figure 2. The *Davidov* cello boasts a succession of
famous players, and its beauty continues to awe admirers.
'Antonio Stradivari made this cello to give us all a
lesson in humility.'

able, but it is the varnish that creates the greatest
impression: 'For a few precious moments towards evening
the sun broke into the airy studio and the cello blazed
with light. Not only did it change colour, it changed in
transparency and depth and like some fantastic natural
hologram it presented a different image with each new
twist and turn.'

THE *Messiah*, the *Viotti*, the *Khevenhüller*, the *Paganini*,
the *Lipiński* and the *Davidov*: these are our six Strads.
Each has its own history. Occasionally two will cross
paths, in the collection of a single owner or at the same
performance, but there is only one man whose life
encompasses all six: Antonio Stradivari himself. And his
story begins at least a century before his birth, with the
emergence of Cremona at the centre of Europe's nascent
violin industry and the royal patron who helped to put it
there.

Chapter Two

'THE INCOMPARABLY BETTER VIOLINS OF CREMONA'

The Amati dynasty

UNDER NORMAL circumstances the French royal family would never have considered tainting its line with the blood of a woman whose family, only two or three generations before, had been in trade. But Catherine de Medici was a cousin to Pope Clement VII, with whom the perpetually belligerent François I sought an alliance, and her new husband-to-be Henri was only a second son with little prospect of inheriting the throne. So the marriage in October 1533 was quickly arranged, and the wedding night observed by the King, who noted afterwards that 'each had shown valour in the joust'.

Pope Clement's death in 1534, less than a year after the nuptials, was therefore a bitter blow. It meant, according to a contemporary Venetian report, that 'all of France disapproved of the marriage'. Worse was to come. Henri's older brother, the Dauphin, died in 1536, apparently from drinking ice-cold water immediately after a game of tennis. Catherine, still only seventeen, was destined to be Queen of France, responsible above all else for continuing the male line. But for ten years she bore no children, while her husband fathered enough offspring outside his marriage to demonstrate that the problem clearly was not with him. Stuck in a medieval court that followed its monarch around the country, chasing the latest reports of a hart fit to be hunted by a king, Catherine could hardly be blamed for surrounding herself with servants and artists from her native Florence. Even before she acquired any political influence, her cultural connections were starting to be felt.

Over the next twenty years a series of births and deaths transformed Catherine from devoted but neglected wife into the ruler of France. In 1544 she finally gave birth to her first child – what is more, a son. Thoughts of putting her into a nunnery, freeing Henri to take a second, more fertile wife, were finally shelved. Several more sons and daughters were to follow. Her father-in-law's death in 1547 made Catherine Queen, even if her husband elected to spend most of his time with his mistress. Then, in 1559, Henri himself died following a jousting accident. The widowed Catherine was Queen Mother, a powerful influence over her sickly son François II, who at fourteen was deemed able to rule alone. A year later François' own death brought his younger brother to the throne. Deft political footwork ensured that Catherine was named as Charles IX's regent, and she retained her power even when he was judged to have reached his majority in 1563. By then France's religious wars had already begun. Catherine was unable to stop them and she must bear some responsibility for the infamous St Bartholomew's Day massacre of Huguenots in 1572. So while she may have planned her lavish festivals and ballets as peaceful diversions, they only served to cast her in the same mould as Nero, fiddling while Rome burned.

It is an apt analogy; the court entertainments were accompanied by music from an instrument that had only recently emerged from Italy: the violin.

At the time the violin had a distinctly questionable reputation. The accepted view was that it might provide a good accompaniment for dancing, but it was not something in which true musicians should take an interest. In parts of Italy there were even Church edicts directing the destruction of this licentious object. Viols, another recent invention, were considered far more suitable for both courtly and religious music. With fretted fingerboards like the lute and guitar, but played with a bow, the various members of the viol family were softer-voiced than their violin equivalents. Ultimately this was to prove their undoing, but initially it was an advantage. In 1556 Philibert Jambe de Fer, writing in Lyon, praised the viol, expressing only opprobrium for the 'harsher sound' of the violin, which (the ultimate insult) 'few persons use save those who make a living from it through their labour'.

For the violin to flourish, the support of someone as influential as Catherine de Medici was crucial. An Italian dance band of violinists, headed by the marvellously named Balthasar de Beaujoyeux, had first arrived at the French court around 1555, before Henri's death but under Catherine's patronage. The band's original instruments have not survived, but some of their immediate successors do. Soon after Charles IX reached his majority, he and his mother set off for a tour of the kingdom, one that would last two years. At around the same time Catherine ordered a set of thirty-eight string instruments from Italy. Whatever her faults as a ruler, she knew how to buy. The entire set was made in the northern Italian town of Cremona. It included that small violin from 1564 that now lies on the floor of its case in the Ashmolean Museum, the earliest surviving violin in the world. And all the instruments were made by Andrea Amati. He and his family would dominate violin-making for the next 100 years.

THE VIOLIN is one of the great products of the late Renaissance, the result of a process of evolution, rather than a moment of inspiration. At the end of the fifteenth century there were only primitive instruments, good for providing dance music or accompanying voices but not for carrying their own tune. By 1535 Gaudenzio Ferrari was painting the ceiling of Saronno Cathedral to show not just violins (or possibly what we would now regard as violas) but also a cello, although both have just three strings. A workshop serving the courts of Mantua and Ferrara in northern Italy had probably made the crucial breakthroughs, combining the pegbox of the *rebec*, a lute-like instrument of Moorish origin, with the sound-box of the *lira da braccio*, itself a development of the Renaissance fiddle. Although he cannot have been the violin's inventor, Andrea Amati's delicacy and aware-ness of geometric principles established the blueprint for others to follow; everything of the instrument's form and function can be seen in that 1564 violin.

Before even hearing a violin one has to be conscious of its beauty. Comparison with an idealized female sil-houette – narrow-waisted and voluptuous – is unavoid-able. Man Ray's 1924 photograph, superimposing a pair of f-shaped soundholes on the back of a naked model, indicates the similarity with erotic simplicity. And the violin has always been described in anthropomorphic terms. Its hollow 'body', or soundbox, has a 'back' and a 'belly', held apart by 'ribs' around the side, and a 'neck' rises from one end towards the 'head' of the instrument. Even in Amati's original instruments that head took the modern form of the scroll, the spiralling volute whose only function is as a hook when the violin is hung in storage, but whose beauty cannot fail to inspire. A modern violin-maker, Roger Hargrave, recently described the scroll on Amati's 1564 violin, as 'softened but not ravaged by time'. Its 'concept was mathematically and optically so perfect that what followed over the centuries could only be steady degeneration'.

Perhaps the most remarkable aspect of that oldest surviving violin is that it is in no sense a prototype. The way the instrument works has not changed since 1564. Four strings, held under tension, travel its length, from the tailpiece, over a bridge that supports them above the soundbox, and along the neck to the head. They are made to vibrate, usually by rubbing with a horsehair bow, but also by plucking, or by striking with the wood of the bow. The bridge transmits these vibrations to the soundbox, which acts as an amplifier, so that we hear notes. The head contains the pegbox, whose pegs wind the strings and adjust their tension, thus tuning the violin. Glued along the neck's flat upper surface, between it and the strings, is a fingerboard against which the violinist can press a string with a finger of his left hand, effectively shortening it and changing the note it produces.

That fairly basic description may be enough to indicate

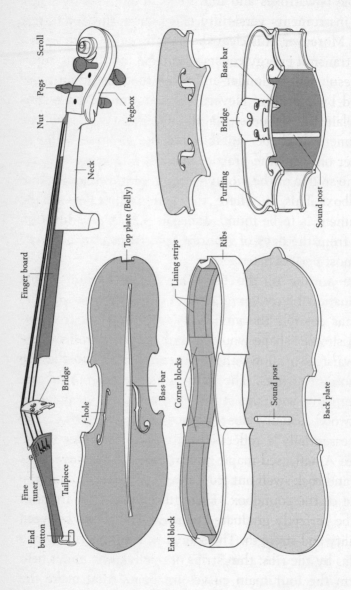

Figure 3. The apparent simplicity of the violin masks the considerable complexity of a design unchanged for more than four centuries.

what makes the violin family unique: the variety of possible bowstrokes and infinity of finger positions give these instruments versatility of a different order to any other. Moreover, it is clear that bowing allows the violinist to transmit energy constantly to his instrument: notes that result will be louder and more sustained than those created by plucking. Nevertheless, nothing even begins to explain the richness of a violin's sound, nor why one instrument may be suitable for the concert hall and another only for the practice cubicle. The heart of it all, and the source of the violin's power and mystique, is that soundbox. This is where the true complexity of the instrument is to be found, and where form and function have, from the days of Andrea Amati onwards, achieved an almost perfect marriage.

The outline of the body is not just beautiful; its combination of convex and concave curves equalizes as much as possible the violin's resonances at all frequencies; a simpler shape would favour one note over others. The waist also allows the bow easier access to the top and bottom strings. The belly must be able to vibrate in sympathy with the strings and is therefore made of a softwood, usually close-grained European spruce. The back, essentially a reflective plate, is of a harder wood; Andrea Amati used maple and so have all his successors. Belly and back swell out from the edges, plateauing in the middle of the soundbox. Their thicknesses and archings must be perfectly graduated to achieve a balance between flexibility and strength. The soundbox is completed around its sides by the ribs: thin strips of maple, bent under heat to form the four main curves or 'bouts' that make the hourglass shape of the body. Just inside the edge of both belly and back, accentuating the outline in a sublime demonstration of the craftsman's skill, but also protecting against cracks, lies the 'purfling'. Again Amati's 1564 violin sets the standard which almost all others have followed: three narrow strips of inlay, the outer two of pearwood stained black and the inner of poplar.

Only within the body has symmetry been sacrificed to function. Beneath the left-hand foot of the bridge, glued along the underside of the belly and running almost its entire length, is a long, thin piece of wood, tapering towards its ends, called the bass-bar. Beneath and slightly behind the other foot, wedged like a prop between belly and back, is a wooden rod, the soundpost. These two objects are crucial to both strength and tone: the soundpost creates a pivot point around which the belly can vibrate; and the bass-bar adds power to those vibrations. They are the only really counter-intuitive part of the violin: an indication of the process of trial and error that Amati's nameless predecessors must have put into perfecting the design.

And what about the soundholes? Symmetrical cursive fs, with circular finials at each end, they are perhaps the most recognizable part of the violin. They have such grace and beauty that it is easy to imagine that they owe little to functionality. Yet the more one considers them, the clearer it is that few other shapes would work so well. Some sort of aperture is necessary to allow sound to escape, but the middle of the belly must remain intact to support the bridge, hence the holes' positions towards the sides. Their narrowness means removing as few grains of spruce as possible – again important for strength – and the curves into circles at each end prevent splits developing. Finally, the outward curve into the lower corners places the bottom finials in dead wood, not wasting any potential source of amplification, while the narrow waist of the violin forces the holes to curve inwards at the top ends. In short, no one has conceived of a better basic design for the soundholes than the original, seen to perfection in Amati's work.

Finally, there is the varnish. No element of violin construction engenders more debate than this last apparently simple component. None doubt that it is a crucial part of the look of a good violin, enhancing the natural beauty of the materials in a way that only increases with age. All also agree that the wrong varnish can kill a

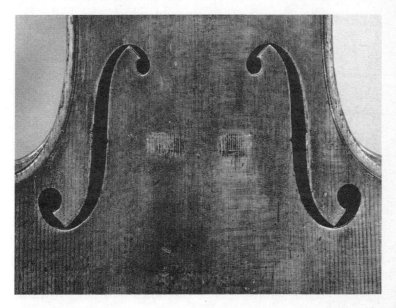

Figure 4. The tops of the soundholes curve in towards the centre of the violin, and their bottoms curve out towards the violin's outer corners.

violin's sound, deadening the vibrational quality of its wood. But is there more to it than that? Legendary qualities have been ascribed to the Cremonese varnish that Andrea Amati was apparently the first to use. Whether the best recipes actually enhance the tone, perhaps by acting as a filter, or are merely neutral, remains one of the central arguments in violin-making.

THERE IS another noteworthy aspect to Andrea Amati's legacy. He made not only the earliest surviving violin but also examples of both its sister instruments, the viola and the cello.* All follow the same principles of construction, the only real difference between them being the pitch at which their strings are tuned. The violin's four strings start at the G below middle C, and go up through D and A (the note around which an orchestra tunes) to the top E string a little under two octaves higher. Nine of Andrea Amati's violins survive: four 'small' and five 'large'. Violas are pitched a little lower, beginning with the C an octave below middle C, and then with three upper strings – G, D and A – that match the three lower strings on the violin. Four large Andrea Amati violas still exist. Finally, there is the cello, nowadays with four strings that repeat the notes of the viola, but an octave lower. Six by Andrea Amati survive. They include the world's oldest cello. Dated 1572, it also bears the arms of Charles IX and was probably presented to him by Pope Pius V.

---

* Although similar, the double bass appears to be more directly descended from the viol.

Amati made his cellos with only three strings and soundboxes 31 inches long, against the modern 29 inches. All the survivors have been cut down and had a fourth set of holes inserted in their pegboxes. The 1572 Amati cello accommodated the changes with singular success. At the end of the eighteenth century it was the favoured instrument – before he later acquired a Stradivarius – of Jean-Louis Duport, one of the most influential cellists of his time. When Roger Hargrave heard one of Amati's cellos recently in a large concert hall, it 'seemed to power its way into every corner of the auditorium. It simply blew away the younger but still highly commendable competition.'

ANDREA AMATI died in 1577, leaving his business to two sons, Antonio (b. 1540) and Girolamo (b. 1561). Antonio seems to have left the partnership in 1588, but the instruments made by the workshop until the 1620s are still labelled as the work of 'The Brothers Amati'. They are more substantial than Andrea's, but there is no mistaking his influence, which was already extending further than his immediate family. Imitators of the Amati style were springing up throughout northern Italy as lute-makers, or 'luthiers', turned their attention to the new instrument.

The most important were in Brescia, 30 miles north of Cremona. Here, Gasparo Bertolotti, always called 'da Salò' after his birthplace, built violins with a powerful tone but in a style so primitive that he was once thought to be the instrument's inventor. The honour has had to be taken back with the fixing of his birthdate at 1540;

he is simply too young. The violins made by da Salò's pupil, Giovanni Paolo Maggini, retained his overall shape but flattened the archings. For many listeners these two makers' violas, in particular, have never been bettered.

By the end of the sixteenth century the power and the versatility of the violin were undeniable. In 1581 Balthasar de Beaujoyeux composed the first music specifically for the new instrument, a ballet to celebrate the marriage of Catherine de Medici's daughter. From about 1600, paintings by Caravaggio and others depict the full beauty of the violin: it had emerged from the shadows, a work of art, but also the most advanced technology of the age.

The Amati dynasty continued into a third generation with the birth of Nicolò in 1596. He was one of several children to Girolamo, born twelve years after his second marriage to Laura de Medici de Lazzarini. As her name suggests, Laura may have been a distant cousin to the French Queen. It seems unlikely that Catherine, who died in 1589, ever became aware of her relationship with her former supplier. Always keen to forget the Medicis' origins in trade, she would hardly have appreciated being reminded of the fact. Connected to royalty, scion of the greatest family of luthiers in Europe, by the time Nicolò joined Girolamo in the workshop a bright future beckoned.

The late 1620s, however, were to bring calamity. The death of the childless Duke of Mantua in 1627 prompted a struggle for control of his dominions in which Venice, France, Spain and the Holy Roman Empire all became embroiled. Part of the Duchy of Milan, Cremona came under Spanish influence and was plunged into the fray. The effects were disastrous. As a 1630 Cremonese parish book recorded: 'rich people have by this time been reduced to such a state of poverty, caused partly by the quartering of soldiers in their houses and partly by the heavy taxes imposed . . . that were it not for the shame of it, they would go begging'.

In the same year plague swept from the ruined city of Mantua through the whole of Lombardy. By August Cremona was deserted. Its citizens returned to their homes later in the year, but two thirds of the population had disappeared, either dead or remaining in outlying villages. The town's wealth had all but evaporated. Among those who died were Girolamo and Laura Amati, as well as two of their daughters. In Brescia Giovanni Maggini would be dead by 1632. Of all the great master luthiers in the two cities, only the young Nicolò Amati survived.

The demand for violins had not slackened off. Louis XIII's foundation of his famous 'Vingt-Quatre Violons du Roi'* is indicative; the instrument was taking the position of orchestral workhorse that it still holds today. Violins were needed in ever greater numbers. Nicolò rose to the challenge. Unmarried and childless, he made a decision that was to have far-reaching consequences: to take on apprentices from outside his family. By 1632 these included Francesco Rugeri and Andrea Guarneri; later, Giovanni Battista Rogeri joined the workshop. Violins by any of them are now highly prized. Amati even employed apprentices from outside Italy. Leopoldo'di

---

* A court orchestra of twenty-four string instruments.

Tedesco' ('the German') was one. Another may have been Jacob Stainer, of Absam in the Tyrol, whose violins would be the main challengers to Amati's for much of the seventeenth century.

Nevertheless, in 1637 Nicolò Amati cannot have had any Cremonese rivals when, on 20 December, Father Fulgentius Micanzio, a monk at the Servite Monastery in Venice, wrote the following words:

> Concerning the violin which your nephew on passing through here wishes to buy, I have spoken to the Maestro di Concerti di San. Marco, who tells me that I can easily find Brescian violins, but that those of Cremona are incomparably the better – in fact, they represent the non plus ultra; and by the medium of the Cremonese Signor Monteverdi, Chapel-Master of St. Mark's, who has a nephew living in Cremona, I have given the order for a violin to be sent here. The difference in the price will show you the superiority, for those of Cremona cost at the lowest twelve ducats [£300]* each, whilst the others can be had for less than four ducats. As your nephew is in the service of His Highness of Bavaria, I think he will prefer by far the one ordered to be sent to Venice as soon as possible ...

The importance of the letter lies in the price it gives: it plots the first marker on a graph whose trend ever

---

* Throughout the text, the figure in the square brackets gives the approximate current sterling equivalent, for indication only, of the sum stated. For a discussion of methodology and sources see Appendix Three.

since has been one of almost uninterrupted increase. It is also hard to resist the reference to Claudio Monteverdi. There can be no doubting his credentials as an adviser: his opera *L'Orfeo*, written in 1607, contained some of the most complex music for violins then written. The real joy of the correspondence, however, is that the letter's recipient was none other than Galileo Galilei. The great astronomer-mathematician was by then seventy-three and blind. On the orders of the Inquisition he would spend the rest of his life under house arrest in Arcetri, just outside Florence. There is something rather wonderful about the violins of Nicolò Amati being the link between the founder of astronomy and the first composer of modern opera.

Nicolò Amati's career encompassed the emergence of violin virtuosi. It was probably in response to their need for increasing power that Nicolò developed his grand pattern, wider than his predecessors' violins and with more pronounced corner-points. These instruments came close to perfection. They can still inspire love in those who play them: '[Its sound] gently surrounds me with a depth and multi-dimensional quality that is at once rich and beguiling,' says Thomas Bowes of the grand-pattern Amati for which he re-mortgaged his house. Only the archings of the front and back plates can be criticized: full in the middle, with scoops down towards the edges that restrict flexibility and inhibit amplification.

Nicolò was almost fifty when he married Lucrezia Pagliari. One son, Girolamo, born in 1649, would continue the Amati tradition into the fourth generation. The few violins by him that still exist are a testament to his abilities. It was Girolamo's misfortune, however, to reach adulthood at the same time as another Cremonese craftsman, destined to outshine all other luthiers, the greatest of them all: Antonio Stradivari.

Chapter Three

'HE WAS A GENIUS ALREADY'

The origins and development of
Antonio Stradivari

'I THOUGHT, WELL, it'll be like an Amati, a rather sweet and contained little sound, but not a bit of it, like a laser beam. It was a Strad. I mean, he was a genius already, he had the ability.' Leader of the Aberni Quartet and violin teacher at London's Royal Academy of Music, Howard Davis has encountered many Strads; the Academy's own collection is one of the most extensive in the world. Even so, he feels a special sense of wonder when he remembers playing Stradivari's earliest known violin, made in 1666. 'It really was astonishing, it had a clarity and a sweetness at the same time but also a projection of that sound, I could hear it hitting the back of the hall.'

That same violin represents the earliest evidence of Antonio Stradivari's existence. Cremona has no record of his birth, although there are surnames similar to Stradivari in Cremonese histories dating back to the twelfth century. Most probably Antonio's parents were among the many who fled the city during the disasters of 1628–30, so that the great luthier would have been born in some outlying parish. Although we can deduce from later violins that Stradivari was born in 1644, we have to accept that he arrives in the history of violin-making at the age of twenty-two, and is already a force to be reckoned with.

The question of who taught Stradivari his trade compounds the mystery. Once again, that early violin provides what seems to be a crucial piece of data. Its label bears the words 'Antonius Stradivarius Cremonensis Alumnus Nicolaii Amati, Faciebat Anno 1666' ['Made by Antonio Stradivari of Cremona, pupil of Nicolò Amati, in 1666']. The evidence seems incontrovertible: Stradivari had been taught by Nicolò Amati and was now setting out on his own. If further proof were needed, then the style of the violin and its successors should be enough to convince anyone of Amati's influence over Stradivari's work: there is the same golden-brown varnish, the overall similarities of design, the differences that suggest a master beginning to develop his own way of doing things.

Nevertheless, something does not quite add up. That 1666 label was certainly intended to be one among many: apart from the final handwritten '6', it is printed from a specially made stamp. Yet the very next violin by Stradivari to have survived uses entirely different wording: 'Antonius Stradivarius Cremonensis Faciebat Anno 1667'. What made the young luthier abandon his first stamp so quickly? Why do Stradivari's earliest violins actually bear less resemblance to Amati's than those he made a decade or so later? If he really had been Amati's apprentice, why do the annual census records never show him living in his master's house? We can see the hands of Andrea Guarneri, Giovanni Battista Rogeri and Francesco Rugeri in the output of the Amati workshop; why not Antonio Stradivari's?

Many answers have been proposed to these questions,

but the simplest of all is that Stradivari was never apprenticed to Amati. Cremona's census returns show that from 1667 to 1680 he lived in the Casa Nuziale, owned by a wood-carver and inlayer, Francesco Pescaroli. The young luthier could not have lived off his violin-making alone in this period. The implication is that he continued to work for some other master, and the most likely candidate would be the man in whose house he lived. Antonio Stradivari, unchallenged as the greatest violin-maker of his or any other age, may originally have been a woodworker.

The theory would seem far-fetched, except that it is supported by Stradivari's own violins. Even the early instruments are carved amazingly well. The purfling, in particular, is inserted with such skill that it is hard to imagine that the craftsman responsible does not have some special expertise. But there is another, more intriguing clue. Towards the end of the 1670s Stradivari started to produce decorated instruments of immense artistry. Beautifully inlaid, these violins carry elaborate purfling and elegant tracery around their sides and on their scrolls. Of Nicolò Amati's entire output only one or two violins from the mid-1650s compare with them; their designs, in fact, are strikingly similar.

What if the ornamentation on those Amati violins was the work of the young Antonio Stradivari? No older than thirteen, he would have been an apprentice for only a year or two at most, but long enough for his master to appreciate his pupil's skill with the gouge and knife. Pescaroli could easily have suggested to Amati, his near-neighbour, that he employ a talented youngster to decorate some of his famous violins. The few weeks this implies Stradivari spent in Amati's workshop would explain his familiarity at a distance with the Amatisé style. It might have been all that was necessary to show him that violin-making was both more interesting and more lucrative than his chosen trade. Later, of course, Stradivari must have learnt more about the actual business of building violins, but even then he may not have had Amati as his master. Francesco Rugeri seems more probable: there is at least one technique to do with thickness gradation that he shares with Stradivari but that neither luthier derived from Amati.

And so we come back to that first surviving violin from 1666. It would have been natural, if a little cheeky, for the young Stradivari to paste a label in his early experiments that overplayed his link with the great Amati, and equally natural for the older luthier to demand that he drop the reference the moment he found out about it. We start to see Stradivari not as a dutiful apprentice who eventually outshone his master, but as an independently minded genius with an entrepreneurial streak. We can also begin to understand the background and character that would eventually lead him to rethink every aspect of the violin's soundbox. He understood and respected the Cremonese tradition that Amati represented, but he was not bound by it.

Sketchy as they are, the few details we have of Stradivari's private life also suggest a man who was prepared to take risks. On 4 July 1667 he married Signora Francesca Feraboschi. Their first child, Giulia, was born the following October, less than four months later. This was not particularly unusual; the church had been happy to cooperate with an accelerated reading of the banns. But there was more than that to make the marriage remarkable. Francesca was the widow of a relatively wealthy Cremonese burgher, Giacomo Capra; their short marriage had surely not been a happy one. It brought two daughters and was based on a substantial dowry of 3,500 lire [£15,000], but after less than two years, on 28 April 1664, Capra was murdered by Francesca's brother, Giovanni Feraboschi – shot with an arquebus in the Piazza Santa Agata, in front of one of Cremona's many parish churches.

The motives concealed by this bald statement of the facts can only be imagined. Feraboschi must have been acting for his sister's welfare at least, perhaps on her instructions. He seems to have been scarcely censured, let alone punished, for his crime. Initially banished from Cremona, he would be pardoned by all less than three years later. Meanwhile Capra's father, a prominent architect, had taken in his grandchildren and Francesca had successfully sued him for the return of her dowry (1,437 lire remained in cash and personal items). Free to marry she may have been, but Francesca undoubtedly came to Antonio Stradivari with a past.

Soon after their wedding the young couple moved into the Casa Nuziale. For thirteen years it would be not just Stradivari's home but also his workshop. It was a classic Cremonese artisan's house, long and narrow, incorporating a small courtyard, with a shop and workspace on the ground floor and living quarters on the two floors above. A covered roof-terrace could be reached through a trapdoor from the second floor. Known in the Cremonese dialect as a *seccadour*, the terrace would normally have been used to dry clothes and foodstuffs before winter storage. This must have been where the newly varnished violins were hung out to dry. The floors underneath would have accommodated Antonio and Francesca's growing family. Giulia was the oldest of six children. The first son, Francesco, died in 1670, only twelve days after he was born. Less than a year later, however, another Francesco arrived, to be followed over the next eight years by another sister, Caterina, and two brothers, Alessandro and Omobono.

As a father Stradivari may have been close to prolific, but the same can hardly be said of his initial output of violins. From his first fourteen years as an independent luthier until 1680, by which time he was thirty-six, only eighteen violins are now known to exist, along with a viola, a guitar and a cello that was originally a viol. Some may show the spark of genius but overall they suffer by comparison with the authoritative instruments emerging at the same time from Nicolò Amati's workshop. Stradivari was still finding his feet, no more than a marginal figure in Cremonese luthiery, itself facing new challenges from German makers. Taking only the commissions that Amati could not fulfil, the small number of instruments Stradivari produced simply reflects a lack of demand for them.

So it seems inescapable that Stradivari's instrument production alone could not have sustained his family. Prices cannot have risen that much since the days of Galileo. It is hard to imagine Stradivari receiving any more than 15 ducats [£400] for a violin; half that seems more likely. Even if he sold four violins a year (assuming that many have since been lost), his profits from the instruments would never have been enough to account for the increasing prosperity that he came to enjoy. He must have had another source of income. One theory is that he was independently wealthy, able to experiment with new designs as his violins gradually came towards perfection. But there is little else about Stradivari's life to suggest dilettantism. It is more likely that he was continuing to work for his master, Pescaroli.

One way or another, by the end of the 1670s there are signs that Stradivari's fortunes were decisively improving. His earliest decorated instruments date to this period. The second to have survived is distinctive not just for its ornamentation. Although Stradivari made it in 1679, he only sold the violin to its first owner, Sir Edward Hellier, many years later. It is hard to avoid the implication that it was not made for any specific buyer but rather as a statement. The artistry is there for all to see, its impact is immediate in the way that the more understated qualities of a good violin can never be. Stradivari was announcing his presence in the way he knew best, through the quality of his inlay.

Stradivari's investment in the *Hellier* is not the only evidence that he was moving above the level of a poor journeyman. In 1680 he bought his first house, agreeing a price of 7,000 lire imperiale [£40,000], a down-payment of 2,000 lire with the balance to be paid over four years. This house, at No. 1 Piazza San Domenico, had a similar layout to the Casa Nuziale, but was more substantial, with large cellars and an attic between the living quarters and the *seccadour*. Tradition has it that it was in this attic that Stradivari made his most famous violins.

Around the same time as the move, Stradivari produced the violin that would go on to be called the *Paganini*, the earliest of our six instruments. It is typical

Figure 5. Stradivari's house in Piazza San Domenico
(now Piazza Roma) is no longer standing but is captured here
in a nineteenth-century engraving.

of the period in every respect: influenced by Amati in overall model and in its golden-orange varnish, but with Stradivari's original style visible in the more angular soundholes and less rounded curves. The violin would probably have taken about two weeks to make, as Stradivari followed traditional Cremonese techniques by then already over a century old.

CONSTRUCTION BEGAN with an internal mould. At this stage in his career Stradivari probably had two, which he coded 'MB and 'S'. The assumption is that MB stands for 'Modello Buono', the independent luthier's first successful attempt at creating his own mould, and S for 'Secondo'. The moulds themselves are little more than flat pieces of wood, with the shape of the outline of a violin without its internal blocks. Stradivari designed them with few tools other than a ruler and compass, but even so they incorporate some fascinating mathematical relationships. The most striking of these is the recurrence of the 'golden mean' – the number used by the ancient Greeks to give perfect classical proportions – as the ratio between several key widths and heights.

First on to the mould, lightly glued for future removal, were the violin's end and corner blocks. Next, Stradivari used a heated iron to bend the ribs around the mould, fixing them to the blocks with glue and clamping them in place so that the four thin strips of maple formed the uninterrupted outline of the *Paganini*'s body. This became Stradivari's template for tracing out the violin's shape on to the planks of spruce and maple that were to form, respectively, the instrument's belly and back. For

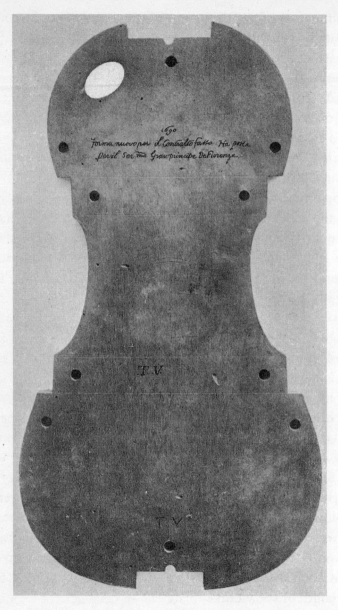

Figure 6. One of Stradivari's internal moulds,
in this case for a tenor viola.

both, at least in the case of the *Paganini*, the plank actually consisted of two wedges of wood cut 'on the quarter'. Think of two vertical 'cake' slices from the trunk of the tree glued together at their thicker ends. After 1670, Stradivari almost invariably used this technique to make his violins' bellies, so ensuring that their treble and bass sides were in balance. With the backs, Stradivari varied his approach according to the wood available. Many of his earliest violins have their backs made from maple cut 'on the slab', taking slices in planes at a tangent to the tree's growth rings. This loses the classic 'figure' of quarter-cut maple – apparent horizontal stripes caused by ripples in the wood's grain – and gives a different sound to the resulting violin, richer perhaps, but less highly focused. Later, he usually used quarter-cut wood: two pieces for the *Paganini*, often only one, if he had a large enough piece of maple.

The shapes that Stradivari had cut out from the spruce and maple were now ready for working on to create the front and back plates of the violin. First the external archings: Stradivari probably used guides, cutting channels to match them with a long rounded gouge. Connecting these channels gave the rough exterior. A succession of finer tools finishing with a hard steel scraper led to the perfect smooth curves of the final surfaces. The interior followed, as Stradivari gradually brought each plate down to its ideal thickness, thinning out from the centre towards the edge and taking great care to make front and back as thin as possible without compromising the strength of the violin.

To carve the two soundholes in the *Paganini*'s belly Stradivari started with the circular finials at each end of

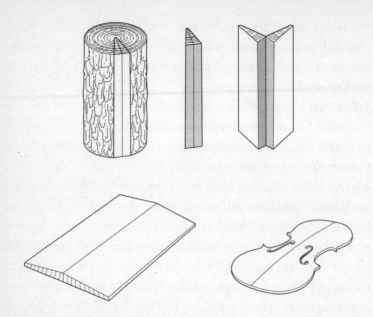

Figure 7a. Quarter-cut wood is cut as a wedge from the tree trunk. Stradivari used it for almost all his violins' bellies and most of their backs. This example shows the wedge being re-sawn and glued at the thicker end, creating a symmetrical plank for shaping into the violin's belly.

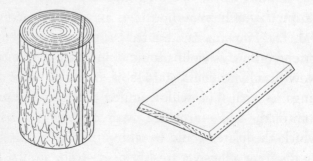

Figure 7b. Slab-cut wood, by contrast, is cut as a section from the tree trunk.

the holes, placing them with a compass and drilling them out using a cylinder with cutting wings. A template specific to the *Paganini*'s mould then gave the outline of the f that connected the finials. The simplicity of Stradivari's soundholes is deceptive: try drawing one freehand. Their grace and perfect proportions, together with the flawless carving, are part of what an expert looks for when distinguishing a Strad from a copy.

The belly also needed a bass-bar attached to its interior surface. It ran about three-quarters of the length of the instrument, at its thickest in the middle and tapering down towards the ends. At this point Stradivari may have tested the 'tap-note' of back and belly to find its resonant frequency. If so, he seems to have aimed for something around the F below middle C for each. Alternatively, or perhaps as well, he may have tested the feel and flexibility of each plate in his hands. In either case, subsequent thickness adjustment would have achieved what experience told him was ideal. It is in this kind of crucial detail that Stradivari's innate genius comes through. He made his violins not according to a specific formula but by taking account of the specific properties of the wood he was using. Even he may not have fully understood what he did. The *Paganini* is an early example; as Stradivari's experience grew his violins could only improve in quality.

Now Stradivari could start to assemble the soundbox. 'Linings' – strips of willow glued along the top and bottom of the ribs – provided, with the blocks, a surface to which the plates could be glued. First was the back, using a strong adhesive, freshly made from animal hide. Now was the time to tap out the internal mould, its job done. Two further internal attachments remained before the closure of the body: the *Paganini*'s neck, by means of glue and three hand-forged nails through the top block; and the label, with its date and seal, clearly visible through the left-hand soundhole of the violin. Then, finally, he glued on the belly, using a weaker adhesive to allow for future repairs.

Many hours had gone into producing that neck, carved together with the pegbox and scroll from a single piece of maple. Stradivari probably made a batch of them in advance. Again there is mathematics behind the scrolls. The Italian architect Giacomo Vignola had laid down principles for spirals in the sixteenth century, building on Archimedes' work almost two millennia before. Stradivari's scrolls show that he knew the work of both men, as the central volute comes out in an Archimedean spiral, with relatively tight windings, before changing to a more expansive Vignola's spiral on its outer curve. On some cellos the connection is not seamless, but on the violins it is a glorious single sweep of two parallel grooves, narrow at the scroll's top, and expanding effortlessly in both directions away from it. The apparent inevitability of the scroll's lines, the way they draw the eye along them from every direction, and the sheer confidence and artistry underlying the carving, are again all crucial to what sets Stradivari apart from the mere artisan. The genius is unmistakable.

The instrument was far from finished. Stradivari had cut out the back and belly so that they overlapped the ribs. This now gave him the opportunity to contour round slight irregularities in the shape of the ribs, where for example these were slightly thicker than normal, or had not perfectly followed the line of the mould. The

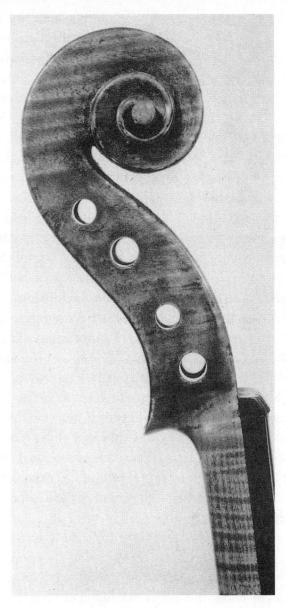

Figure 8. One of Stradivari's scrolls: they
cannot fail to please the eye.

result is an instrument whose outline initially appears flawless; only the most careful examination reveals the imperfections inevitable in any handmade object.

With the final shape of the violin complete, Stradivari applied his last piece of artistry: the purfling. After first tracing and then cutting the grooves around the edges of the instrument, front and back, he inserted the inlay in strips that he had previously glued together. It is probably at the corners that Stradivari's skill is most apparent; the *Paganini* shows the characteristic 'bee-stings' of his mitres, points remarkably thin while remaining beautifully and precisely formed. The result is both delicate and confident, ornamentation that adds elegance while avoiding frippery.

The *Paganini* was now ready for varnishing. This is one process where simple deduction is insufficient; nor do surviving records tell us anything directly about the recipe for any Cremonese maker's varnish. All we have in Stradivari's hand is an apology for a delayed repair having had to wait for the varnish to dry. The way is therefore left open for endless speculation, both as to the formula Stradivari used and as to its resulting impact on tone. The varnish on the *Paganini*, however, cannot have been much of a secret: every luthier in Cremona was using something similar. Its golden-yellow colour, and faint softness to the touch, owe everything to Cremonese tradition.

STRADIVARI made the *Paganini* during one of the most important periods of his life. The relocation to Piazza San Domenico had a significance beyond the house's greater

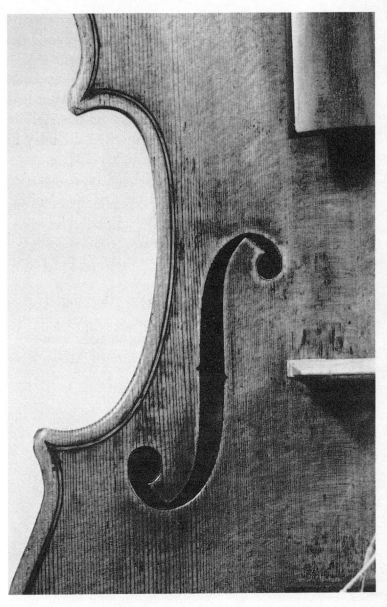

Figure 9. The delicacy of Stradivari's purfling
emphasises his skill as an inlayer.

size. It was only a few steps away from the Amati and Guarneri workshops, a clear statement that Stradivari now considered himself on a par with Cremona's best. More than that, he was breaking his links with Pescaroli. From now on Stradivari would concentrate on his instruments. As many Strads survive from the period 1680–85 as from the previous fourteen years. They are not just violins. A harp dated 1681 seems to be authentic. Its elaborate carvings of children, satyrs and women provide further evidence of Stradivari's woodworking skills, not to mention a taste for the flamboyant that he could not display in his violins. A year later Stradivari made a second guitar. More important, it was around now that he produced his first true cellos. They are as large as those Andrea Amati had been producing over 100 years before and most have suffered a similar fate, being cut down to modern requirements.

One instrument is missing from this period, although Stradivari would go on to make a very few more: the viola. Throughout his life, and in common with his Cremonese contemporaries, Stradivari never seems to have devoted particular attention to this third member of the violin family. The reason probably lies in the changing fashions among musicians. Given the violin family's original role as an accompaniment to singing, and the lower, male, vocal registers that prevailed in the sixteenth century, it is probable that the viola was the first of the family to develop. It was left in the cold, however, by rising registers and the increasing popularity of the higher-pitched, more audible violin. When Stradivari was at his peak, violas were hardly played. Demand for them only revived with the development of the string quartet after 1780.

Nicolò Amati died in 1684, aged eighty-eight. The violins emerging from his workshop in the last few years of his life do not look like the product of an old man, and must largely have been the work of his son Girolamo. Nevertheless, it was his death – following on the heels of that of his great German rival, Jacob Stainer, in 1683 – which removed the final barrier between Stradivari and international recognition. It can hardly be a coincidence that this was also the point at which Stradivari came into his full powers as a craftsman. The improvement in his workmanship is so marked that later historians could only assume that Stradivari displaced Nicolò's own son as the inheritor of the dead luthier's tools. It seems unlikely. Nevertheless, the beauty of the instruments Stradivari produced in the late 1680s is unsurpassed; he would never cut f-holes, insert purfling or carve scrolls more skilfully. At the same time he was changing the design of his violins, increasing their dimensions so that he moved closer to Amati's grand pattern. Royal commissions were quick to follow. James II of England apparently ordered one set of instruments in 1685. Five years later Cosimo de Medici, Grand Duke of Tuscany, bought another. His family might no longer be the power-broker it had been in the days of Queen Catherine but its appreciation of Cremona's skills was clearly undimmed.

In 1688 Stradivari's eldest daughter Giulia married Giovanni Farina, a Cremonese notary who would frequently act as the luthier's representative in future business. Stradivari had been able to provide Giulia with

a generous dowry and was surely behind the match.
He seems to have played the patriarchal role in all his
children's lives. Francesco, the eldest son, probably joined
him as an apprentice at eleven, perhaps a bit older. At the
close of the 1680s his teens were coming to an end. Fully
trained, Francesco must have contributed to the increasing output of his father's workshop. The second son,
Alessandro, was destined for the priesthood; his education
would continue. Of the two remaining children Caterina
was still only sixteen in 1690; there was plenty of time
to choose her a husband; and Omobono, eleven, would
have to be found a trade. In the meantime he too could
continue his education.

Stradivari should have been content. Only his violins
suggest restlessness, as he embarked upon a decade of
almost ceaseless experimentation. The starting-point
must have been what Stradivari heard from violinists
themselves. Perhaps the era's greatest, Arcangelo Corelli,
made his requirements clear. Composer-violinists of his
breed were attracting followings in all Italy's cultural
centres. Their concerti and sonatas showcased technical
prowess that would have been inconceivable to their
predecessors, used to accompanying voice or dance, or to
playing in ensembles. But to achieve their full effect as
soloists in front of large audiences they needed violins
with a stronger tone.

Stradivari set about trying to meet this demand. By
now he had already produced violins whose outlines were
based on at least five different internal moulds, three for
full-size instruments and two for smaller examples, probably for children. In 1689 he came up with a sixth mould,

his largest yet, that he called 'PG', probably 'Più Grande' ('Bigger'). Its dimensions bear a marked similarity to those of Amati's grand pattern. Two years later a seventh mould had almost the same length as the 'PG', but a significantly narrower width. Six months on and yet a further mould kept the narrow bouts but increased the length and the width at the waist. Finally, at the end of 1692, a ninth mould maintained these widths but shortened the length back to that of Stradivari's earliest violins.

The pace of experimentation is startling. There can scarcely have been time for the varnish to dry on a newly designed violin before Stradivari started thinking about how it might be changed. He did not settle on any one form; the soundboxes of the violins he produced until 1697 have lengths as great as 14$\frac{5}{16}$ inches against the standard 14 inches, and widths as little as 8 inches, compared to a more 'normal' 8$\frac{1}{4}$ inches. Neither variation seems huge, but in the narrower instruments in particular the appearance of length was exaggerated. That is not to say that these 'Long Strads' are in any sense out of proportion; they are as graceful as any Stradivari made. And they have one other important characteristic. As Stradivari developed his long pattern, he started to reduce the archings of his violins' backs and bellies. This eliminated the need to reduce height in a dramatic scoop towards the edges. The resulting instruments are not appreciably thinner when viewed side on, but are flatter than anything previously produced in Cremona. The most obvious antecedent is the work of Maggini in Brescia almost a century earlier. Stradivari may have drawn inspiration from him, but it seems more likely

that the gradual decrease in archings was simply part of
his overall quest for tone, seeing what he could achieve
with incremental changes.

Long Strads are still beautiful. Their varnish is redder
and tougher than on earlier violins, with an almost
bottomless depth of colour. Stradivari was at his peak as
a craftsman when he made them; and his long pattern
pushed the design of the violin further than anything
achieved before. But the form was not ultimately successful. The greater power came at the cost of some
sweetness; and players may have found the instruments
unwieldy. Corelli is said to have owned an especially fine
Long Strad from 1693; yet he preferred to play his
Albani, made in the Tyrol to Jacob Stainer's model.

Over the period 1695–7, almost as though he was
struggling with the form, Stradivari's production slowed
significantly. Then, in 1698, he reverted to the old Amatisé design, producing violins with an outline similar to
those Nicolò Amati had been making fifty years before.
The long pattern had been a dead end.

That same year, on 20 May, Francesca Stradivari
died. Whatever the circumstances that brought her and
Antonio together, they had been married for thirty years,
Stradivari's entire career as an independent luthier. The
list of funeral expenses is one of the few personal documents to survive from Stradivari's life. It probably sheds
more light on Cremonese ceremonial than Stradivari's
feelings for his wife, but it seems clear that he gave her
a good send-off. Three lines from the total bill of 182
lire [£700] give an indication: fourteen Priests and one
Choirboy: 7 lire; thirty-six Dominican Fathers: 18 lire;
sixteen Franciscan Fathers: 15 lire, 10 soldi. Stradivari

himself was now fifty-four years old. Francesco would have been working with him for fifteen years. Andrea Guarneri and Francesco Rugeri had both retired in favour of their sons. Perhaps it was time for Stradivari to do the same?

Chapter Four

'HIS COSTUME SCARCELY EVER VARIED'

Stradivari's golden period, decline and death

THE YEAR 1698 was indeed a critical one for Stradivari, but not because there is any hint of him slowing down, or retiring in favour of Francesco. Almost certainly, however, his sons played a part in what was to follow. Very few facts can be ascertained over a distance of 300 years, and they all require interpretation. Nevertheless, there do seem to be two other crucial developments that can be traced back to that same year.

The first is the return of Stradivari's youngest son, Omobono, to Cremona. We only know that he had been away in Naples from a statement made by his father in his will thirty years later. We can only place 1698 as when he was there because that is the single year of his adult life when he does not appear on the census records for his father's house. The first draft of the will makes it clear that Stradivari did not approve of his son's Neapolitan adventure: 'If he insists on something, then let him have the debt which is the three thousand lire I spent for him when he was in Naples and since his return.' Later drafts both reduce the 'debt' to 2,000 lire, and specify that Omobono was away for two and a half years, while the census returns for 1699 show Omobono already back in Cremona. The discrepancy over the period he was away can only be reconciled through disbelieving either the parish priest who acted as census-taker, or Stradivari's memory after thirty years. It seems likely, however, that Omobono only ever went to Naples under his mother's protection, with her insistence that their youngest son should be allowed to make his own way in life. When she died he was summoned back to Cremona to be his father's junior apprentice.

The other change that we can detect from 1698 is subtle, but equally important. From this time on, Stradivari's scrolls, that sublime example of his artistry and craftsmanship, appear to be the work of another hand. The implication is that with the advent of a younger assistant, Francesco, by now twenty-seven, finally achieved more responsibility. The cutting of scrolls is an easily separable task, a natural for delegation: teachable, inherently satisfying, and with no impact on the violin's tone. The idea raises, of course, the uncomfortable question of how something so characteristic of Stradivari could in fact be the work of an assistant. There are two answers. The first is that Stradivari's genius extended not just to his own carving, but to the way he was able to standardize and supervise, ensuring that his sons produced work of the highest quality. He can hardly have been an easy taskmaster. From 1698 onwards, in fact, we should probably think of Stradivari's violins as being the product of a workshop rather than a single man. The second answer is that, to a purist, Francesco's scrolls are not as good as his father's. There is a hesitancy and a squareness to them, by comparison with those on earlier

Strads. This is a minor criticism, however, unimportant when set against the flowering of genius that the violins themselves display.

For the presence of two helpers seems to have liberated Stradivari. The 1690s had seen him conduct every possible experiment with the size and shape of the traditional violin, and now he was able to bring it together. He returned to the 'PG' template that he first constructed in 1689, but this did not constitute total regression. His years working on the long pattern had generated one key insight: a flatter body gives greater tonal power without making the violin itself unacceptably fragile. The elimination of that tone-weakening scoop to the sides – the only real flaw in Amati's design – would prove to be crucial. By the early 1700s the workshop was producing violins whose soundboxes remain a model for those being made today. Stradivari himself would continue to experiment for the rest of his life, but it was always around this basic form; he must have known he could not do better.

The additional manpower also had an immediate effect on the workshop's level of production. At least twenty-five violins and four cellos survive from the two years 1698–9. Perhaps Stradivari was seeking solace through work for the loss of his wife. If so, the treatment seems to have been effective: on 24 August 1699 he married Antonia Zambelli, a Cremonese woman who was by then thirty-five. It would be easy to cast this marriage in a sentimental light: grieving but still vigorous widower of fifty-five finds consolation and love with sympathetic younger (but mature) woman. Stradivari's violins themselves, however, portray an obsessive search for excellence that is hard to reconcile with the idea of the luthier paying very much attention to his wife. There was probably more reason than romance to the arrangement. From Stradivari's point of view he had much left to achieve; a settled home life would be a distinct advantage. To Antonia, who brought no dowry to the marriage, the famous craftsman and the security he represented must have seemed infinitely preferable to the spinsterhood that would have been the destiny of most thirty-five-year-olds in her position.

So began the 'golden period', when Stradivari's drive for perfection led to the violins, and later cellos, that remain the most highly prized in the world. From about 1700 the workshop produced them in ever greater numbers. Acoustically, of course, that final redesign of the soundbox is their most important attribute, but there is far more to them than that. The deep red of the varnish – another innovation dating to the Long Strad years – makes the golden-yellow of the Amatis and of Stradivari's earlier instruments appear insipid by comparison. The scrolls are emphasized with black edging that when new would have proclaimed the carver's skill but has now largely worn away on nearly every example. Broad edges and wider corners give the violins an almost masculine appearance. Everything about them speaks of confidence, of the luthier's desire to draw attention to his brilliance.

The term 'golden period' may usually be applied to Stradivari's instruments, but it might just as well be used of his personal circumstances: wealth and contentment far removed from the struggles and uncertainties of his earlier life. Whether or not that second marriage was a love match, Stradivari's will would later remember the 'affection which [Antonia had] always demonstrated towards him', and his second family would be almost as numerous as the first. Francesca was born a little over a year after the wedding. She must have been named for her father's first wife, a touching remembrance and by no means an uncommon habit, but also a permanent reminder to her mother of her predecessor. Four sons followed, of whom three survived infancy: Giovanni Battista, Giuseppe and Paolo, the last of them born in January 1708, when his father was sixty-three and his mother forty-three.

Cremona's greatest luthier might have been flourishing, but the same could not be said of his rivals. With the Stradivari workshop now approaching its peak, there was little business left for others. Stradivari's second son, Alessandro, became the priest of the altar of San Raffaele in Cremona in 1705. Part of the benefice was a 3,000 lire [£10,000] mortgage his predecessor held over the Amati workshop. Nicolò's sons had sunk into debt following their father's death; they would never pay Alessandro the 5 per cent interest he was due each year, so that he eventually took possession of part of the Amati house itself. It is a stark illustration of how the fortunes of the Stradivari family increased while those of other luthiers went into decline.

The year 1705 was also when Stradivari adopted a new 'P' ('Prima'?) internal mould to supplement the 'PG' form he first made in 1689. The two have very similar dimensions and the workshop used both in parallel until its master's death. The purpose of the new mould therefore provokes some speculation. It would certainly have helped to keep production flowing as output rose, but one further possibility is suggested by the way modern luthiers work: Francesco was now being allowed to make his own violins. It makes sense for different craftsmen in a workshop to have their own moulds; each can then proceed at his own pace. A third 'G' ('Grande'?) mould was to follow, probably in 1708. It was slightly larger than the other two, but again did not displace them. Perhaps Omobono too was finally being granted more responsibility. If the theory is correct, then we should, one might think, be able to work out who used which form. That this has so far proved impossible is partly a tribute to the workshop's standardization, and partly a reflection of the fact that Stradivari, having delegated scrolls to Francesco, kept the other fine work to himself.

One further characteristic of Stradivari's golden period instruments is that they are made from superb wood. It may be that Stradivari could now afford to buy the best materials, or it may simply have been luck. However it happened, around 1709 he acquired a particularly good block of maple, large enough to make backs of one piece, even when cut on the quarter. Its figure is especially striking and can be seen recurring in violins made by the workshop for the next six or seven years. The *Viotti* was one of the first of them. Made in 1709 on the 'PG' mould, its tiger-striped back still catches the eye. What must it have looked like when newly made, the varnish iridescent, glowing a fathomless red? It is the second of our five violins.

By this time the Stradivari workshop had started to produce cellos again, following a six-year gap. The hiatus is easy to understand. Stradivari must have been so

excited by the capabilities of the violins made according
to his new model that for a time he concentrated all his
energies into their construction. After a few years, however, he started considering what principles he could carry
across to their larger siblings.

The result was a radical redesign of the cello: soundboxes whose flatter archings reflect what Stradivari had
learnt from his violins and whose length, at 29 inches, is
now regarded as ideal. These cellos not only meet the
challenge of tone projection common to all string instruments, but also strike the ideal balance between sonorous
bass and vibrant treble that is a more specific problem
for cellos. They would become a template for generations
of cello-makers.

Stradivari continued to use the 'B' ('Buono'?) mould
around which these cellos were constructed for more than
twenty years. In 1712, he used it to produce the third of
our six instruments, the *Davidov* cello. Bought by one
of the last of the Medicis to rule Florence, the incompe-
tent and intolerant Cosimo III, this gorgeous orange-red
instrument probably represents the final chapter in that
family's long association with Cremona.

IN 1714 Stradivari turned seventy. He had been the
greatest luthier in Europe for thirty years. No one
would have predicted the semi-deification that would
be accorded to him by posterity, but he had certainly
become one of Cremona's most substantial citizens. In
1714 alone he made two separate investments totalling
12,000 lire [£50,000]. One was in a pastry shop that soon
failed, although Stradivari did not lose his entire stake.

The other was a loan which gave Stradivari a mortgage over a substantial garden outside the walls of Cremona. It is easy to imagine that the saying 'as rich as Stradivari' really did become current on the streets of his city, as nineteenth-century writers claimed.

The most interesting aspect of that pastry-shop investment is the man whose witnessing signature appears on the partnership deed. Gasparo Visconti was born in Cremona, and went on to study the violin with Corelli for five years around the end of the seventeenth century. He had subsequently been a popular soloist as far afield as London. The presence of his signature on that document is the first proof that Stradivari was friendly with some of the great musicians of his era. One similar piece of evidence comes in 1731, seventeen years later, when Omobono Stradivari helped to arrange a marriage between a neighbour and the daughter of another virtuoso, Tommaso Vitali. He travelled to Vitali's home in Modena, about 100 miles away, to do so. Moreover, in 1715 Dresden's Director of Music, Jean-Baptiste Volumier, arrived in Cremona. Another fine violinist, friendly with Johann Sebastian Bach, he waited for three months until the twelve violins he had ordered from Stradivari were ready. We can begin to see the workshop in the Piazza San Domenico as a meeting-place for musicians, discussing ideas and making suggestions to the great master.

So it seems fitting that production was not only at a peak during the decade that began in 1710, but that its middle years saw a greater concentration of Stradivari's masterworks than any comparable period. We will follow two. The *Lipiński* was produced in 1715. Made on the 'G' mould, it was one of the largest violins the workshop ever produced. The back required four pieces of maple: the two standard slices cut on the quarter had to be augmented with two further inserts in the lower, wider, 'hips' of the instrument. The way in which Stradivari made do with the materials available is typical. He was only a perfectionist in the areas that mattered, and he must have known that this would not: the *Lipiński* would be in continuous employment for over 200 years.

Stradivari's greatest biographers, the Hill brothers, may have been thinking of the *Lipiński* when they wrote: 'Stradivari seems to have awakened to the fact that his work had assumed an air of breadth and solidity through-out, which, treated by less skilful hands, would have bordered on the clumsy. He therefore determined to retrace his steps, and immediately gives us, amongst others, an example which for lightness of build takes us back ten years.' They are describing Stradivari's decision in 1716 to make the *Messiah*, the fourth of our violins. Made on the 'PG' mould, with a two-piece back and covered in Stradivari's classic red varnish, the *Messiah*'s flatness, especially in the belly, sharp edges and 'slanting, youthful soundholes' seem to have set it apart from the rest of the workshop's output. It would become the most famous Strad of all, seducing successive owners in a way that seems almost mystical. Perhaps the first of them was Stradivari himself. In 1715 he had needed three months to meet Volumier's order; yet the *Messiah*, made one year later, would never be sold. It was still in the luthier's possession on the day he died.

*

By 1720 Stradivari was entering his late seventies and the golden period was coming to an end. The violins start to show signs of age in their craftsmanship: the corner points are shorter, the carving clumsier, and the sound-holes placed less exactly. Moreover, they are made with inferior materials. From 1722 the workshop returned to using native maple, or *Oppio*, whose smaller curls do not show off the varnish so well. This may have been an attempt to cut costs. The whole of northern Italy experienced an economic slowdown in the 1720s and luthiers were as badly affected as any other trade. Demand fell behind production. From this time on a significant proportion of the workshop's output went into stock.

Perhaps if conditions had been better Stradivari would have considered handing over the reins to one of his sons. It is more likely that neither Francesco nor Omobono had shown the aptitude or ambition to take over. The former was at least dutiful. Stradivari's will describes him as 'the principal support of the profession of the said Testator, having always been, as he is, obedient and obsequious to the Testator's demands'. Omobono, on the other hand, was better educated than his father, a man about town and frequenter of at least five different religious confraternities, the only real social organizations of the period. Every now and then he performed some service on his father's behalf, chasing an unpaid debt, or helping to arrange that marriage to Vitali's son. But he could clearly be spared by the workshop in a way that suggests his value to it was only marginal.

Given the opportunity to spread his wings, would either brother have flourished, or were they really best employed as closely supervised workmen? Was it really their choice to remain unmarried, living in their father's house, for their entire lives? It must have suited Stradivari to have two trustworthy workers, free from external distractions. Even so, he must occasionally have wondered what would happen to his expertise and business after his death. One possibility is that he had his eye on a third helper in the workshop. For there is a striking curiosity about the violins from the 1720s: an apparent narrowness to their soundholes. It seems to be the result of the knife that cut the holes being held at a different angle from before. Stradivari was finally trusting someone else to take responsibility for his soundholes.

That someone cannot have been Francesco or Omobono; their occasional examples of f-holes do not look like this. The most likely possibility is Giovanni Battista, eldest son of Stradivari's second marriage, born in 1703 and now entering his maturity. It would have been characteristic of the old patriarch to determine that the children of his second family should follow similar careers to those of his first. The eldest daughter, Francesca, was to become the bride, not of a Cremonese burgher like her predecessor, but of Christ. In 1719 she joined the Convent of the Holiest Annunciation of San Giorgio, in a suburb of Mantua, as Sister Rosa. The second son to survive infancy, Giuseppe, would become a priest like Alessandro. He was ordained in 1728. That left the oldest and youngest sons of the second marriage, Giovanni Battista and Paolo. The latter would eventually be found a trade – Stradivari probably had the same plans once for Omobono. Giovanni Battista, on the other hand, was almost certainly always destined for the workshop, where he would have started as an apprentice some time between eleven and thirteen, around 1714–16. If so, and if his father really was trusting him to cut soundholes only a few years later, something that he scarcely ever delegated before, then the idea that he saw him as a potential successor seems entirely possible.

Within a few years, however, and before he was even twenty-four, Giovanni Battista was dead. Whatever hopes Stradivari had for his son were buried with him in the newly acquired family tomb, in the Church of San Domenico's Chapel of the Rosary. A devastating blow for any father, the loss must have given the octogenarian luthier intimations of his own mortality. Around this time he finally passed on responsibility for cellos to Francesco. The larger instruments simply required more effort than he was able to give them. Within two years he was ready for his own death. The date 1729 is carved on his tombstone, together with his name, in lettering that only partly conceals the name of the grave's previous occupants.

If the premature gravestone alone were not indication enough of Stradivari's frame of mind, 1729 is also the year he drew up his will. It is a remarkable document, consisting of a handwritten draft, the longest autograph manuscript left behind by any of the great classical luthiers, together with three increasingly elaborate legal versions. That first draft is what truly catches the attention. The writing is vigorous; whatever the evidence from his violins, the author can still wield a pen. The contents, however, tell a different story. Stradivari designates Francesco as the master or owner (*patro*) of the workshop, the storeroom (and therefore its contents) and, touchingly, 'the room where I sleep where I am now'. For the first time he had truly named a successor.

That first draft of the will has only vitriol for Omobono, Stradivari's other luthier son; the trip to Naples still rankled. By the final notarized version he does receive something, along with all the other children: modest competencies, enough to pay a small income, but hardly sufficient for independence. A suggestion in an intermediate draft that gave Omobono the right to choose some tools did not make it to the final version. Francesco remained, in all ways, his father's anointed heir, exhorted above all, and many times, to keep the family together.

The will reached its final version in the convent of Augustinian Fathers attached to the Church of San Agostino in Cremona on 6 April 1729. Stradivari signed it in the presence of a notary and two assistants, and seven Augustinian priests. This was the only time he used this firm of notaries; and the decision to formalize the will in a convent was itself unusual: the normal venue would have been the notary's office. It seems clear that Stradivari wanted to keep the existence of the will secret from its beneficiaries. The desire to control, to spring surprises from beyond the grave, is all at one with the dictatorial tone of the will itself. No other document sheds as much light on the character and life of the world's greatest luthier. It even gives us the best contemporary valuation of his instruments: a proportion of the cash legacies is in the form of violins; and Stradivari values six at 1,000 Cremonese lire. To the Master himself, therefore, one of his violins was worth 166 lire [£700]. The whole bundle of documents was only discovered in 1995, by researchers on the trail of an entirely different Cremonese luthier. It was still in the archives of the notaries with which it was originally lodged.

Prepared for death, freed of many responsibilities, Stradivari continued to work. The routine was all he knew. Did he even consider, as he began a violin, that he might never finish it? If so, he must have been energized by the thought, rather than inhibited. For the violins he made after 1730 are among the most powerful of all. There was a time, in the first half of the twentieth century, when if a great soloist played a Strad, it was from the 1730s. Perhaps, as some have suggested, increasing deafness led Stradivari to search for an ever more vibrant sound; more probably he was galvanized into action by a far greater motivator – competition.

For the early part of the eighteenth century the Stradivari workshop had all but eclipsed its Cremonese rivals. Even so, some families had managed to keep going, among them the Guarneris. The first of them, Andrea, had been a pupil of Nicolò Amati. Two of his sons followed him as luthiers; one, Pietro, went to Mantua, while the other, Giuseppe, remained in Cremona; born in 1666, he would spend his whole working life in the shadow of his famous neighbour. Giuseppe too taught his craft to two sons; the elder of them, also called Pietro, again would leave for greener pastures, in his case Venice. The other, Giuseppe Guarneri 'del Gesù' (his labels carry the cipher 'IHS' – the Greek abbreviation for Jesus – underneath a cross) would remain in Cremona.

Compared to Stradivari's seventy years, del Gesù's decade and a half of brilliance was brief, but it began

around 1730. He was clearly influenced by both Stradivari and his own father (whose hand, in a poignant
reversal of the Stradivaris' practice, can be seen in the
scrolls of many of his son's instruments), but he went
further than either. Del Gesù are the only consistent
alternatives to Strads for the virtuoso soloist: dark,
powerful and responsive. Roughly worked, occasionally
even slipshod, there is little evidence that they were
much valued in their maker's lifetime, at least by most
purchasers. Stradivari, however, must have known differently. Conscious of his younger rival, he determined to
maintain his own standards.

The *Khevenhüller*, the fifth and last of our violins,
proves the longevity of Stradivari's genius. Made in 1733,
on the 'G' mould, the largest of them all, with a single-
piece back and a reddish-brown varnish, it is tonally
magnificent. Among the Stradivari workshop's later
violins, it seems to be one of those that are almost
entirely the work of the Master himself. Perhaps that is
connected to its other remarkable, though not unique,
characteristic, the handwritten annotation on its label,
'Anni 90' ('ninety years old', or 'in the ninetieth year').
The labels on about ten violins carry similar inscriptions,
the earliest from 1727 with its 'fatto de Anni 83'. Most
probably they were made by a later owner of the instruments, although he would have had to possess every one.
But the tantalizing possibility remains that it is the old
luthier himself addressing us down the centuries: 'Yes,
I may not be as young as I was, yes, I may have had to
hand on most of my business to less talented sons, but
I can still make my own violins.' Later addition or not,
and in the absence of any official record of Stradivari's

age, it is these proud but shaky scrawls that give the first indication of his birthdate.

It must be to around the time Stradivari made the *Khevenhüller* that we owe the one even vaguely authentic eyewitness account of the master luthier. According to François Fétis, Stradivari's first biographer, writing in the mid-nineteenth century,

> Polledro, late first violin at the chapel Royal of Turin, who died a few years ago, at a very advanced age, declared that his master had known Stradivari, and that he was fond of talking about him. He was, he said, tall and thin. Habitually covered with a cap of white wool in winter, and of cotton in summer, he wore over his clothes an apron of white leather when he worked; and as he was always working, his costume scarcely ever varied.

It is a powerful image of the workaholic genius. Only a spoilsport would complain that Polledro's master, Gaetano Pugnani, seems to have remembered an awful lot for someone who was no more than ten when Stradivari died.

Meanwhile, Stradivari continued to direct his family's affairs. In the same year that he made the *Khevenhüller* he paid 20,000 lire [£80,000] to make Paolo, his youngest son, the junior partner of a Cremonese cloth-merchant. Four years later, in September 1737, he found Paolo a wife, or at least approved the match, overseeing the formal transfer to him of Elena Templari's dowry. At last he could expect future generations of Stradivaris, their fortunes built on the money he had earned from his violins.

The dowry transfer was to be the ageing luthier's last formal act. He had already buried his second wife Antonia in March that year; and now death was approaching for him too. Since 1734 Stradivari's pace of work had finally slowed. But it had not come to a halt. Three violins are known to exist even from that last year. Posterity has assigned to one of them the status of being his last work, and given it the appropriate title 'Chant du Cygne' (swansong). Antonio Stradivari died on 19 December 1737. He was buried beside his wife in the Church of San Domenico, opposite the house where they had lived together for almost forty years.

Chapter Five

'SO SINGULAR AND SO BEAUTIFUL'

The violins of Giuseppe Tartini and Paolo Stradivari

I dreamt one night in 1713 that I had made a compact with the devil for my soul. Everything went at my command; my novel servant anticipated my every wish and surpassed all my desires. Finally I thought of handing him my violin to see what he would do with it. Great was my astonishment when I heard a sonata so singular and so beautiful, played with such superiority and intelligence, that I had never heard the like, nor even conceived that something so lovely might be possible. I felt such pleasure – rapture, surprise – that my breath failed: the violence of the sensation awoke me. I immediately seized my violin, trying to reproduce the sounds I had heard, but in vain. The piece I then composed is truly the best I ever wrote, and I called it 'The Devil's Sonata', but it is so inferior to what I heard that if I could have subsisted on other means I would have broken my violin and abandoned music for ever.

GIUSEPPE TARTINI'S story of how he came to write his most famous composition evokes an image of violinists

Figure 10. 'Finally I thought of handing him my violin to see what he would do with it.' Tartini's dream, from an engraving by L. Boilly, 1824.

in league with Satan that still resonates today. It is probably responsible for a large part of Tartini's continuing fame, although there are better reasons than that. But it is his ownership of one of our five violins that brings him into this narrative – the massive *Lipiński*, made by Stradivari in 1715. He may even have been its first purchaser.

Tartini was born in Pirano in 1692, the son of a pious noble. He received his first musical instruction at ecclesiastical school, before abandoning thoughts of the cloth and going to study law at the University of Padua. Here he kept up his violin playing and began to teach the instrument, but appears to have spent most of his time fencing – his skill was enough to see off any challenger. He even considered a future career teaching sword-play in Naples.

All these interests, however, were put on hold when Tartini secretly married a pupil. Both parties were still under twenty. Moreover, Elisabetta was the daughter of a dependant of the Archbishop of Padua, Cardinal Giorgio Cornaro, who took a dim view of the marriage. Cut off by his parents and subject to proceedings from a vengeful cardinal, Tartini fled both Padua and his bride, eventually finding refuge in a monastery at Assisi, where a relative had taken the vows.

As tradition has it, the serenity of monastic life instigated a complete change in Tartini's character. He eschewed martial pursuits and devoted himself to his violin, so that his musical contribution to services in the monastery chapel came to be welcomed. Still fearing retribution from the Cardinal, however, Tartini remained hidden behind a curtain, from which the other-worldly sounds of his violin would emerge. It took two years for him to be exposed, when a gust of wind blew aside the drapes during a well-attended service. A Paduan native recognized the object of Cornaro's wrath and reported back. But time had mollified His Eminence; he gave retrospective consent to the secret marriage. Husband and wife were reunited and the career of the eighteenth century's most influential violinist was back on track.

One year later Tartini set off for Venice, where he had been invited to compete with the great Francesco Veracini, famous for his phrase 'There is but one God, and one Veracini.' That was more than mere bravado. When Tartini heard Veracini he realized how much he had to learn, particularly when it came to bow-control, and retired mortified. Once again Elisabetta was to lose her husband. She was sent to Tartini's brother in Pirano, and the violinist himself headed for Ancona on Italy's Adriatic Coast, and a further period of study.

It was around this time, probably in 1716, that Tartini made a pilgrimage to Cremona to hear Stradivari's friend, the violinist Gasparo Visconti. The virtuoso made a deep impression on Tartini, who would later say that Visconti's unique God-given style of playing had been born and died with him. Once in Cremona, the ambitious young violinist must have sought out Stradivari himself. I imagine him joining the workshop conversation, trying out various violins, finally settling on the *Lipiński*. The evidence for his ownership of it is third-hand, but Tartini could not have had a better violin than this as he went on to develop the techniques that were destined to bring the best out of the Stradivari model.

When Tartini returned to Padua from Ancona, armed

with the *Lipiński*, it was as one of the most complete
violinists of his era. In 1721 he was appointed to the
post of first violin at Padua's Cappella del Santo. The
letter of appointment calls him an extraordinary violinist and states that he need not provide any proof of his
excellence in his profession. That was a rare concession,
an indication of the reputation Tartini already enjoyed.
So was another unusual privilege, the right to play elsewhere. In 1723 Tartini used it, going to Prague to play at
the coronation of the Emperor Charles VI. His prime
motivation for the trip was probably to avoid scandal: a
Venetian innkeeper had accused him of fathering her
recently born child.

Tartini's success in Prague was proof enough of his
virtuosic abilities. He was to remain there for three
lucrative years, but in 1726, finding, as he wrote to his
brother, that 'the skin is nearer than the purse', he
returned to Padua. He never left Italy again. Posterity
has blamed the nervous disposition of his wife for this
unwillingness to travel. If that is true, one might think
she could scarcely be criticized for it.* In any case, Tartini
was to have a pan-European influence not as a player
but as a teacher, for in 1728 he established one of the
first serious training programmes for young violinists,
in an academy that came to be known as the 'School of
Nations'.

With no children of his own, Tartini had an almost
paternal regard for his students. At least seventy of them

---

* Few biographies, however, have a kind word for her. In later years,
supposedly embittered by childlessness, she would acquire the reputation of a shrew.

have been identified from all over Europe, and they returned the devotion. The most famous, Pietro Nardini, whose playing was said to bring tears into the eyes of stony-hearted courtiers, returned to Padua to attend to his master during his final illness in 1770; an attack of 'convulsive paralysis' in 1768 was subsequently complicated by a cancerous growth in Tartini's foot. Another student was Maddalena Lombardini, one of the first female virtuosi. Tartini's letter of instruction to her, written in 1760, was still being used as a basis for tuition in the twentieth century.

Gaetano Pugnani, witness as a child to Stradivari's labours, was not a formal student of Tartini, but at one time went to him for guidance. The story has it that he began to play, to be interrupted almost at once with a cry of 'No, too loud.' Pugnani recommenced, only to hear an immediate 'No, too soft.' There must have been more to the lessons than this. Pugnani had an ego to match Veracini's – 'with a violin in my hand I am Caesar' – but reputedly regarded his time with Tartini as the making of him. Finally, there is one other student whose name has simply been handed down as 'Signor Salvini'. He has made no particular mark on history, unless he is the Salvini who had printed, in 1785 in Florence, six duos for violin and viola. Apparently one of Tartini's 'most promising pupils', it was to him that the 'Master of Nations' passed on his Stradivarius, the *Lipiński*, and it is in his possession that we will encounter the violin again, in 1818.

*

TARTINI'S ACCOUNT of composing The Devil's Sonata was first published by a French traveller, Hubert Lalande, in 1769. His book, *Voyage d'un François en Italie*, is something like an early Baedeker, recording its author's impressions of all Italy's major towns. Lalande sought out Tartini; he was clearly interested in violins; so it is natural to turn to his pages on Cremona to see what he found of note in the greatest of all violin-making towns. The answer is – its Torazzo, the highest medieval tower in Italy. There is not a word about the industry that had made the town famous for more than 200 years. Its traditions were practically dead.

The seeds of the decline must surely have been apparent even as the Stradivari family gathered around their father's deathbed on that gloomy December day in 1737. They may have been surprised by the existence of the will, drawn up so secretly almost a decade before, but they can hardly have been shocked at its contents. Omobono would have been long aware of his father's displeasure at his Neapolitan adventure; one imagines a rueful smile as he hears that his 5,000-lire inheritance is to be reduced by a 2,000-lire debt assigned to the time he spent away. Alessandro had died five years before, and Caterina, Sister Rosa and Giuseppe were presumably reconciled by now to their lives as, respectively, spinster, nun and priest. Their small inheritances gave them a little more independence, but not enough to change their lives. One returned to the convent; the others continued to live in their father's house. Paolo presumably accepted his legacy gratefully; newly married, he was surely expecting his expenses to increase. For the time being, the cloth-merchant and his wife also remained in the Piazza San Domenico.

And what of Francesco, the ever-faithful son? Left everything else – house, cash, instruments and tools – and named his father's executor, he was now a rich man. Presumably he would have ensured that the six masses his father requested were said over the body. It was a matter in which Antonio had placed himself 'entirely in the piety and love of Francesco, in whom he especially confides', and the request was eminently reasonable; contemporary Cremonese testators made much more elaborate dispositions. Dutiful as ever, he seems to have obeyed his father's admonishment to prevent the dispersal of the family 'if it will be possible': his newly inherited house would not be his own after all. And then what?

Francesco had been his father's assistant for over fifty years: 'the principal support of the profession of the said Testator, having always been, as he is, obedient and obsequious to the Testator's commands'. Who would grudge him his retirement? Already sixty-six and without his father's energy or single-mindedness, he was past any realistic age of marrying or of gearing up the workshop by taking on apprentices. He seems to have settled down to a well-deserved rest. Francesco survived his father by less than six years, dying in May 1743; by then Omobono too was dead. Since their father's death each had only made a handful of violins.

Antonio Stradivari's career had spanned over seventy years. He is estimated to have made at least twelve hundred instruments, from tiny 'pochettes' used by dancing masters to the enormous 'churchbass' cellos of his early years. He fathered eleven children, of whom nine survived infancy; five were still living in his house the year after his death and two had worked with him for upwards of fifty years. He had brought the craft of violin-making to a peak which no predecessor could have imagined, and in doing so had gained the recognition of archbishops, dukes and kings across Europe. He had not, however, created a violin-making dynasty. By living to such a great age, and by keeping a tight hold of the reins for so long, the old patriarch had, ironically, ensured that his commitment to excellence died with him.

On Francesco's death, the house and all its contents, including about a hundred unsold instruments, were all inherited by the lucky Paolo. Within three years he had moved his young family and his surviving siblings out of the Piazza San Domenico. The new occupants, luthier Carlo Bergonzi and his children, must have been Paolo's employees as well as tenants. Those unsold violins were unplayable; each would have needed a tailpiece, strings, bridge, soundpost and pegs at the very least. Paolo needed the Bergonzis simply to help him prepare his inheritance for sale. His family's knowledge of violin-making was truly lost.

It may seem difficult to understand now why Stradivari did not try harder to record his methods – 'secrets' is probably too strong a word – for succeeding generations. The consequence may be his immortality, through having produced instruments that have never been matched, but he could hardly have been planning for that. In fact he was meticulous about keeping records of his experiments, storing each mould with associated drawings that gave details such as the position of the soundholes. They were good enough for anybody trained by him to follow. Francesco and Omobono's instruments certainly have an excellent tone. The real problem was the breaking of the master–apprentice chain after Stradivari's death. Nicolò Amati had been very much the exception in taking on apprentices outside his family; he was forced to do so by plague and demand. Antonio Stradivari had his sons to assist him. As a bachelor, Francesco did not. The workshop he inherited had no apprentices.

More puzzling, perhaps, is why some of the more general techniques known to all the Cremonese luthiers – most famously that formula for varnish – were lost so soon after Stradivari's death. The simplest answer lies in technological progress. Cremonese varnish is soft to the point of fragility: grip a Strad too firmly and the palm-print is clearly visible on its surface, too much rough treatment and the bare wood is exposed. Moreover, the necessary drying time had been bothering the Cremonese since the time of Galileo, whose nephew ended up with an old violin because Father Micanzio would not wait for 'the strong heat of the sun' to bring a new one 'to perfection'. These disadvantages were felt by other wood-workers, who in the course of the eighteenth century moved to a tougher and quicker-drying varnish that used a spirit base. Nothing would have been more natural than for luthiers to follow their lead. One suspects that Stradivari, with his innate knowledge of acoustics, would have known better than to coat his violins in such a rigid substance. But he and his contemporaries were all dead.

Underlying all this is the final reason why there was such a rapid fall-off in the quality of Cremonese instruments after the death of Stradivari. The slackening in demand that had started in the 1720s continued. In the almost 200 years since the violin form had been perfected, the towns of northern Italy and their competitors over the Alps had produced thousands of the highest-quality instruments. It had been known for at least fifty years that wooden instruments produced a better tone after a period of ageing. Why waste money on a modern master-piece, when a fully mature equivalent was available for the same price? In a few decades, of course, this equation would change spectacularly, but for most of the eight-eenth century, old violins would remain relatively cheap.

Moreover, Strads were not even the most sought-after or expensive of the old violins. The need for a bigger tone that Stradivari had been anticipating from his Long Strad period onwards had still not really arrived. A virtuoso might give the occasional public performance, probably acting as his own impresario, but he would generally remain dependent on the patronage of a court or great noble family. In these circumstances, playing for select gatherings in small private rooms, the relatively young Strads performed probably rather worse than the famously sweet-toned Amatis. Even these, however, were generally felt to be inferior to the violins made by Jacob Stainer in the Tyrol. High-built, with small grace-fully curved soundholes and a silvery tone, by 1770 Stainers were regarded as the epitome of their craft.

IT WAS a propitious time for the first great accumula-tor of Strads, and archetype for many that followed, to come on to the scene. Count Cozio di Salabue was born in Casale in Piedmont in 1755. Educated at the Military

Academy, he became an ensign in the Saluzzo cavalry. Like Tartini, however, his thoughts soon strayed from this conventional career as he started to take an interest in violins. The spark seems to have been his inheritance of a 1666 violin by Nicolò Amati. Cozio had wealth and connections, and subsequent generations of collectors could only envy his luck at being in the right place at the right time.

The Count was only eighteen when he came into contact with Giovanni Battista Guadagnini, a sixty-three-year-old almost itinerant luthier who had fetched up in Turin. An odd relationship ensued. On the one hand, Cozio conceived it as his duty to reverse the decline in the art of violin-making and would not shirk from telling the older luthier how to do his job; on the other, he depended on Guadagnini for much of the knowledge he was seeking to preserve. Perhaps not surprisingly, the two parted company after only four years, but it was a time that saw the luthier produce some of his best work, and his patron develop an appreciation for Strads that was decades ahead of his contemporaries. Cozio soon understood, as he later noted: 'They still say of Antonio Stradivari in Cremona "while other makers did what they could, Stradivari did with violins as he wanted".'

It was not long before Cozio was in touch with Stradivari's youngest son. Paolo had been making a tidy living from his inheritance. Of the violins left to him by Francesco only thirteen remained by the time he first heard from the Count in 1775. All ended up in Cozio's collection. Among them was at least one of our violins, the *Messiah*. Made in the Stradivari workshop in 1716, it had been passed on first to Francesco and then to Paolo.

So pristine as to be apparently freshly made, it must have been one of the violins that led the Count to demand from Paolo an affidavit confirming that all were the work of Stradivari and his sons. Cozio recognized his 'most large and beautiful violin of 1716' as a masterpiece, later writing of its exquisite workmanship, perfect quality of wood, and powerful, even tone.

Paolo had sold all the violins, but the Count still wanted more. He pestered Paolo for information about his father, to the cloth-merchant's increasing exasperation; in one reply he suggests the Count goes to ask his questions at Stradivari's grave. One piece of information the Count gleaned was that Antonio was ninety-three when he died: some have suggested that it is his handwriting that gives the Master's age on the labels of later instruments.

Finally, in May 1776, Paolo offered Cozio all his father's tools and drawings, asking 28 gigliati [£1,000] for them. The Count's response was to offer 5; Paolo eventually accepted 6, to be paid at once into the hands of a silk-stocking manufacturer, 'to show you the desire I have to please you, and so that not a single thing belonging to my father be left in Cremona.' It is an odd sentiment to hear from a son who owed so much to his father. Perhaps it was a final flash of resentment at the way Stradivari had controlled the lives of all his sons. Perhaps Paolo simply wanted to bring the correspondence to a close. Or perhaps he realized that for his father's relics to be treasured they had to be in the hands of a connoisseur; Cremona was no longer the place for them.

Paolo did not enjoy the fruits of the final liquidation of his father's legacy for very long. He died in October that same year, before the tools had even been dispatched. His son Antonio attempted to extract more money from the Count, claiming that a newly discovered chest had not been included in the sale. Whether or not he was successful, everything that had remained in the Stradivari family's possession was soon in Cozio's hands.

There is no record of what Cozio paid Paolo for the violins themselves. We know from other correspondence between them, however, that a Strad could be bought in 1775 for 10 gigliati [£400]. Prices had fallen since Stradivari's own valuation in 1729; Paolo's offloading of his inheritance over the years can hardly have helped. By comparison, an Amati was sold in the same year for 40 gigliati. Within twenty years, however, all was to change. A new era in violin playing was dawning, and it was heralded by the ground-breaking talent of one remarkable man.

Chapter Six

'MY VIOLIN SHOULD REALIZE A LARGE SUM'

Viotti and his Strad

ON 13 MARCH 1782 *Mémoires Secrets,* a Parisian news-paper, carried an intriguing notice: 'Monsieur Viotti, a foreign violinist, who has not yet appeared in public here ... will be making his debut at the Concert Spirituel over the next fortnight.' The writer little knew it, but he was alerting his readership to a series of concerts that would change the course of violin playing for ever, not just in Paris, but throughout Europe. The concerts would also, almost incidentally, ensure that Stradivarius violins finally deposed their weaker-toned rivals as the instruments of preference for both players and audience.

Of course, Giovanni Battista Viotti's audience would not have known this. What it did know was that the Concert Spirituel was the place to be heard and seen in Paris, and the premier musical venue in Europe. London or Vienna might have rivalled the French capital as cosmopolitan centres, but they did not have the same music publishing industry or pan-European influence. An artist who succeeded at the Concert Spirituel could expect success anywhere. On the other hand, secure in the knowledge of its own influence, the Parisian public also knew what it liked; this was not likely to be Viotti. The French had a deep distrust for Italian performers, and extended that distrust to the use of the violin itself as a solo instrument. The tradition of violin playing in France had been built on the Vingt-Quatre Violons du Roi, as much an ensemble as its name suggests and the very antithesis of individual virtuosity. As late as 1740 Hubert Le Blanc, a French writer, had published his defence of the bass viol 'contre les entreprises du violon et les prétentions du violoncelle'.* In his opinion, 'Sultan Violin' was 'undersized, a pygmy', which 'not content with Italy, its inheritance, proposed to invade the neighbouring states'.

Le Blanc may have been an anachronism even as he was writing, but he was not alone in his opinions. A few years later the French violinist André-Noël Pagin, a pupil of Tartini who played at the Concert Spirituel from 1747 to 1750, was hissed by audiences for 'daring to play in the Italian style'. There was little doubt that over the preceding century Gallic amour-propre had caused French violinists and audiences to miss out on the enormous uplift in technique that had been set in train by Corelli and Tartini and their followers.

It was time to shock the Parisian public out of its complacency, and Viotti was the man to do it. Since its foundation in 1725, the Concert Spirituel had been based at the Tuileries Palace, originally built by Catherine de Medici as her Paris residence. The Salle des Suisses, one of the first-floor state rooms, was certainly imposing, but it can hardly have been designed for acoustics. Its

---

* 'against the ventures of the violin and the pretentions of the cello'.

3,000 square feet could accommodate an audience of several hundred, standing, in tiered banquettes and in boxes around the room's perimeter. These last would house society ladies, there to see and be seen. Stepping on to the stage at the end of an already full programme, the young virtuoso must have seemed a forlorn figure, barely visible through an atmosphere already hazy from the room's nine chandeliers, each containing up to sixteen candles. Nevertheless, there must have been a sense of anticipation, the same buzz that fills a modern concert-hall. A report of a single private performance that Viotti had given since his arrival in Paris a few weeks before had declared that he 'knocked the bow from the hands of all our great masters'. He would hardly have been booked to play on Good Friday – the biggest date in the Concert Spirituel's whole year – if great things had not been expected of him.

Presumably the hush spread from the front as the maestro prepared to play. The best-placed may have noticed his violin: a little over seventy years old, the varnish hardly worn, just entering its maturity. Their eyes would have been caught by the back, a single piece of maple with a glorious tiger-stripe pattern. Only the most knowledgeable would have noticed its shape: the flatter arch of the belly, compared with the more rounded Stainers and Amatis that were usually played in the Concert Spirituel. Perhaps one or two realized it was a Stradivarius.

That first programme from 17 March 1782 simply tells us that Viotti played a concerto of his own composition. Listening, his audience must have become aware that they were hearing something quite unlike anything they had witnessed before. Some would have realized that violins would never sound the same again; others were simply nonplussed. In the subsequent press reports there was no disagreement about Viotti's technique; his virtuosity was a given, but he was not really pushing these boundaries. The real controversy was over his tone. Disoriented by the novelty of Viotti's sound, at least one listener described his playing as 'abrupt and halting, sacrificing the feeling and the spirit of his sub-ject to his desire to draw extraordinary sounds from his instrument'.

Such criticisms did not persist. With further perform-ances, audiences were repeatedly struck by the expressive richness of Viotti's tone, by the way he made the violin resemble a voice in song, by his particular exploitation both of the sonorous qualities of the lowest string and the soaring aspiration of the highest. By April 1783 *Le Mercure* was prepared to say, 'It seems that other artists are beginning to forgive him for not having been born in France': high praise indeed. Viotti's influence among French violinists was assured. They all wanted to imitate his sound, and that meant playing on a Stradivarius.

VIOTTI's violin was vital to the beauty of his tone. We last encountered the *Viotti* in Stradivari's workshop, built in 1709 for an unknown client using that single block of maple whose curls can be seen in the backs of so many of the Master's greatest instruments. There is no record of whose hands it had passed through on its way to apotheosis in Paris, nor do we know how Viotti himself came to acquire it. The most romantic theory would make

Figure 11. The tiger-striped back
of Viotti's Stradivarius.

it a love token to him from the Empress Catherine the Great of Russia.

Viotti had arrived in Paris following a series of concerts with his master Pugnani in most of the principal cities of Europe. Their time in St Petersburg had been particularly triumphant, and it was there that Viotti had caught the Empress's eye, introduced by her former lover, and sometime procurer, Prince Potemkin. Viotti was handsome, elegant and charming – attributes only multiplied by his virtuosity with the violin. Catherine would have been fifty at the time, but her predilection for young men was famously undiluted. Although she was then midway through her relationship with the twenty-five-year-old Alexander Laskwi, court gossip at the time never hesitated to link her with multiple lovers. Moreover, she already had a reputation for dalliances with Italian violinists. Her affection for Antonio Lolli during the ten years he had spent at court excited much comment at the time. It was a relationship that almost ended in disaster for the violinist, when Catherine's chief of police misinterpreted his absolute monarch's desire to have her pet spaniel, also called Lolli, stuffed and put into a glass case. Not surprisingly, Lolli left Russia soon afterwards, so his sojourn there did not overlap with Viotti's.

After his initial success with Pugnani in St Petersburg, Viotti left for a short tour of the Russian provinces. On his return an illness apparently forced him to spend twelve months in the capital convalescing. The period seems excessive; but even so the Empress showered him with presents in an effort to persuade him to stay even longer. There is no doubting Catherine's generosity: one lover received at least 100,000 roubles [£2 million] and

5,000 serfs in the course of a two-year relationship. Eventually, however, Viotti brought himself to leave and continue the tour, still with Pugnani, in Berlin and possibly London. Stradivari's instruments had found their way to the Russian court by then and it is quite conceivable that one of Catherine's presents was the superb violin with which Viotti made his – and its maker's – name.

The Russian Empress did not represent Viotti's first encounter with either celebrity or royalty. On an earlier occasion, in Geneva, he and Pugnani had played in front of Voltaire at the very end of the philosopher's life. Viotti's skill was such that their one-man audience confused master with pupil and persisted in calling Viotti 'le célèbre Pugnani' during their entire conversation. The real Pugnani could only mutter, in Franco-Italian patois, 'Cette Voltaire, il est oune bête, il ne sait faire que des traxedies.' ('That Voltaire, he is an idiot, he only knows how to write tragedies.') In Warsaw, Viotti's success was such that he became the hunting partner of King Stanislaus-Augustus himself. Only in Berlin had Viotti's reception been less than triumphant. In a contest between him and Jarnowick (until Viotti's arrival the most celebrated violinist in Europe, and the particular favourite of the Concert Spirituel) the latter was judged to have matched him; Viotti must have been off song.

Viotti could have acquired his Strad at any point on his European tour, but it is equally possible that he found it in his native Italy. He was born in Fontaneto in Piedmont in 1753. His father, a blacksmith with a talent for the horn, first bought him a violin when he was eight at the Crescentino Fair. We can assume that this was not

the *Viotti*. Nevertheless, it was good enough for young
Giovanni who, apart from one year of lessons from a
wandering musician, taught himself until he was thirteen. This was when he appeared in front of a bishop
from Turin, as part of an impromptu orchestra in which
his father was also playing. The bishop knew that the
Marquis of Voghera was looking for a violin-playing
companion for his eighteen-year-old son Alphonse, and
the young Viotti caught his eye and ear. He was given a
letter of recommendation to take to the Marquis in Turin.

We know what happened next from the testimony
of Alphonse himself, who remembered it all more than
sixty years later in 1830. The thirteen-year-old Viotti
arrived in Turin, but was almost sent away immediately
by the Marquis, whose perception of the five-year age gap
was probably rather more realistic than the unworldly
bishop's. By chance, however, a royal chapel musician,
Colognetti, entered during Giovanni's audience with the
Marquis, and insisted that he should at least be heard.
Viotti promptly and perfectly sight-read a relatively easy
Besozzi sonata. Upon being complimented for his prowess, the adolescent merely replied in the local dialect – we
can imagine the shrug – 'That's nothing.' To put him in
his place, therefore, the Marquis demanded that Colognetti test him with something much more difficult. A
sonata by Domenico Ferrari, one of Tartini's most celebrated pupils, was placed in front of the boy, who was
again triumphant. Realizing that there was something
here, Colognetti took him to visit the orchestra, where
Viotti proceeded to sight-read an entire opera. On his
return to the palace, he was asked what he'd enjoyed
most on his tour and reproduced from memory the over-

ture and several themes. His place as a court musician was assured. Furthermore, the Marquis and his son took responsibility for Viotti's musical education, so that he eventually gained no less a master than the virtuoso Pugnani himself. On hearing him, even the phlegmatic Viotti was impressed – 'He is a Jupiter' – and the relationship between master and pupil was to prove remarkably close.

Alphonse estimated, with no regrets, that Viotti's musical education had cost his family 20,000 francs [£70,000]. One small component of that was probably the purchase of the *Viotti* Stradivarius. Pugnani may well have helped to choose it. The prosaic option, perhaps, but it seems most likely that in the sixty or so years before Viotti acquired it, the great instrument had never left northern Italy.

There is one other story of Viotti purchasing a violin, worth repeating because of the light it sheds on his character. It takes us back to Paris in the 1780s, and the period of Viotti's greatest triumphs. Strolling on the Champs-Élysées with a friend, he could not avoid hearing the terrible noises that a blind street musician was producing on what proved to be a tin fiddle. Intrigued by the instrument, which produced a sound closer to a clarinet than a violin, Viotti offered 20 francs [£70] for it. Before the deal was transacted, however, he took the violin out of the old man's hands and played upon it, producing a remarkable and beautiful tone. Meanwhile, his quick-thinking friend passed the hat round the audience that swiftly gathered, and gave the collection to the street musician. When Viotti got his purse out to hand over the 20 francs, the old man thought better of it – 'I did not know the violin was so good. I ought to have at least double the amount for it.' Viotti, pleased with the implied compliment, came up with the greater sum and walked off with his prize, only to feel a tug on his sleeve: it was the musician's tinker nephew, offering to make him as many fiddles as he liked for 6 francs apiece.

So VIOTTI was the toast of Paris. Young violinists were attempting to copy his style; older ones simply acknowledged his greatness. His evenings at the Concert Spirituel were sell-outs and he was sufficiently confident in his position to stalk off the Versailles stage in front of Marie Antoinette when a newly arrived member of the aristocratic audience proved too noisy. Then, quite suddenly and only eighteen months after his first triumphant appearance, Viotti gave up public performance. His contemporaries had numerous theories about this, of which the most reasonable is that he simply didn't enjoy it and the money was not good enough: a whole season might net him no more than 1,200 francs [£4,000].

As it turned out, Viotti's abandonment of the stage only served to deepen his influence. It gave him time to compose and take pupils. Including Alday, Cartier and Rode, while both Kreutzer and Baillot were disciples, the list reads like a recital of the great French violinists of the late eighteenth and early nineteenth centuries. They all started playing on Cremonese instruments, mostly acquired for them by Viotti himself. Many Strads today still bear the name of Viotti somewhere in their pedigree; it is a mark of pride.

*

THERE WAS another way in which Viotti influenced violin playing, again to the benefit of the fuller-toned Stradivarius model: his playing style and compositions demanded the use of a modern bow. And it was around the time that Viotti first arrived in Paris that François Tourte – 'the Stradivarius of the bow' – was putting together the final elements of the design that is still used today.

From a family of bowmakers, Tourte kept a shop in Paris. As the story goes, this was where Viotti came to explain his requirements for a new type of bow. His *cantabile* style required more control and power than was offered by the old model. Tourte's solution incorporated a number of improvements, building on work that had started with Tartini. For the shaft he used a Brazilian wood, Pernambuco; its inward curve, in contrast to the previous convexity, gave the bow greater strength and elasticity, so that the horsehair could be kept at greater tension. This could be adjusted by a nut at the foot of the bow, to which the horsehair was attached by a wedge and metal band, or 'ferrule'. The weight of this arrangement, counterbalanced by a bigger head, added to the bow's momentum. The result gave the violinist greater control, and the increased tautness allowed a greater range of styles, from seamless *legato* to abrupt *sforzando*. Moreover, the bow's greater weight and tension, together with one other change that Tourte made – an increase in width from ¼ to ⁷⁄₁₆ inches – put much more power at the player's disposal. Only with the new bow, indeed, could the full potential of a Strad be realized.

It is possible that these developments would have come together without the inspiration of Viotti. For example, John Dodd in London was producing a similar

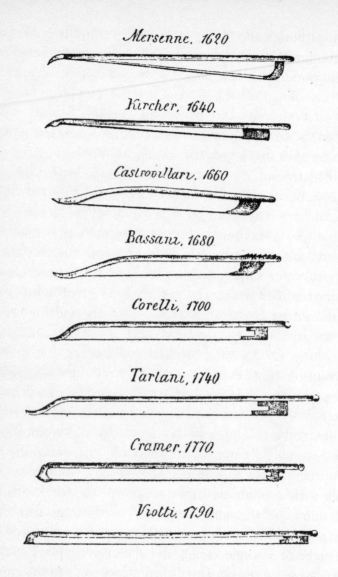

Mersenne. 1620

Kircher. 1640.

Castrovillari. 1660

Bassani. 1680.

Corelli. 1700

Tartani. 1740

Cramer. 1770.

Viotti. 1790.

Figure 12. This sequence of illustrations, from
The Violin and its Story by H. Abele, shows the
changing shape of the violin bow from the beginning
of the seventeenth century to Viotti-Tourte.

bow, although too short, at the same time. It is hard to doubt, however, that the *Viotti* was one of the first violins to sing under the new bow.

Viotti's disappearance from public life does not mean that he gave up playing for friends. He set up in lodgings with his friend, the composer Cherubini, and continued to give masterclasses there every Sunday. As the only place where it was still possible to hear the great man, invitations were hugely sought after. They had to be limited as the apartment was hardly spacious, but their scarcity value only increased Viotti's reputation. Quite apart from his violin playing, all who knew him were impressed by his idealism, his sensitivity and his artistic integrity. An elegiac little book by A. M. d'Eymar, *Anecdotes sur Viotti*, which came out after the French Revolution (it is dated 'An VIII' of the new calendar), paints the best portrait we have of Viotti in this period. The tone is set by an opening statement, grieving both for his absence in exile – 'France, has she therefore lost you for ever?' – and for the death at the guillotine of many who heard him play. Most of the book, however, deals with a single day the author spent with Viotti at the home of the pianist Hélène de Montgeraut: the afternoon in her garden, with the maestro enraptured at the sight of a single violet; and the evening playing the most beautiful music. Later chroniclers were to interpret d'Eymar as implying that the violinist was 'a little more than an admirer' of the pianist.

In about 1788, Viotti's career really did start to take a different turn when he founded an opera company in partnership with Leonard, Marie Antoinette's entrepreneurial hairdresser. The company was initially successful. Under the patronage of the Count of Provence, it commenced performances in the Tuileries. Talented in so many ways, Viotti proved to be a gifted administrator and impresario; he even made a bid for control of the Paris Opera itself.

Viotti was becoming a public figure, but it was the wrong time for that. At first the impact of the Revolution on the music world seemed almost incidental. The particular effect was the removal of the Royal Family from Versailles to the Tuileries, and the consequent displacement of the opera company. Undaunted, Viotti and his backers decided to build their own venue. Accordingly, the Théâtre Feydeau had its opening night on 6 January 1791. Its orchestra included some of the greatest musicians in Paris and the singers were drawn from around Europe. Again there was initial success, but it could not last. Growing political instability led to ever-decreasing audiences, and by August 1792 the theatre was closed. Of more personal importance was the presence of Viotti's name in the infamous 'red book'. At one stage in his career he had held the title of 'Accompanist to the Queen', with the right to an annual stipend of 6,000 livres [£20,000]. He was a marked man, and at the end of 1792 he fled, with the *Viotti*, to London in fear of the guillotine. With his entire fortune sunk into the unsuccessful theatre, he was penniless.

EVENTS HAD conspired to ensure that Viotti would be heard by an entirely new audience. With no money, he was forced to turn back to public performance, appearing at concerts in Hanover Square organized by Johann Salomon, the German violinist who had moved to London in 1782. Salomon's arrival had already revitalized the London music scene, drawing Joseph Haydn to the British capital in 1791 and leading to a request for violin lessons from King George III himself.*

Salomon knew what he was doing when he engaged his Italian rival and the British press was quick to endorse his choice. In the words of *The Oracle*, in February 1793, Viotti was 'original and sublime – he reaches at unattempted grandeur'. According to *The Morning Chronicle*, 'Viotti, it is true ... astonishes the hearer; but he does something infinitely better – he awakens emotion, gives a soul to sound, and leads the passions captive.' In short, and almost despite himself, Viotti ensured that Londoners became as aware of the necessity of owning a Stradivarius as Parisians had ten years before. For the next 100 years Great Britain, as the most prosperous economy in the world, was to act as a magnet for Strads from around Europe.

Reconciled to public performance, and with a growing circle of English friends, Viotti's life at last appeared to be gaining some sense of stability. From 1795 he was employed as a conductor at the King's Theatre, becoming leader of the orchestra at £300 [£20,000] per annum when the previous incumbent retired. His personal life

---

* When the King asked his teacher how he was doing, Salomon is said to have replied: 'There are three levels of skill in violin playing: an inability to play, the ability to play badly, and the ability to play well. Your Majesty, I am pleased to say, has already reached the second level.'

revolved around his friendship with William and Caroline Chinnery, a wealthy couple who adopted him into their family and introduced him to smart society. It was not to last, however. In March 1798, in what seems like a particularly cruel twist of fate, he was arrested at dinner with his friends, accused of Jacobin sympathies and ordered to leave the country. The charges were probably unfounded, but Viotti had been unwise in some of his associations. Britain was at war with France and facing rebellion in Ireland. Realpolitik took precedence over art.

Protesting his innocence, Viotti went into exile near Hamburg, staying with an admirer in Schoenfeld. The only requirement this benefactor, a Mr Smith, placed on his famous guest was that they dine together on Sundays. Music lovers should perhaps be grateful to the British authorities; Viotti's enforced absence from London gave him time to concentrate on his compositions, writing of them, 'This work is the fruit of leisure which misfortune procured for me. Some of the pieces were dictated by Pain; others by Hope.' His letters back to the Chinnerys from Schoenfeld show him to be articulate and affectionate, chiding the daughter to keep up with her practice, and always asking to be remembered to the governess.

Only in 1801 did Viotti's exile come to an end. During the Peace of Amiens in 1802, he was even able to travel to Paris, where his disciples found that his playing was as good as ever. Baillot later remembered the visit: 'The quality of his tone had become so soft, so sweet and was at the same time so full and so energetic, that one would have supposed it a cotton bow controlled by the arm of Hercules.' One year later, in 1803, Rode, Kreutzer and Baillot collaborated on a book of violin instruction –

Méthode de violon – that effectively codified the Viotti style. Immensely influential, it alone justifies thinking of Viotti as the father of modern violin playing. He himself, however, was by then back in England, again unable to travel to Paris following the resumption of war.

Free to perform in London, Viotti once more chose not to do so, but he did at least give lessons. His teaching led to a curious story which first appeared in the journal *The Musical World* in 1839, after all the named protagonists were safely dead. It was said that one day a new, aristocratic pupil arrived, bearing a violin picked up during continental travels. It was a superb Strad, although its owner, a fairly incapable musician, had no idea of this. Viotti failed in every attempt to buy the violin, but was allowed at least to borrow the magnificent instrument, finding it superior even to his existing Strad. So matters continued, until the death of the nobleman's father called him away to the country for an extended period. He left his violin in his teacher's care. At around the same time Viotti had taken another pupil, whose own brilliant replica of a Strad had been made in the workshops of his father, John Betts. It gave Viotti an idea of which we cannot be expected to approve, and he lost no time in approaching Betts to make a copy of the nobleman's Strad. Betts guessed his game, and instead asked his workman, Fendt, to make two replicas. In due course 'milor' (as *The Musical World* calls him) returned to take possession of a fake, none the wiser for the substitution. Viotti, however, found his own supposed original sadly disappointing, realized what Betts had done, but was unable to challenge him. Viotti and Betts subsequently avoided each other until, the story goes, Viotti was forced

to flee London, dying soon afterwards. That much must
be wrong; and the entire anecdote paints a picture of
Viotti entirely different from that portrayed by his contemporaries. *The Musical World*, however, swears to the
truth of the account, claiming it to have been well known
in London at the time.

There is another interesting aspect to the story. Viotti
did have a Betts as a pupil – Arthur, who was in fact a
brother to John. Arthur Betts is remembered for his 1820
purchase of a Strad for £1 [£50] from a seller who arrived
in the shop and did not know any better. It is a famous
story, both for what it says about the morals of some
violin dealers and because the *Betts* Stradivarius, made
in 1704, is one of the greatest and most celebrated of
them all. It is at least conceivable that Viotti might
have preferred it to his own 1709 Stradivarius, raising
the possibility that Betts acquired his eponymous Strad
in a way even more reprehensible than that related in
the authorized version.

Viotti's circumstances were not as seedy as this story
implies. He was one of the founders of the Philharmonic
Society in 1813 and continued to move in aristocratic
circles. The letters to him from the Duke of Cambridge,
tenth child of George III, in unashamedly poor French,
are a testament to their intimacy. One of them, from
1817, details the arrangements for Viotti to send a violin
on to Hanover, where the Duke was Viceroy. It cost 50
guineas [£2,500]. At that price the violin was probably a
Strad; values were rising, though hardly radically. Viotti
had by now been the most influential advocate of the
great luthier's works, first in Paris and then in London,
for thirty-five years.

Nevertheless, and to the astonishment of the Parisian friends who re-established contact with him after Napoleon's abdication in 1814, Viotti's main occupation following his return to London was as a wine merchant. This seems extraordinary, even for someone as multi-talented and apparently unenamoured of his sublime skills as Viotti. He had in fact been building the business since before his exile to Germany. Mrs Chinnery had recommended it to him, and even bankrolled the venture. As far as the French were concerned, it was simply proof of the violinist's corruption by the nation of shopkeepers.

No matter, Viotti made a brief trip to Paris in that same year and an evening at the Conservatoire was hastily arranged. Once again his disciples were able to hear him play and once again he was triumphant; his playing seemed only to have improved in the previous twelve years. Meanwhile, the virtuoso's absence from Paris had turned him into a figure of legend. He was greeted as a god by pupils who otherwise only knew him through his compositions, which themselves had become the subject of an annual competition. Nevertheless, he could not be persuaded to stay and soon returned to the London wine trade.

Only in 1818 when his business collapsed was Viotti, deeply in debt, once again forced to consider a career in music and a return to Paris. It should have been a triumphant homecoming. Viotti's old patron, the Count of Provence, had taken the throne as Louis XVIII and with his backing Viotti was, in November 1819, appointed Director of the Opera, the very position he had tried to gain thirty years before. We can only wonder at his continuing reluctance to perform. He could surely have

commanded huge fees from a public brought up on
stories of his brilliance. Perhaps, at sixty-six, his dexterity
had started to leave him. Or perhaps he really did feel
that performance was in some way beneath him, an
unworthy way to use his talent. I prefer to think that
Viotti relished the idea of one last challenge, a chance to
show that it was only the atmosphere of revolutionary
Paris that had caused his first failure as an impresario.

Sadly, Viotti was never to get the opportunity to show
off his entrepreneurial talents. Just as before, politics
were to prove his downfall. The assassination of the Duc
de Berry at the Opera early in 1820 lost the institution
both its public and its royal patronage. Viotti attempted
to turn the situation round, then moved briefly to the
Théâtre des Italiens, but in November 1821 he finally
retired. He spent his last few years mainly in France,
comfortable enough with an annual pension of 6,000
francs [£15,000] but deeply distressed by the knowledge
that he could never now repay his English friends. It was
on one last visit to the Chinnerys in 1824 that he died.
His will shows the distress he felt at the way his life had
turned out. He states that his soul is torn to pieces in the
agony of feeling that he dies owing Mrs Chinnery 24,000
francs, and requests that 'If I die before I can pay off this
debt, I pray that everything I have in the world may be
sold off, realized, and sent to Madame Chinnery, or her
heirs, praying only that they shall pay to my brother,
André Viotti, the sum of 800 francs that I owe him.'

Among his belongings he mentions his Stradivarius,
the 1709 *Viotti*, with the plaintive hope that it 'should
realize a large sum'. By the standards of his time he
was correct. Auctioned at the Hôtel Bouillon in Paris, the

violin went for 3,816 francs [£10,000]. It was probably a record at the time, a measure of the impact this one man had on the value of Stradivarius violins, but it was not enough to repay his debts.

The violin passed into something like obscurity. Remaining in France, by the middle of the century it was owned by a Monsieur Brochant de Villiers, who, we can assume, did not extract the best tone from it. Even so, Viotti's violin was not forgotten. At around this time François Fétis named it, with incongruous certainty, the 'third best' Strad in existence. It would be another fifty years, however, before the *Viotti* came back to the attention of music lovers around the world. In the meantime, and in its wake, all the other instruments we are following would have come to some sort of prominence.

Chapter Seven

'TO THE VIRTUOSOS OF VIOLINS'

Prince Khevenhüller, Count Cozio,
Joseph Böhm and Tarisio

ON 4 NOVEMBER 1800 Prince Johann Sigismund Friedrich de Khevenhüller-Metsch made his second highly aristocratic marriage. Already sixty-eight, he must have thought of his union with Maria Giuseppina, Countess of Strassoldo and less than half his age, as a new beginning. His gift to her of a violin, a year younger than himself but only just mature, seems almost symbolic. Moreover he had the taste, wealth and connections to ensure he bought the very best: the large violin made by Stradivari in 1733, when he was nearly ninety. It would come to be called the *Khevenhüller*.

The eldest son of one of Vienna's most influential families, Prince Khevenhüller had grown up accustomed to the idea that he would be a member of Austria's ruling elite. A cousin, General Ludwig Khevenhüller, had saved Maria Theresa's throne at the very beginning of her reign in 1744. The Prince's father, Johann-Joseph, was the Empress's Chamberlain and one of her closest advisers. His diaries remain the best source of information on life at her court. The Prince himself married for the first time when he was only twenty-two. His seventeen-year-old wife, Marie-Amélie, Princesse de Liechtenstein, was, if anything, even more aristocratic; and two years later he began his diplomatic career.

The Prince's initial postings were as ambassador to the courts first of Portugal and then Turin. After five years back in Austria, he became in 1775 the Empire's representative in Italy, in essence governor of the Duchy of Milan, in which Cremona lay. Then, in 1782, he gave up his public duties. The reasons are no longer easy to divine, but it is interesting that even as a private citizen the Prince was to remain in Milan and its surroundings for most of the rest of his life. It seems to have been a self-imposed exile; he simply preferred the culture and lifestyle of Italy to Vienna, then in its imperial heyday.

Marie-Amélie is an even more shadowy figure than her husband. She bore nine children, of whom four survived infancy, and then died in 1787, not yet fifty and only one month after her oldest son, Johann-Joseph. Even this double loss did not send the widowed Prince back to Vienna; he stayed in Italy, where he developed a reputation as a man of culture and knowledge. And so, thirteen years later, we find him in Vienna marrying Giuseppina Strassoldo, from the town of the same name in northern Italy.

The courtship, what drew each to the other, must all now be speculation. But it seems fair to assume that the Prince first noticed his future wife on account of her skills on the violin. She is said to have been an accomplished player, and it is easy to imagine him captivated at a Milanese soirée. Or perhaps both had fled to Vienna from Napoleon's invasion and were able also to share reminiscences of their beloved Italy. In fact, we only know one thing, that Prince Khevenhüller gave his wife that violin.

The Prince could have read, of course, the 'Anni 90' inscription on the violin's label giving its maker's age. Still over twenty years younger than that, he might have drawn comfort from the implications as he embarked on a new life with the thirty-one-year-old Giuseppina. Within a year, however, he had died, finally back home at Klagenfurt in Carinthia, where his family estates lay. So the Prince only owned the violin for a year and was never its player, but still the *Khevenhüller* bears his name. He did, after all, leave a permanent reminder of his ownership on the violin, a black seal towards the top of its back which represents the combined coat-of-arms of Khevenhüller-Metsch and Strassoldo. It means that the Prince's name is still occasionally remembered, long after his other claims to fame have faded from memory. The violin is also the only memento of that brief marriage: there were no children, nor have I found any trace of what happened to Giuseppina, by then Princess de Khevenhüller-Metsch, after 1801.

As for where Prince Khevenhüller acquired the great Strad, his Italian connections mean there could be any number of possible sources. One possibility, however,

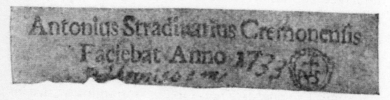

Figure 13. The bottom of the label of the *Khevenhüller* just shows the annotation of Stradivari's age when it was made.

stands out: Count Cozio di Salabue. The Count's fortunes had waned in the twenty-five years since he bought the *Messiah* and other violins, as well as tools and templates, from Paolo Stradivari. His estates had been in the path of Napoleon's invasion of Italy. They had suffered accordingly, although his instrument collection, being portable, had at least been removed to Milan for safekeeping. Their absence, however, seems to have reduced the Count's affection for his treasures. So 1800 – the year of Prince's Khevenhüller's second marriage – is also the year when the Count started to consider selling instruments. The combination of date and location is striking. Might one of the Count's first customers have been Prince Khevenhüller, an inhabitant of Milan then looking for a suitable violin for his fiancée?

For students of Stradivari, the possibility that Cozio owned the *Khevenhüller* is important. It gives support to those who believe that he, and not Antonio Stradivari, wrote the latter's age on the labels of later instruments, based on the information he had received from Paolo Stradivari. My interest comes from a different perspective. Cozio was also, of course, the owner of the *Messiah*. So two of our instruments may have crossed paths in his collection. They could have been kept together, unplayed but admired, for as long as twenty-five years. As far as I can establish, however, they have not met again since 1801.

THE NEW Princess de Khevenhüller-Metsch must surely have retained her violin after her husband's death. Most likely she remained in Vienna. For that is where the

Khevenhüller next surfaces, around 1820. Joseph Böhm
was a Hungarian violinist, inspired and briefly taught
by Pierre Rode, one of Viotti's most distinguished pupils.
He began his public career with a tour of Europe, accompanied by the pianist Johann Pixis. His success was
immediate and universal, but it was in Vienna, where
he first played in 1815 aged only twenty, that Böhm
received the warmest reception. He decided to settle
there, becoming Professor of Violin at the newly established Conservatoire in 1819. Within a couple of years,
as a member of the Imperial Chapel orchestra, he had
revived a Viennese institution: the 8 a.m. quartet mati-
nees at the First Coffee House in the Prater-allée. This is
where the *Khevenhüller* was first heard in public performance. It had probably not travelled far from one
Viennese home to another.

Böhm began his career in Vienna at a time when
that of its presiding musical genius was coming to an
end. Ludwig van Beethoven was by now almost totally
deaf, yet he was turning his sublime talent towards the
compositions that are to many his life's masterpieces:
the late string quartets. Böhm and the *Khevenhüller*
turned out to be in the right place at the right time.
The first of Beethoven's late quartets, the Eb Op 127,
was premiered on 6 March, 1825 by the quartet led by
Ignaz Schuppanzigh. It was far from satisfactory. Beethoven had subverted the classical form with surprises,
introducing unprecedented textures and sonorities. The
audience scarcely knew what to make of it and the players themselves were probably underprepared for such
difficult music, having received the score only two weeks
before.

Beethoven blamed Schuppanzigh's excessive stoutness for the failure, and insisted that the next performance should be given by the same quartet but led by Böhm. The violinist later remembered the commission:

> Beethoven could have no peace until the disgrace was wiped off. He sent for me the first thing in the morning – in his usual curt way, he said to me, 'You must play my quartet' – and the thing was settled. Neither objections nor doubts could prevail, what Beethoven wanted had to take place, so, I undertook the difficult task.

Böhm found rehearsals a disquieting experience:

> It was studied industriously and rehearsed frequently under Beethoven's own eyes. I said 'eyes' intentionally for the unhappy man was so deaf that he could no longer hear the heavenly sound of his compositions. And, yet, rehearsing in his presence was not easy. With close attention, his eyes followed the bows and therefore he was able to judge the smallest fluctuations in tempo or rhythm and correct them immediately.

Even so, Böhm was able to exert some influence:

> At the close of the last movement of this quartet there occurred a *meno vivace** which seemed to me to weaken the general effect. At the rehearsal, therefore, I advised that the original tempo be maintained, to the betterment of the effect. Beethoven, crouched in a corner, heard nothing, but watched with strained

* Italian for 'less quick', therefore an instruction from the composer to slow down.

attention. After the last stroke of the bows he said laconically, 'Let it remain so,' went to the desks and crossed out the *meno vivace* in the four parts.

Another story tells how at an early run-through of one quartet (almost certainly this one) Böhm was brave enough to declare a passage to be unplayable. 'Böhm! He's an ass!' was Beethoven's immediate rejoinder. Nevertheless the composer responded with alterations, coming back at the next rehearsal with a 'Na, Böhmerl,* are you satisfied now?'

It may have been the extra rehearsal time, or Böhm's natural affinity with the music, and the 'powerful, mellow and sweet' *Khevenhüller* no doubt played a part, but the second and subsequent performances of the quartet were all huge successes. Böhm led four of them: once in front of a small audience, twice in one evening at a public concert, and once at a well-deserved benefit for Böhm himself. Encouraged, Beethoven was to devote the remainder of his life to producing the four further quartets that make up the group. Posterity could scarcely owe any violinist or violin a greater debt.

AT AROUND the same time, Count Cozio was finally bringing himself to sell the *Messiah*. He had continued looking for buyers for his collection from the early 1800s, even going so far as to issue advertisements, first in French and then in English, as follows:

---

* A piece of informal friendliness which could be translated as something like 'Böhm, my old mate'.

To the Virtuosos of Violins

A Virtuoso having done a large, and choice collection of Violins of most famous ancient Cremone's Authors, vis, of A'NTHONY, JEROM, AND NICOLAS AMATIS, A'NTHONY STRADIVARIUS, FRANCIS RUGER, called PER, ANDREAS and JOSEPH GUARNERIUS, CHARLES BERGONZI, and JOHN BAPTIST GUADAGNINI, and being now disposed to sell that collection both by wholesale, and separately here into Milan, at discret price, invites all virtuosos who will buy them, to apply in this City to Merchant A'nthony Clerici at house Cavanago in the street of that name, N. 2334 since twelve o'clock until two, and since four, until six.

The announcement does not appear to have attracted many purchasers. The Count was undoubtedly right to consider that the English were in the best position to pay high prices; but there can have been few English 'Virtuosos' in Milan during the Napoleonic Wars. The French version of the advertisement is both more detailed and more grammatical, but it too seems to have excited little immediate interest.

As time passed, however, the fame of the Count's collection spread; many musicians would come to see it. One was the great German composer-violinist Ludwig Spohr, who was responsible for the development of the chin-rest. His diary for 22 September 1816 mentions a trip to the Conservatoire in Milan, where he met 'Count Gozio [sic] de Solence'. He had

four Stradivari's which have never been played upon, and which although very old look as though they had

only just been made. Two of these violins are the
production of the last year of that artist, 1773[sic],
when he was an old man of ninety-three years of
age. But it is immediately perceptible on the violin
that it was cut by the tremulous hands of an infirm
old man; the other two are however of the best days
of the artist, from 1743 and 1744, and of great beauty.
The tone is full and strong, but still new and woody,
and to become fine, they must be played upon for ten
years at least.

Given that Stradivari died in 1737, we clearly cannot
trust the dates that Spohr assigns to Cozio's collection.
Nevertheless, one of the violins from 'the best days of
the artist' must surely have been the *Messiah*, which was
exactly a century old then and still looks as though it has
only just been made. Even Spohr's comments on its tone
were to be echoed by later witnesses towards the end of
the century. By the Count's death in 1840, however, the
Messiah had been sold. Its purchaser could hardly have
been more unlikely: a peasant's son from Fontaneto,*
Luigi Tarisio.

It seems amazing that a man from such humble
origins should have ended up owning a collection that
put even Cozio's in the shade. Tarisio probably trained
as a carpenter. This knowledge gradually combined with
his violin-playing hobby to become an obsession with
Cremonese masterpieces. It is difficult to imagine how
he first translated this infatuation into acquisition. Tarisio
spent no money on himself, and violins were certainly
cheap in comparison with later values, but properly priced

* Also, by one of those curious coincidences, the birthplace of Viotti.

they would still have been way beyond his means. Presumably he had a few strokes of luck which, combined with his eye for a masterpiece and a conscience unlikely to be troubled by paying below the odds, were enough to set him on his way.

One way or another, by the 1820s Tarisio was on the road in Italy, playing the violin to support himself, and sniffing out treasures wherever he could. He used the tricks of any modern antique dealer. On arrival in a village he would ingratiate himself with the locals to find out if anyone owned a violin, or he might visit monasteries and other likely prospects, and offer to repair their instruments. Armed with information, he could gauge the situation, perhaps simply buying cheap, or, more subtly, offering new violins for old. Even if no purchase resulted, knowledge was still useful to him; and Tarisio gradually became both connoisseur and collector. He had the great advantage, as later dealers noted ruefully, of coming across violins while they still had their original labels in them, so that he was able to build a picture of different luthiers' work without being misled by false information. Those who bought violins from him were not necessarily so lucky: he does not seem to have been averse to increasing an instrument's value with a little judicious forgery. Even contemporaries who realized what he did, however, still did not think of him as crooked. If he had been seeking material gain, he would surely have lived a more luxurious lifestyle.

Probably the best insight into Tarisio's character comes from Charles Reade, a novelist and violin connoisseur, who had several dealings with him: 'The man's whole soul was devoted to violins, he was a great dealer, but greater amateur.' This was certainly the prevailing view in Tarisio's lifetime. It is hardly likely that Count Cozio would have had much to do with him otherwise. What is certain is that at some point after 1823 Tarisio persuaded the Count to part with the jewel of his collection, the 1716 Strad still in impeccable condition, the *Messiah*.

The outside world first became aware of Tarisio in 1827, when he made the first of his now famous trips to Paris to sell parts of his hoard. Leaving, as always, his best instruments at home, Tarisio made the first journey from Italy on foot, choosing a Parisian luthier, Aldric, as his first potential customer. The latter must have thought his fortune made when the scruffy Italian peasant arrived, bearing masterpieces. Tall and thin, and looking distinctly ordinary, Tarisio spoke French indifferently and dressed badly. The long walk had left his face dirty, his clothes in rags, and his heavy shoes with no soles. Sensing an opportunity, Aldric offered a fraction of what the violins were worth, and was disconcerted to realize that this tramp was perfectly aware of what he was selling. Tarisio probably knew more about violins than anyone else alive; he would end up educating his customers. Nevertheless, negotiations had commenced in such a way that Tarisio was forced to accept a lower price than he had expected, even if one several times the original offer. He did not make the same mistake again.

On his return to Paris two months later, Tarisio appeared well groomed and fashionably dressed. He hired a coach and, avoiding Aldric, made the rounds of the younger generation of Parisian luthiers, men like Georges Chanot and his friend Jean-Baptiste Vuillaume. Not just paying the prices Tarisio asked, but outbidding each other, they did all they could to persuade him to bring more of his collection to Paris. Like any good salesman, he in turn would whet their appetites, teasing them with the existence, back in Milan, of his perfect 1716 Stradivarius. It was on one such occasion that Delphin Alard, Vuillaume's son-in-law and himself a great violinist, responded with understandable exasperation: 'Ah ça, votre violon est donc comme le Messie; on l'attend toujours, et il ne parait jamais.' ('So, your violin is like the Messiah, always expected, and it never appears.') The *Messiah* was not only famous, Alard had now given it a name.

As an instrument, however, the *Messiah* was fast becoming an anachronism. Treasured by collectors rather than players, it was one of the few Strads to escape adjustment in the early years of the nineteenth century. For the shift that its maker had begun to anticipate a century before was finally occurring; instrumental music was following opera from the private chambers and ballrooms of the aristocracy to the public arena. Dependent on a fee-paying audience for their income, soloists had to produce a tone that could reach the back of the largest halls.

Tourte's bow helped, but there was a further way to increase an instrument's power and brilliance: to raise its pitch. From about 1800, the frequency of middle A, the third string on a violin around which an entire orchestra tunes, increased from about 420 vibrations per second (Hertz) to around 435 Hertz by the middle of the nineteenth century and as much as 460 Hertz today. What Stradivari called A would nowadays sound more like the G one note below it. The resulting increase in string tension raised the pressure on the bridge, leading to a risk that the belly would collapse. To prevent this, the old bass-bar had to be replaced by a longer and stronger one. The soundpost would also often be thickened.

In a parallel development instigated to keep pace with advances in technique made by virtuosi, the necks on all old violins had to be adjusted. Violinists were seeking a greater range and versatility of fingering, requiring the ability to move the left hand up and down the neck from pegbox to bridge with ease. The old style of neck, in the same plane as the soundbox and with a wedged fingerboard, did not allow this. It got thicker and less easy to grasp as the left hand travelled along it. The solution was to tip back the neck by means of an insert, so that it ran parallel to the strings, and replace the wedged fingerboard with a flat one. Normally the changes to both bass bar and neck were made at the same time. In one sense the violin had been transformed, but the core element of its design – the size and shape of the soundbox – remained inviolate.

Every concert violin went through this kind of alteration. It is clear evidence of how, already antiques, the classical violins and cellos were valued not for their age but for their playing qualities. Stradivari's later instruments, designed for power, responded magnificently. The sweet-toned, high-arched violins of Amati and Stainer, and indeed those of the eighteenth-century luthiers who had followed their lead, did not. The superiority of Stradivari's model could no longer be challenged, and the

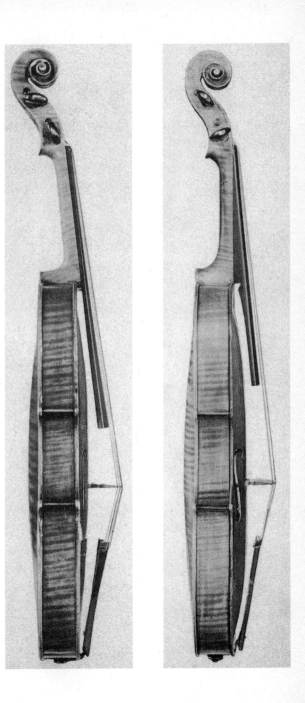

Figure 14. A violin by Jacob Stainer (top), still in its original set-up with wedged fingerboard, compared to a Strad adjusted for modern playing. The photo also shows the fullness of Stainer's archings compared to Stradivari's.

old order would never be re-established. It is hard to imagine a more thorough vindication of the Master's years of experiment. It all presents us, however, with a supreme irony: the brilliant and powerful tone for which Strads are famous, and which is most responsible for their value, is very different from what their maker himself must have heard.

Chapter Eight

'THE TURNING-POINT IN THE HISTORY OF VIRTUOSITY'

Paganini, showman and dealer

THE NAMES OF violinists and cellists jump off the page in any musical history of the nineteenth century; only the quality of their compositions and the enthusiasm of contemporary reports now enable us to distinguish them. In the days before recording, appreciation of a performer could only be ephemeral. It is all the more remarkable, therefore, that the name of Nicolò Paganini remains so resonant. The associations – feverish talent, technical brilliance and dramatic excess – are as strong now as in the days when audiences believed him to be in league with the devil.

Paganini was not the first travelling virtuoso, but he showed how profitable violin playing might be. No contemporary could match his combination of ability and chutzpah and all successors have been condemned to undergo comparison with the great maestro. In Robert Schumann's memorable phrase, he was 'the turning-point in the history of virtuosity'. Paganini's story is therefore intimately entwined with that of Stradivari. He owned one of our five violins, and encountered another; and by creating and satisfying the demand of a large audience for solo violinists, he did as much as Viotti to ensure the supremacy of the Stradivari model. So it is paradoxical that the instrument with which he was most associated was not a Strad at all, but a violin made by that other Cremonese master, Guarneri del Gesù. The story of how Paganini acquired it is one of the central myths within his legend.

Paganini was introduced to music at the age of five, when he began to learn the mandolin from his father, a shipping agent in Genoa. Two years later he was taught the fundamentals of violin playing and, as he later said, 'within a few months I was able to play any music at sight'. Early lessons followed, and in 1793, at the age of eleven, Paganini gave his first public performance. Its success gave his father pause for thought. For the next six years he was to supervise his son closely, insisting on ten hours' daily practice around a schedule of lucrative concerts, first in Genoa and then further afield. Only when he was eighteen did the young virtuoso finally escape, following his elder brother to the Tuscan city of Lucca.

Freed from parental control, Paganini embarked on a life of famous excess. As he later put it, 'When at last I was my own master I drew in the pleasures of life in deep draughts.' He would spend the next twenty-seven years in Italy, filling his life with music, love affairs and gambling, interrupted by long periods of utter exhaustion. His first four years away from Genoa were spent establishing himself, giving concerts in Lucca and neighbouring cities. By the end of his life, Paganini was angrily denying reports that he spent these years in prison for the murder of a rival in love, honing his skills on a smuggled violin. Equally exotic, but sadly equally untrue, is the story that he was in a Tuscan castle, learning the guitar and using it to serenade an aristocratic paramour.

It was during this period, however, that Paganini acquired his del Gesù. The violin was presented to Paganini in Leghorn, in the early 1800s. Its donor, a French merchant called Colonel Livron, owned a theatre there at which Paganini had been contracted to play. Quite why he ended up giving the virtuoso his 1742 del Gesù is unclear, but the popular story has it that it was originally a loan. Paganini had arrived in Leghorn without a violin, having pawned his previous instrument to pay off a gambling debt. Once he had heard Paganini play, the Colonel realized that his violin had found its true master and insisted that it remain with Paganini: 'Never will I profane strings which your fingers have touched; that instrument is yours.' The vibrant, powerful sound of the del Gesù was perfect for Paganini's style. It soon acquired an evocative nickname – the *Cannon* – and violin and virtuoso became inseparable.

FROM 1805 TO 1813, Paganini was attached to the court of Napoleon's sister, Elise, first in Lucca and then in Florence. Gossip did not hesitate to link him with his royal mistress. Madame Laplace, lady-in-waiting to Elise, was almost certainly a conquest. She seems to have had a predilection, if an eclectic one, for geniuses. Her cuckolded husband was one of France's most celebrated mathematicians and astronomers; the uses of 'Laplace Transforms' are still learnt by university mathematics students.

Madame Laplace may have been the intended target

of Paganini's 'Scène Amoureuse', which he first played –
on only two strings – at the Lucca court. The bottom G
string was to represent Adonis, the top E string Venus.
The goddess's initial love-lorn melody on the high notes
is answered by Adonis' romantic passion on the G string,
with both voices joining in a jubilant and climactic finale.
Its success was such that Princess Elise, in Paganini's
words, 'lauded me up to the skies; and then said in her
most gracious manner: "You have just performed impos-
sibilities on two strings; would not a single string suffice
for your talent?" I promised to make the attempt. The
idea delighted me, and some weeks later I composed my
military Sonata for the G string entitled "Napoleon"
which I performed before a numerous and brilliant court
audience.'

The performance, if not the composition, of the Napoleon Sonata, covering over three octaves on one string,
is a striking technical achievement. It is consistent with
what contemporaries say of its composer – that musicianship took second place to displays of virtuosity. String-
breaking stunts, *scordatura** and raising the pitch of the
violin by a semi-tone for increased brilliance: all were
part of Paganini's dramatic stock in trade. The *Cannon*
still bears the scars today.

From 1812 Paganini was on the move in Italy, building
a reputation both as his country's most accomplished
violinist and as a lothario. One adventure resulted in a
suit for breach of promise that cost 3,000 francs [£7,000].
This notoriety is what probably led a doctor in 1823 to
regard Paganini's cadaverous form and persistent cough

---

* Deliberate mistuning of strings.

as symptoms of 'hidden' syphilis. The standard treatment was mercury, taken both as an ointment and orally, in what even Paganini described as 'murderous doses'. Hand tremor and eyesight deterioration are classic side-effects of the regime and after five years he was beginning to exhibit just these symptoms. Yet he chose this moment to launch his European tour.

PAGANINI WAS responding to a long-standing invitation. Count Metternich, the Austrian Chancellor, had invited him to Vienna as far back as 1817. It was the violinist's lover, the dancer and singer Antonia Bianchi, who finally persuaded him to take up the offer. She and their two-year-old son Achillo accompanied the virtuoso and the *Cannon* on their first trip out of Italy, in the early spring of 1828.

It is hard to exaggerate the impact Paganini had on the Austrian capital. The timing was perfect. Enough rumours of his skill had filtered out from Italy in the preceding twenty years to ensure that everyone wanted to hear him; and he arrived on the international stage still close to the peak of his powers. Seats for his first concert in the Imperial Ballroom were priced at five times the going rate, so that a 5-gulden [£40] note rapidly became known as a 'Paganiner'. Even so, the enormous hall was filled to capacity.

Paganini appeared after a short orchestral introduction that included the overture from *Fidelio*. Emaciated and deadly pale, he could, recalling that opera's most famous scene, have been an emerging prisoner himself. When he bowed it was as though his body was detaching itself from his legs; but he was not a figure of fun. From the moment he started to play the audience was enthralled. He began with his Violin Concerto in B Minor, composed two years before. Its opening movement makes huge demands on both instrument and player, alternating passages of intense lyricism with bravura displays of the virtuoso's art: flying staccato, amazingly rapid double stopping,* trills in runs, or maintained on one string while another carries the tune. Paganini had taken Viotti's development of the concerto form and added a level of technical difficulty that only a violinist with perfect intonation and bow control, and apparently superhuman dexterity, could achieve.

The *Adagio* second movement, by contrast, is songlike in its simplicity, relying for its effect on purity of tone and feeling. Franz Schubert, a repeated member of Paganini's Vienna audience, was to say of it that he heard an angel sing. The final *Rondo* changes mood again. Known as *La Campanella*, it both incorporates a popular melody and has become one of the prime exhibition pieces for any virtuoso. By the time the last chord rang out the audience's adulation was unconfined. Paganini received it with characteristic sangfroid. 'He stood before us', wrote one critic, 'like a miraculous apparition in the domain of art.' The rest of the concert had a similar impact. The final applause was led by the orchestra itself in a frenzy of enthusiasm. No one had witnessed virtuosity on that scale before.

Poor Antonia Bianchi, in an appearance sandwiched by her lover's, had been quite ignored. It is hardly surprising

---

* Playing on two or more strings at once.

Figure 15. Paganini in full flow: part of a series of pictures
by Sir Edwin Henry Landseer that capture something
of the maestro's showmanship.

that within six months she had left him. For 2,000 Milanese scudi [£30,000] she renounced all rights to Achillo, who was to become the focus of his father's life. Visitors to the maestro's dressing-room would be struck by how the violinist, despite his avaricious and diabolic reputation, became soft and playful in the presence of his son.

Paganini's Viennese debut had been on 29 March 1828. His second appearance on 11 April was attended by every member of the Imperial Family who was in Vienna. The ballroom was full three hours before the beginning of the concert, and thousands had to be turned away. By the middle of August Paganini had given his twentieth performance. His picture appeared on snuffboxes, napkins, ties, pipes, billiard cues and powder boxes. In one day he had displaced in the public's affections the giraffe presented to the Viennese court by the Pasha of Egypt.

The effect Paganini had on Austria's musicians was equally decisive. One member of that Vienna audience was Joseph Böhm, who had no doubt that the Italian was the greatest virtuoso of all time. But the encounter did not spur him to greater achievement. With a temperament unsuited for performance, Böhm may even have suffered from stage fright. He retired from the concert stage. In his hands, the *Khevenhüller* would not be heard in public again.

THE WITHDRAWAL of Böhm and his Strad in the face of Paganini and his del Gesù was one example among many. As the maestro continued his tour from Vienna, violinists became obsessed with discovering his 'secret'.

Many convinced themselves that it lay in his violin. For a century, del Gesù had been underrated by comparison with Stradivari; Count Cozio had regarded him as no more than an unsuccessful imitator of his Cremonese contemporary. Paganini's success was to change all that. For the first time since Viotti's Parisian debut half a century before, a rival to Stradivari had finally emerged.

Not all musicians, of course, were as self-effacing as Böhm. So the rivalry between Stradivari and del Gesù was often to be expressed on the concert stage itself, as violinists set themselves up to challenge Paganini's preeminence. One was the Polish virtuoso Karol Lipiński, who was in Warsaw when Paganini visited the city in 1829. There should not have been any antagonism. The two violinists had known and admired each other for more than ten years; in 1827 Lipiński had even dedicated his 'Three Caprices for the Violin' to the Italian maestro. Events during 1829, however, were to test this friendship to its limits.

Both virtuosi were in Warsaw for the coronation of Czar Nicholas I as King of Poland. Lipiński had made the journey from his base in Dresden with the expectation that, as his country's pre-eminent violinist, he would lead the orchestra. He had not reckoned on Paganini's presence. In the C Major Mass, specially composed for the occasion by Ksawery Elsner, it was the Italian who took the lead, with the Pole relegated to a supporting role. Patriotic sentiments were inflamed and Lipiński himself was clearly upset. When Paganini scheduled concerts for 3 and 6 June, Lipiński announced one on the 5th, rebuffing all attempts to persuade him to change the date.

The stage was set for a confrontation, a comparison of

the two violinists' styles and talents. It was also a contest between luthiers. For while Paganini would be playing his *Cannon*, Lipiński's violin was a Strad. Moreover, it was one that Paganini had heard him play before. Indeed, the last encounter between the two violinists had taken place just after Lipiński's acquisition of the violin in 1818, as he himself related at the end of his life.

Many years have elapsed since I was challenged to play with Paganini in Italy, and numerous were the letters of introduction forced upon me by kind friends. Amongst others there was a letter from Spohr, to an old gentleman living in Milan, who in his youth had been one of the most promising pupils of the great violin-master Tartini, who died in 1770. After I had slept the first night in Milan and recovered from the fatigues of the journey, I, provided with my letter of introduction, and my violin, betook myself to the house of Signor Salvini; he gave me a very kind reception, and as I did not speak Italian, carried on a lively conversation with me in French. In all his movements Signor Salvini showed the quiet dignity of age, but, when listening to music, his eyes sparkled from an intensity of feeling and hardly seemed to belong to the feeble old man, and his whole being seemed rejuvenated as if with some sparks of life from by-gone times.

After telling him that I had hitherto chiefly occupied myself with the works of Beethoven, Mozart, and Weber, he asked me to play to him, and sat down to listen. I chose some selections from [Weber's] *Der Freischütz*, but the old gentleman stopped me and said, 'Play something of Beethoven's,' and, after hearing me for about a quarter of an hour, he got up, looked intently first at me, and then my violin, and cried out 'Vasta.' This 'enough' made me tremble, for I concluded from it that he had formed an unfavourable opinion of my playing. But I was somewhat reassured when Signor Salvini said to me in the most kindly manner: 'Come and see me again tomorrow morning at ten o'clock.' On the way back to my hotel all kinds of doubts and fears arose within me.

In this sad mood, I almost regretted having consented to play with Paganini, for I knew that to a certain extent it was to be trial of skill between us. On the next day, with much fear and hesitation, I went to Signor Salvini's house at the appointed time. He received me with great cordiality, and before I had unfolded my music he said, 'Please give me your violin.' I handed it to him and was amazed to see him grasp it firmly by the neck and strike it with all his might on the edge of the table, on which it fell, smashed to atoms. But with the greatest coolness and tranquillity the old gentleman then opened a violin-case which was on the same table, and carefully taking from it a violin, said to me, 'Try this instrument!'

I took it, and after I had played one of Beethoven's sonatas, Salvini held out his hand to me, and said with some emotion, 'You are doubtless aware that I was once formerly a pupil of Giuseppe Tartini, my famous fellow countryman, and one of the greatest violinists of the time. On one occasion he gave me this large and genuine Stradivari violin, which I have cherished as a souvenir of his memory. You, Herr Lipiński, know how to use such an instrument, and to give expression to its hidden power.' 'But,' cried I, 'there is the world-famed Paganini.' 'Don't speak to me of him,' cried out the old man excitedly. 'I have heard him, that one-stringed magician, who has no real musical depth, but who can merely astonish those who listen to him by his great mechanical dexterity, without being capable of any noble or mighty colour of tone. Paganini is admired, but your playing thrills and transports one. You alone are a worthy follower of Tartini; therefore take this violin as a present from me, and at the same time as a souvenir of Tartini.'

It is not a good idea to examine this account too closely. Lipiński's memory must have embroidered the facts through the years, colouring them with his later antipathy for Paganini. It is true that the two violinists first played together in 1818. On that occasion, however, Lipiński was unquestionably the junior partner, grateful for Paganini's friendship and his reputation enhanced simply by being allowed to share the Italian's concert stage. Moreover, Weber did not complete *Der Freischütz* until 1820, after Lipiński claimed to have played it for Salvini. And Lipiński also told an entirely different story of meeting another pupil of Tartini in Italy, called Dr Mazzurana. In this version, Mazzurana was dissatisfied with Lipiński's performance of one of Tartini's sonatas, but unable on account of his extreme age (ninety) to correct him by demonstration. So instead he gave Lipiński a poem he had written to explain his teacher's intentions. By declaiming the poem in response to Mazzurana's promptings, Lipiński was said both to have mastered the sonata and to have infused all his future performances with a poetic spirit.

Figure 16. Karol Lipiński – 'a worthy follower of Tartini' – with his newly acquired Strad, painted in 1822 by Walenty Wankowicz.

Whatever the truth of the detail, Tartini's old Strad, the massive violin which we saw being made in 1715 when the Master was at his peak, had come down to Lipiński. It would take his name. And so, in Warsaw in June 1829, the *Lipiński* was set against the *Cannon*. By the 13th, local critics were clear: 'His [Lipiński's] bowing is far superior to Paganini's and he is also his superior in power and fullness of tone.' It was a verdict that has led some to dub the *Lipiński* 'the fiddle which fought Paganini'. It is hard to escape the feeling, however, that Polish sentiment was swayed by patriotism. Lipiński was one of his era's pre-eminent composer-violinists. His successful tours took him as far as Moscow in one direction and London in another, where *The Musical World* was highly complimentary. His classical style gained him the reputation of being his era's Bach player *par excellence*. Lipiński did not, however, have Paganini's star quality; he spent the last half of his career in Dresden as concertmaster of the royal orchestra. Little now differentiates him from the army of other nineteenth-century virtuosi. Perhaps we should leave the last word about this encounter to Paganini himself, who when asked who was the greatest violinist of the age replied: 'I do not know who the first may be, but assuredly the second is Lipiński.'

PAGANINI WAS to tour for another five years. Illness prevented a trip to Russia, but Germany, France and England all fell under his spell. In London, where he was initially signed up for five concerts, demand was such that he had to announce numerous 'final' performances, so that in four months he gave fifteen concerts, all in the

Royal Opera House. His share of the takings was a monumental £6,000 [£500,000]. Some of the proceeds went on purchasing one of the few great Stradivarius violas, made in 1731. Its effect on the maestro was such that he almost abandoned the violin for its deeper-voiced sibling, commissioning a piece for the viola from the composer Hector Berlioz.* Paganini's subsequent visit to London in 1834 was a relative flop but productive in another way. By then fifty-two, he was only just prevented from eloping with the eighteen-year-old Charlotte Watson, daughter of his impresario, with whom he had been lodging.

That same year Paganini finally returned to Italy. His lifelong friend and notary, Luigi Gugliemo Germi, had been investing the proceeds of his European tour, purchasing several houses and estates on his behalf. One was the Villa Gaiona, near Parma, which the virtuoso chose as his favourite residence. Here he planned to publish his compositions and to found a conservatoire, where he was to teach the violin class himself.

It should have been a fulfilling retirement, but Paganini seemed congenitally incapable of enjoying one. Within eighteen months he was back in France, apparently on his way to America, where he had been offered huge performance fees. That idea was quickly superseded by a promise to be the main attraction at Paris's 'Casino Paganini'. In an inevitable breach of contract, the violinist hardly played; the subsequent failure of the enterprise

---

* Paganini ended up rejecting the result, *Harold in Italy*, a symphony with substantial viola solos. There were too many rests for the soloist.

cost him 50,000 francs [£100,000] and an exceptionally vindictive lawsuit. The simple truth is that by now ill-health meant that little was left of Paganini's virtuosic talent. In retrospect it is remarkable that he carried on as long as he did.

Paganini had continued to suffer at the hands of the medical profession and his own hypochondria since that original diagnosis of syphilis. Told in 1828 that he was consumptive and would be dead within the year, he had unfortunately ignored the advice of the one physician who told him to abandon doctors. Instead he was bled and prescribed horse-riding, presumably to relieve constipation. He also began taking 'Leroy's Purgative', a laxative whose power derived from its toxicity. It seems hardly surprising that the violinist was commonly regarded as taciturn and disagreeable. By the time Paganini returned to Paris in 1836 his illnesses included chronic cystitis and orchitis.* Within a year he was unable to speak, and used conversation cards to communicate.

Paganini still had two years left to live. His health might have gone, but his desire to make money had not. No longer able to play violins with his old skill, he turned to dealing in them. He knew that his mere association with an instrument would add value to it. That would be to his advantage when he came to sell, but first he had to add to his collection. Paganini began to establish a network of agents around Europe through whom he could act anonymously. They searched for instruments

---

* A letter from Paganini to Germi describes the second of these conditions all too clearly: 'the left testicle had swollen to the size of a large pear, or a little pumpkin'.

by all the Cremonese masters, but above all for those by Stradivari. Whatever Paganini's own predilection for del Gesù, there were simply far more Strads to be found. In 1828 he had left two for safekeeping in Milan; by the time he died he had acquired a further nine.

One of Paganini's agents was the violinist Vincenzo Merighi, based in Milan. On 20 March 1839 Paganini wrote to him from Marseilles, where he had gone for his health: 'I am glad to have the beautiful violoncello, which I always keep with me along with the Stradivari violin, *that completes the quartet* [my italics] . . . The belly of the Stradivari violin has ceded around the bridge but it's not too bad and it's a beautiful instrument.'

The cello that the letter refers to must surely be the 1707 *Countess of Stanlein*. This was in Paganini's possession when he died and had been discovered in 1822 by Alessandro Pezze, a pupil of Merighi's, being wheeled in a barrow along the streets of Milan. And the violin 'that completes the quartet'? All the evidence points to it being the *Paganini*, the earliest of our five violins, made in the Master's workshop around 1680.* We cannot be certain about that date because at some point in the century and a half of the violin's obscurity the year on its label had been changed to 1696. This attempt to increase the violin's value could only be successful with an ignorant buyer: the violin is so clearly Amatisé in style that it could not be from the heart of the Long Strad period. There is something undignified about the crude attempt at forgery: the violin trade's equivalent of an unsuccessful

* Although usually assigned to 1680, it may date to the following year, from which it has a twin, the 1681 *Fleming*.

facelift. The implicit insult – that a Strad from 1680 is less valuable than its younger siblings – is no less wounding for being true.

Paganini, however, had found a more creative way of increasing the violin's value than tampering with its label. His name added lustre, but his true genius was to think of marketing the violin as part of a Stradivarius quartet, bringing together the world's greatest luthier and most celebrated violinist in an almost impossibly rare combination. He already had the trickiest piece, the 1731 viola bought in England a few years before; first violin would play a 1727 Strad he had bought from Count Cozio; the cello would be, presumably, the *Countess of Stanlein* (not a name he would have used: that owner lay in the future). Second violin could have played any one of four or five Strads, judging from the list of violins in Paganini's possession when he died. Presumably he regarded the violin he bought from Merighi as completing the quartet because he knew that to fetch a reasonable price the 1680 violin needed more than just his name.

It was a good plan, one that would surely have worked if Paganini had been able to see it through. All too soon, however, decrepitude took over. He never made it to Paris, or even back to Italy. He died on 27 May 1840, while in Nice, where he had gone still hoping to write a violin manual. He was fifty-eight. Contemporaries blamed tuberculosis of the larynx, but it seems more likely that it was an over-reliance on doctors and quack medicines that did for him.

Even in death, controversy did not abandon the virtuoso. His failure to receive the last rites meant that the Church refused to bury him on consecrated ground. A petition to the Pope had little effect; it can hardly have been helped by the popular rumours of a pact with the devil. Nine years elapsed before Paganini's body was finally interred in the village church adjoining the Villa Gaiona. Over the next few years it was to undergo several further moves as cemeteries closed and graveyards fought for the honour of being the virtuoso's final resting-place. As late as 1893 there was a report of his grave being opened for an inspection by the violinist Frantisek Ondricek, then touring Italy. It was probably a hoax, but Paganini's remains were said to be still clearly visible in a glass casket.

Paganini's material legacy was substantial. His estate was valued at £80,000 [£5 million]. After bequests to his sisters, and an annuity to Antonia Bianchi, Achillo Paganini was declared sole heir. Already legitimized, he had the added benefit of a hereditary barony, which had been conferred on his father in Germany. A substantial proportion of Achillo's inheritance consisted of the violins his father had bought in his last years. With no talent for the instrument, Achillo himself needed none of them. The *Cannon* Guarnerius was bequeathed to the Municipal Museum in Genoa, where it remains today. The rest of the collection, including the 1680 *Paganini*, went to be sold by Jean-Baptiste Vuillaume in Paris.

Judging Paganini's musical legacy is more problematic. There are the compositions, of course, but unlike other great Italian virtuosi, such as Corelli, Tartini or Viotti, Paganini founded no great tradition. He only ever took one pupil. Camillo Sivori studied under him, or was at least guided by him, from the age of seven to twelve, just before Paganini left Italy for his European tour. Sivori was later to admit to David Laurie, a Scottish violin dealer and an entertaining but unreliable memoirist, that his former master was probably the worst teacher of the violin that ever lived, short with his pupil and bitter if he showed any deficiency.

There is, however, one area in which Paganini's influence is indisputable. He may have produced one of the most famous of all quotes about Stradivari – that he 'only used the wood of trees on which nightingales sang' – but his own preference for the *Cannon* could not be denied. By the time Paganini died there was a popular conception that the best del Gesù were unmatchable. They were the true concert violins: Strads were better suited to the drawing-room. Violin-makers across Europe set out to copy Guarneri. The supremacy of Stradivari was under threat.

Chapter Nine

'I HAVE 80,000 FRANCS ON ME'

Vuillaume and the Hotel of Delights

PAGANINI'S VISION of a Stradivarius quartet bearing his name did not die with him. Achillo, his fifteen-year-old heir, was as conscious as anyone of the commercial possibilities raised by the juxtaposition of the two names and pursued them with a single-mindedness of which his father could only have approved. To help him in his endeavours he engaged the services of the Parisian luthier who came to exemplify the nineteenth century's growing appreciation for Cremonese instruments: Jean-Baptiste Vuillaume.

Full of contradictions, Vuillaume is to some a genius, whose violins come a close second to those of the great classical luthiers, and to others a charlatan, who was quite happy for his Strad copies to be mistaken for the real thing. He was born in Mirecourt, the centre of French violin-making, in 1798. In later life he managed to give at least one musicologist the impression that an ancestor, Jean Vuillaume, had trained with Stradivari himself. The transparent falsity of the claim meant that after Vuillaume's death all his antecedents were questioned, but it is now generally accepted that his father at least, Claude-François Vuillaume, was a luthier, and that he trained his sons in the craft.

By the time he was nineteen, Jean-Baptiste must have had some sort of reputation, for in 1817 he was brought to Paris by another native of Mirecourt, François Chanot, to assist him in the manufacture of the 'guitar violin'. This novelty, patented by Chanot, enjoyed a brief period of fashionable success until its inventor was called up for military service. It was then soon forgotten, but Vuillaume remained in Paris, having gained a taste for innovation that was to last for the rest of his life. Chanot's business was taken over by Nicolas-Antoine Lété, an organ-builder keen to expand into string instruments, and Vuillaume accordingly entered his employment. Within four years he was a partner. The firm of Lété and Vuillaume persisted for three more years until, armed with capital provided by his new wife, heiress to an ironmonger, Vuillaume set up on his own.

Vuillaume's violins had won him a silver medal at the 1827 Paris Exhibition when he was still under thirty, and golds were to follow in 1839 and 1844. Vuillaume manned his workshop with assistants who produced violins according to his exact specifications. He grew rich on the profits of property speculation and eventually purchased a mansion on the rue des Ternes in Paris. An English visitor in this period later remembered him as a 'tall, well-dressed, dark man, with black whiskers and clean shaved upper lip and chin, rather more like an Englishman than a Frenchman, except as regarded his exceedingly polite manners'.

So this was the man who was formally engaged by Achillo Paganini in November 1846 to sell his father's Stradivarius quartet. Vuillaume set out the terms of the transaction in a letter the following month. Achillo had specified an asking price of 20,000 francs [£50,000]; in Vuillaume's words, 'this price is still very high ... The viola and the violins are ... in the best possible condition but the two violins have a tone which has not been as admired as that of the cello. This is no doubt because they have not been much played.' Vuillaume charged 160 francs for his restoration work, of which 20 francs applied to the 'yellow violin', the 1680 *Paganini*. He had repaired the crack in its belly, renewed the bass-bar, lengthened and raised the neck, fitted a new fingerboard and supplied pegs, tailpiece, bridge and strings. In other words, Vuillaume had brought the *Paganini* (and, indeed, the rest of the quartet) up to modern playing requirements.

The work was to no avail, however. Five years and many letters later the quartet was still unsold. In a final attempt to achieve a good price Vuillaume took the instruments with him to London, when he attended the 1851 Great Exhibition in the Crystal Palace. The event was a personal triumph. Vuillaume was exhibiting two of his own quartets and an instrument of his own invention, the 'octobasse', a massive beast which produced notes four tones lower than the double bass. It has not caught on, but together with the two quartets was enough to win Vuillaume the Exhibition's only Grand Council Medal in any category. There was no interest, however, in the four Strads and Vuillaume took them back to Paris. It seemed that the Paganini name no longer had quite the same magic. Achillo reluctantly decided to break up the quartet, authorizing Vuillaume to accept 5,000 francs [£15,000] for the cello, and 2,500 [£7,500] for each of the other instruments: quite a reduction on his original asking price. Around 1852, the 1680 *Paganini* was sold to a Monsieur Desaint, of Amiens. He would remain its owner for half a century. The other instruments all found separate buyers and the dream of a quartet of *Paganini* Strads vanished into history.

VUILLAUME'S POSITION at the epicentre of the European violin trade gave him a unique opportunity to observe and copy the Cremonese masterpieces, in many cases while they were still in their original state. Replacing the bass-bar naturally entailed taking the violin apart. When Vuillaume did so, he could take every conceivable measurement, gauging the thickness of the belly and back at minutely spaced intervals. With these measurements as his guide, he would be in a position to produce an exact copy of the original. If a violin was beyond repair, then at least its parts might form a basis for scientific study. Using materials from old violins supplied by Vuillaume, the nineteenth-century acoustician Félix Savart concluded that the dominant tap tone of the back plate of a Strad was always a semitone to a tone higher than the belly's. It was one of the first scientific investigations of Stradivari's methods and is an example of the efforts Vuillaume expended in his attempts to reproduce the Cremonese model. He extended this approach to the wood he used, reputedly scouring the flea markets and junk shops of Paris to find furniture of an age which would ensure that its timbers were fully mature.

In other ways, however, Vuillaume seems to have been more concerned with how his violins looked than how they sounded. One example is the way he and other French luthiers constructed their violins using an external mould, rather than around the internal mould favoured by the Cremonese. The technique may make it easier to reproduce the appearance of a violin, but the way the pieces are slotted into place, rather than held under tension by clamps and glue, has implications for sound quality that are only now being understood. There is a similar dichotomy in Vuillaume's approach to varnish. Apparently regarding the Cremonese product as too delicate, he determined to improve on it, creating his own formula based on amber. He does not seem to have reflected that the fragility of the classical luthiers' varnish was one of its key characteristics.

There is little to object to in any of this. Perhaps Vuillaume never really expected that his instruments would, in the words of his advertisements, be as good as Stradivari's 'after a little use', but that is hardly a hanging offence. Unfortunately, his obsession with appearances took him further. Vuillaume found that he could charge more for his violins if he made them look as much as possible like genuine Cremonese instruments, treating them in much the same way as a manufacturer of reproduction antiques would today. The varnish of his new instruments would be worn artistically, perhaps with acid, to resemble the original's more perfectly; violins might be baked to speed up the ageing process; and – the finishing touch – the classic label would be inserted: 'Antonius Stradivarius Cremonensis Faciebat Anno 1717'. Vuillaume always used that date, but he was not attempting to forge Strads; he knew that would be impossible. In fact he would usually sign the instrument with his own name elsewhere. He would also number all his copies in the centre of the violin's back. All these markings, however, can be removed, and now, with 150 years of further wear, it is hardly surprising that only experts can distinguish a Vuillaume replica from a true Strad.

There was a famous anecdote in the nineteenth century of Paganini leaving his *Cannon* del Gesù with Vuillaume for repair and being unable to distinguish it from its newly made copy when he arrived to collect it a few days later. That people believed the story is indicative both of the awe in which Vuillaume's powers as a copyist were held and of his talent for self-publicity. The true story is more prosaic. Paganini was indeed impressed by the copy, and by Vuillaume's speed in producing it, and was extremely keen to purchase it. Vuillaume was equally keen to give the copy to him; and in due course it became the concert instrument of Camillo Sivori, Paganini's pupil. The copy's varnish was a different colour to the original's and its tone was also no match for a genuine Cremona violin. In the hands of Sivori, however, it was transformed; and the story of Paganini being fooled became at least a little more believable. Even so, Sivori's tone has been damned by posterity as 'silvery and clear, but rather thin'.

Other stories raise more significant concerns. In the early years of his career, Vuillaume owned a bass viol made by Gaspard Tieffenbrucker, a sixteenth-century Bavarian who became a naturalized Frenchman. When, around that time, violins apparently made by the Franco-German started to circulate, a number of commentators hailed Tieffenbrucker as the true inventor of the violin. These violins were nineteenth-century impostors, constructions 'antiqued' to look old. Later historians were convinced that Vuillaume had made them. In another vignette, David Laurie tells how Vuillaume would set aside Thursdays for the reception of admirers at the rue des Ternes. There he would sit in public view, applying his varnish to newly made violins and selling bottles of the same to all comers. Later in the day, and safely inside the mansion, Laurie witnessed him removing the worthless varnish before it had time to dry: 'Did you really think I would let my valuable secrets go so easily?'

VUILLAUME never forgot Tarisio's claims for the violin he had bought from Count Cozio di Salabue, the *Messiah*. Such an instrument, unplayed and unaltered since it left the master's hands, would have been the perfect template for Vuillaume the copyist, not to mention its monetary value to Vuillaume the dealer. He must have pressed Tarisio to bring it to Paris many times, eventually realizing that it was a treasure the Italian would never give up during his lifetime. Equally, Vuillaume must have realized that he was by no means the only luthier to be aware of the *Messiah*'s existence. Even in Paris, he knew that Chanot, not himself, was Tarisio's preferred dealer. Moreover, by the 1850s, Tarisio's sales trips were extending to London, where he amazed at least one collector by naming the date and maker of all his violins without even touching them. It was a remarkable feat of recognition rather than magic; Tarisio had been their original supplier. All Tarisio's customers would have coveted the *Messiah*. Vuillaume could only wait and hope that his chance would eventually come.

The story of how Vuillaume achieved his dream has

passed into legend. It begins with Tarisio's neighbours in his Milanese tenement, the curiously named 'Hotel of Delights'. Some time towards the end of 1854 they noticed that the old man had not been seen for a while, or perhaps there was a strange smell. The authorities broke in to find Tarisio lying dead on a tattered bed. Two violins were clasped against him, many more were scattered around the room. Of more interest to the officials was the hoard of securities, banknotes and gold – 400,000 lire [£1 million] – eventually found in a mattress. They traced the heirs, removed the body and obvious valuables, and sealed the apartment. It was only by chance that a commercial traveller in silks heard of the discovery, was on his way to Paris, and knew that Vuillaume was the person there to tell.

So Vuillaume had the luck to be the first luthier to hear of Tarisio's death. Even so, he was right to lose no speed. Who knew what Tarisio's family might have done with his collection? Vuillaume scraped together as much money as he could and caught the train for Italy within an hour of hearing the news. On arrival at Novara, he at once hired a coach to take him to Fontaneto, where Tarisio's nephews still lived on a smallholding bought by their uncle ten years before. Arriving at suppertime, Vuillaume's apprehension was only multiplied by the sight of the relations who assembled 'with every appearance of the most sordid poverty'. He accepted a glass of wine but it was some time before he could enquire as to the whereabouts of the deceased's violins.

'In Milan,' replied one of the nephews, the other adding 'We haven't touched the dirty junk yet.'

As he suppressed his excitement and relief, it must

have been all Vuillaume could do not to leave for Milan that instant. Besides, it was wise to check: 'And nothing has been brought here at all?'

'Oh yes, six violins are here.'

Guided by Tarisio's sister, Vuillaume started to open the drawers of a rickety piece of furniture. Inside he found exquisite violin-cases, made of beautiful wood and adorned with inset arabesques. The first four to be opened revealed as many masterpieces – a Stradivarius, a Bergonzi and two Guadagninis – before Vuillaume came to the last drawer. It was in such a bad state that he had some difficulty opening it without damaging the contents. When he eventually succeeded, all he could do for some time was stare. There was a superb del Gesù, made in 1742 and soon to be christened the *Alard*, but Vuillaume only had eyes for its companion. Tarisio had been telling the truth: there was the *Messiah*, as perfectly preserved as the day it was hung up to dry.

Vuillaume had to spend the night at the farm. The following morning, accompanied by the nephews and with the six violins carefully secured, but not yet purchased, he drove into Milan. In Tarisio's tiny garret, still surrounding the bed where his body had lain, were piles of violins, violas and cellos. Resisting temptation, Vuillaume did not leap straight into examination; it was time to make a purchase. He judged the nephews well. Taking out his wallet, and unbuckling his heavy money belt, he brought out all his cash and counted it, announcing, 'I have 80,000 francs [£200,000] on me.' With these words, Vuillaume sealed the purchase of 150 instruments, including about two dozen Strads. It was the single most important transaction in the history of violins.

Vuillaume was no hoarder like Tarisio. Over the next few years he sold on almost his entire purchase at what would have been a huge profit. At first, he must have intended the same fate for the *Messiah*. He made the same adjustments to it that he did with every old violin to come into his possession, the same alterations that he had carried out on the *Paganini* a decade before, enough to make the *Messiah* ready for concert use. It was probably while he had the violin in pieces for these adjustments that he took the measurements for the copies that duly emerged from his workshop.

Thereafter Vuillaume should have been ready to make a handsome return on his prize. He was, after all, a dealer. In 1865 he seems to have gone so far as to name the *Messiah*'s price, asking a French amateur, Monsieur Fau, for 10,000 francs [£25,000]. In the end, however, and like Tarisio, he could not bring himself to sell. By the end of the century there was a legend that the violin exerted such a hold on its owners that they could only be parted from it by death.*

There may have been a good financial motive for this apparent irrationality. The *Messiah*'s perfection and Vuillaume's story of its dramatic discovery had made it the most famous violin in the world. Owning it added to Vuillaume's lustre as a luthier; his own violins benefited from the reflected glory. There is more, however, to the *Messiah*'s influence than that; it seems to have made its owner question the whole basis on which he had been operating. Soon after he acquired it, Vuillaume shut the

---

* It was probably not generally known that Count Cozio lived on for at least a decade after he sold the *Messiah* to Tarisio.

shop where he and his workmen had made over 2,000 violins and retired to his mansion. Here he continued, on his own, to practise his craft. Every violin he made from then on shows the influence of the *Messiah*. Many would be direct copies. Vuillaume would delight in placing original and duplicate side by side and asking visitors to guess which was which.

The *Messiah* looked destined to remain in a glass case on the rue des Ternes until its owner died. That this might not be a place of safety only became apparent in 1870 with the outbreak of the Franco-Prussian War. By January the following year the victorious Prussians had bombarded, besieged and, eventually, accepted the surrender of the French capital. Vuillaume himself was safe, having fled the city. It must have been a fine judgement as to whether to take his most precious possession with him. Deciding, however, that it was better off hidden until the war was over, Vuillaume then suffered agonies until he could return to Paris and assure himself of its safety.

Vuillaume died in 1875, while making his 3,001st violin. Jeanne-Émilie and Claire-Marie, his two daughters, inherited the entire estate, including the *Messiah*. They offered the violin for £1,000 [£60,000] to their uncle, Nicolas-François, another luthier based in Brussels. The price was too steep, however, and for some time the violin remained in testatory limbo. Eventually Delphin Alard, Jeanne-Émilie's husband, bought out Claire-Marie, and full ownership passed to him. So the man who had christened the *Messiah*, in that conversation with Tarisio half a century before, finally came to own it.

Alard had mixed qualifications for being custodian of

the world's most immaculate Strad. On the one hand, he was a distinguished violinist and composer, Professor at the Paris Conservatoire. On the other, we have the story that Vuillaume himself related to David Laurie. Many years before he had presented his son-in-law with another Strad, made in 1715. Now celebrated as the *Alard*, at the time it had been little played upon and had a relatively poor tone. Alard suggested to Vuillaume that this could be improved by scraping a little varnish off the front. Vuillaume could only expostulate: 'Imagine my feelings, my dear Mr Laurie! How have I sinned against heaven that I should be cursed with a son-in-law who could propose to scrape a Stradivarius?' Alard certainly knew how to wind his father-in-law up, but it is probably fortunate that, like every previous owner, he chose not to play his treasure. The *Messiah* remained unheard.

Chapter Ten

'UNVEILED IN ALL ITS INTACT GLORY'

The *Messiah* makes its mark

EVEN WHEN SILENT, the *Messiah* made its influence felt. It came to world-wide attention at a crucial time in the history of the violin. As the population of Europe and America gravitated towards the cities, old pastimes ceased to be available. Cultured metropolitans had to find new ways of whiling away their leisure hours. Music lovers might go to concerts, but not every day of the week. How much more satisfactory if they could learn to play an instrument for themselves and that skill became the basis for much of their social life. The age of the amateur orchestra had arrived.

Victorian violinists may have been enthused by the example of Paganini and his successors, and even learnt from the artistic descendants of Viotti, but few were expecting any audience for their efforts as soloists. Nevertheless, even indifferent violinists had their place. Those amateur orchestras would have had perhaps thirty violins, covering a wide range of abilities, at the core of their sound. Play the violin and you will always have an opportunity to perform: the same advice is given to children today. There was an inexorable rise in demand for violins.

Towns like Mirecourt in France and Mittenwald in Germany evolved into centres of mass-production. Methods were far removed from the Cremonese tradition of Stradivari: different workers would specialize in fronts, backs, scrolls, assembly and varnishing. Even their input was limited, as machinery was developed for carving or even pressing arched fronts and backs from flat pieces of wood. All this naturally required workers to follow the same template, and the *Messiah*, via Vuillaume's duplicates, was for many the obvious choice. It would become the most copied instrument in the world.

The violins made in Mirecourt or Mittenwald were sent all over Europe. With no initial identification, some would be claimed by dealers as their own work. Others would be labelled as Strads. There may not have been any intent to deceive, simply over-enthusiastic identification of the original model. No one could have expected to sell new violins as genuine Cremonas; but the practice has caused huge problems for modern violin dealers. That Stradivarius violin found in the attic may have been in the family for generations, so it is especially disappointing to be told that it is nothing of the kind. Any dealer is likely to have several encounters like this in a year. 'We have a lot of optimistic violin owners coming along,' says one expert, 'whose response when it is pointed out that their [twentieth-century] "Stradivarius" also carries a "Made in Czechoslovakia" label is to say that "He might have made it while he was on holiday there."'

IN 1872 the *Messiah* was the star attraction of an exhibition of ancient instruments at the South Kensington (now Victoria and Albert) Museum in London. One English commentator marvelled: 'Unveiled in all its intact glory to the gaze of thousands to whom for years it has been a kind of myth . . . stands this matchless new violin amidst its time-worn, rubbed and fractured brethren.' The cult of the *Messiah* was in full swing.

The South Kensington exhibition provided an opportunity for Charles Reade to write a series of articles, in letters to the *Pall Mall Gazette*, on the mysteries of Cremonese violins. They addressed the question which was now beginning to puzzle a wider public: why could modern violins not reproduce the sound of a Stradivarius?

Charles Reade is hardly heard of now, but he was one of the most successful authors of his day. Novels like *Hard Cash* and *The Cloister and the Hearth* cast him as Dickens's natural successor and contemporary critics reckoned him superior to George Eliot. He was also an amateur violin dealer of some note. His purchase of a job lot in Paris in 1848 was almost scuppered by the revolution that broke out between handing over the money and taking delivery, but its significance was probably only exceeded by Vuillaume's encounter with Tarisio's heirs. It was rare for a man of Reade's literary talents to apply them to musicology; and his four letters to the *Pall Mall Gazette* were still being quoted fifty years later. The most interesting of all the theories they propounded was that the Cremonese masters used two varnishes. The first, a slow-drying oil-based varnish that penetrated the pores of the wood, gave the violins much of their colour. The overcoat, spirit-based and quicker to dry, contributed further brilliance and colour but would also be subject to chipping and wear. It was one of the first public references to the importance of Stradivari's varnish, and Reade was in the vanguard of those claiming to have found the secret. Many would follow.

THE *Messiah* was on display to all, stimulating debate and vain attempts at imitation, but another of our five violins was almost as influential. Joseph Böhm had retired from the concert stage after hearing Paganini. He demanded so little of his violin, the *Khevenhüller*, that he never even provided it with modern fittings. Böhm had not, however, given up playing. As Professor at the Vienna Conservatoire he and the *Khevenhüller* continued to be heard, not by Austrian audiences, but by future virtuosos. For Joseph Böhm could make a good claim to being the nineteenth century's most successful teacher of the violin. Many of his pupils would go on to become performers and professors all over Europe. Ernst, Singer, Hellmsberger, Rappoldi and Hauser – all were influential, but the most famous of Böhm's pupils was undoubtedly Joseph Joachim. Born in 1831, he spent three years living with Böhm before he was twelve and by 1860 was the most celebrated violinist of the age, a position he was to occupy for almost fifty years.

Joachim always emphasized his debt to Böhm: 'Severe, earnest and matter-of-fact, he was yet in every way kind and encouraging.' He owed him the freedom with which he bowed, and the unmannered, classical correctness of his playing. As a member of the Böhm household Joachim both heard and played in the private quartet evenings that the professor continued, despite his aversion to public performance, to lead at home. He must have been one of the few people in mid-nineteenth-century Europe to hear Beethoven's late quartets; they had fallen so far out of favour since the composer's death. Decades later the Joachim Quartet would be largely responsible for bringing them back into public recognition.

There was, however, something else that Joachim learnt from Böhm and the *Khevenhüller*. He became the Strad player, and advocate, of his generation. In the course of his life he would own several Strads, almost all either presented to him by admirers or left to him as bequests. The school that Joachim oversaw in Berlin would take up Böhm's baton, producing a generation of violinists who shared their teacher's predilection for Strads. A festival in 1899, held to celebrate the diamond jubilee of Joachim's first performance, centred on his previous pupils: forty-four of their violins, played in the associated concert, were Strads.

By 1888, when the Cremona Society held its inaugural meeting in London, its president could declare that whereas forty years before Guarneri del Gesù was often regarded as the true master, with every violin-maker in Europe setting out to copy him, Stradivari was now back on top. The eulogy praised the Master in words that would resonate with any modern player. His violins offered 'promptness of speech' and 'flexibility under varying pressure to produce tones of all intensity'. They were the models for all violins.

Chapter Eleven

'FIND HIS MAJESTY'S SOLOIST'

Charles Davidov and his cello

STRADIVARI'S VIOLINS might have had to face a challenge from Guarneri del Gesù, but cellos were another matter. Only one has ever been ascribed to del Gesù himself, and those of other Cremonese makers were, like early Strads, originally made too large. Apart from those made by Stradivari in his golden period, the most successful Italian cellos come from Venice. In particular, those made by Domenico Montagnana (1687–1750), the 'Mighty Venetian', are broader than Stradivari's, but of a length that feels comfortable to modern players. They are the only serious rivals to the Master's.

To most players, however, the B-form cellos Stradivari made from 1707 to 1727 remain the *ne plus ultra* of the craft. Only twenty-one have survived and their scarcity value sets them apart even from Stradivari's golden-period violins. Almost every one can boast a succession of great players. Moreover, a debate about which is the best of all is at least possible in a way that is inconceivable for Stradivari's violins. For the first half of the nineteenth century, I suspect, most would have awarded this laurel to a cello made by Stradivari in 1711, the *Duport*. Its eponymous owner was later regarded as the Viotti of his instrument; Jean-Louis Duport made a triumphant debut at the Concert Spirituel in 1768 and had pupils who went on to colonize most of the capitals of Europe.

Duport's position as Napoleon's favourite cellist almost resulted in disaster for his Stradivarius when the Emperor appeared, booted and spurred, at a private recital in the Tuileries. As the French historian Antoine Vidal later recounted, 'He listened with pleasure and, as soon as the piece was over he approached Duport, complimented him, and, grasping the cello with his usual forcefulness, asked, "How the devil do you hold this, Monsieur Duport?" while, sitting down, he squeezed the unfortunate instrument between his spurred boots.' Some say the marks of the spurs can still be clearly seen in the sides of the cello. The legend added to its fame as it passed through almost equally celebrated hands after Duport's death. By 1843 the *Duport* was the treasured possession of another great cellist, August Franchomme, who paid 22,000 francs [£60,000] for it.

The amount seemed unprecedented, justified only by the instrument's celebrity. According to Franchomme's daughter, her father had to make 'strenuous efforts' to raise the money. It must have rather upset him, therefore, to hear that an amateur Russian cellist, Count Mateusz Wielhorski, regarded his Stradivarius cello as superior even to the *Duport*. On 2 October 1843 Franchomme wrote to the Count to query this; the reply, alas, is not preserved. Nevertheless, that letter from Franchomme is the first entry back into history of the *Davidov*, the superb cello we last encountered in 1712, being made by Stradivari for the Medicis.

The *Davidov*'s history before 1843 is obscure. It probably disappeared from the Medici collection in Florence's

Pitti Palace during the occupation by Austrian troops in 1737. The confusion must have created many opportunities for the unscrupulous. There is little to fill the subsequent century. One book, *The Violoncello and its History* by Wilhelm Josef von Wasielewski, published in 1888, implies that the *Davidov* belonged to 'Korczmiet, properly Kaltschmidt, of German descent, an accomplished virtuoso player, [who] lived and worked, from 1811 to 1817, at Wilna'. Apart from that, we know that Wielhorski acquired the *Davidov*, presumably between 1817 and 1843, from another Russian nobleman, Count Apraxin. The price was Wielhorski's Guarneri cello (probably one made by del Gesù's grandfather, Andrea), 40,000 francs [£100,000] in cash, and a pedigree horse from his stud. Compared to that, Franchomme had not, after all, overpaid for the *Duport*.

Wielhorski was clearly a rich man, able to indulge his passions. It was said that in order to have lessons from Bernhard Romberg, founder of the German cello school, the Count lodged him in his palace in St Petersburg for two years. It speaks of his determination to play like an artist; his exuberant purchase of the *Davidov* was no aristocratic whim. Contemporary composers certainly respected Wielhorski. In 1843 Felix Mendelssohn wrote his second cello sonata for him; a year later Robert Schumann declared in a letter that he was the most gifted dilettante he had ever met. The Belgian violinist, Henri Vieuxtemps, wrote his 'Duo Brilliant' for himself and Wielhorski.

In 1838, the Count had even shared a stage with another of our characters, Karol Lipiński, when both appeared as soloists at a charity concert in St Petersburg.

They would not have played together, so we cannot imagine the mingling tones of the *Davidov* and the *Lipiński*, but I find the probable conjunction none the less attractive.

The Count was also one of Russia's first concert promoters. He and his brother Michal were responsible for introducing many western composers to the St Petersburg audience. Schumann's impression of Count Mateusz's talents was formed when he and his wife stayed with the two brothers. Franz Liszt was another guest, and was spotted by the Russian art critic, Vladimir Stasov, strolling with Count Michal at a morning reception: 'The Count, who moved very, very slowly, glowering at everyone with his bulging eyes, was wearing a wig curled *à l'Apollo Belvedere** and a large white cravat.'

A more complimentary account of the Wielhorskis comes from Hector Berlioz, the former beneficiary of Paganini's generosity, who was in St Petersburg in 1847: 'They are brothers, each as intelligent and as devoted to music as the other, and they live together. The prestige of their justly famous taste, the influence of their great wealth and numerous connections, and their official position at court, close to the Emperor and the Empress, combine to make their house a little Ministry of Fine Arts in St Petersburg.'

With all that, it may seem surprising that the Count's Stradivarius cello has not ended up being called the 'Wielhorski'. That it has not is the result of one final act of generosity.

Carl Davidov was being hailed as Europe's greatest

---

* Presumably a reference to the statue in the Vatican that had a profound influence on neo-classical sculpture.

cello virtuoso before he was twenty-five, but he had not taken a standard route to such acclaim. Born in Latvia in 1838, Davidov only began learning the instrument when he was twelve. The late start was compounded by his parents' insistence that before he could contemplate a musical career, he must first finish his formal studies. So he was already twenty and had taken a degree in mathematics from St Petersburg when he arrived in Leipzig to study composition.

Even then, Davidov might have ended up a composer. The extent of his talent for the cello only became apparent when he was drafted in as a last-minute replacement at a private concert given by the Mendelssohn Trio. Davidov's success there, followed by a more public triumph performing his own 1st Cello Concerto, convinced him that his future lay as a musician. In 1862 he returned to St Petersburg, after a brilliant period in Leipzig and concerts around Europe, to take up the post of first cello at the Opera. Within a year he was a professor at the newly established Conservatoire, ready to become a key figure in the development of his country's great cello-playing tradition. To do so, Davidov needed an instrument to match his talent.

THERE ARE MANY stories about how Wielhorski gave his Stradivarius to Davidov. My favourite is the version told by Yo-Yo Ma, the *Davidov*'s current player: 'One night during the winter of 1885–6 Davidov went to visit Count Wielhorski at the court of Tsar Alexander II. "What ails you?" said Davidov to Wielhorski. "You are so excited."

Wielhorski replied, "You are right. For tonight I am celebrating my seventieth birthday, and am doing this by presenting you with my cello." Davidov could not believe this until the following day when the Count's servant brought the cello to his house.' Another version – a letter written to accompany the *Davidov* later in its life – says that the presentation took place at a concert to mark Wielhorski's eightieth birthday, given, with the consent of the Czar, at the Court of St Petersburg. A third account says simply that the presentation took place in 1870.

Wielhorski was born in 1793 and died in 1866, so none of these stories can be quite right. What seems clear, however, is that Wielhorski thought of Davidov as a protégé – he had been involved in the establishment of the St Petersburg Conservatoire, and probably had a hand in Davidov's appointment – and that he knew his own playing days were coming to an end. He regarded his Strad as the best cello in the world; naturally he would want to see it in the hands of his brilliant young countryman.

Most likely the transfer occurred on Wielhorski's seventieth birthday, as Ma's version has it, but this would have been in 1863, around the time Davidov got his professorship. It would be nice to believe the rest of Ma's story, apart from its dates, but to my mind, that goes against what we know of Wielhorski's inclinations as an impresario. Surely he would not have passed up the opportunity he was creating for a very public presentation? The letter must have it basically right, except for adding ten years to the Count's age. There was a concert and its centrepiece was surely the cello itself, played first perhaps by Wielhorski, and then by Davidov, in a symbolic acknowledgement by the older generation that its time had passed.

BY THE TIME Davidov received the cello that would come to bear his name, it would have been largely updated to modern playing requirements. Wielhorski could hardly have played the pieces dedicated to him on a baroque cello. So, just as with violins, its neck would have been tipped back from the body to do away with the wedged fingerboard. The bass-bar, too, would have been replaced with a larger version, strengthening a belly put under greater stress than Stradivari had ever planned. Wielhorski would certainly also have used a modern Tourte-designed bow. In all these developments the violin and cello moved at the same pace. In another, the larger instrument led the way: by 1863 the two lower strings on the *Davidov* would have been of gut half-wound with silver. The result would have been a more penetrating tone, and less tendency to lose pitch during performance, but at the expense of some sweetness. Violins would continue to use all-gut strings until well into the twentieth century.

Davidov was probably responsible for the last change that his cello must have undergone before it was ready for the modern cellist: the installation of an end-pin, allowing him to rest the instrument on the ground. The popularization of this innovation, like so many others, can be credited to a player, although it was being recommended for beginners 100 years earlier. The Belgian virtuoso Adrien-François Servais became celebrated throughout Europe in the first half of the century as 'the Paganini of the cello'. The reference must have been to his technique rather than his demeanour. Towards the end of his life (he died in 1866, aged fifty-nine) Servais grew so fat that he could no longer hold his cello between his knees. An end-pin provided the solution. The invention provoked a revolution in cello technique: the legs could relax, the bow move more easily and the left hand travel freely up and down the fingerboard. Only with an end-pin could women consider becoming cellists: the idea of gripping the instrument between the legs had previously been too unladylike to entertain.

Installing an end-pin simply involves replacing one end-button – the attachment point for the tailpiece – with another that contains a sliding extension; it has no direct impact on tone. There is, however, an indirect result. Ever since the time of Servais, cellos have been connected to the ground, another body with its own set of resonances to consider. Rest the end-pin on a booming stage and the cello's tone quality changes significantly.

IT WOULD BE pleasant to record that Davidov treasured Wielhorski's present, treating it with the care it deserved. In fact, he seems to have regarded his entire career somewhat casually, an attitude he extended to his cello. He had the kind of genius which comes almost too easily. The only time he ever practised seriously was in 1859, for those first crucial concerts. Leopold Aüer, who played first violin in the St Petersburg Quartet with Davidov, said that the cellist would perform without having played for months beforehand. He remembered rehearsals for the 'gaiety, laughter and flood of anecdote' at the 'hospitable table' of Davidov and his 'charming wife', rather than for any hard grind. Pupils recalled Davidov bringing his Strad into class before a concert so that they could play in the new strings because 'I have no time to spare for my cello.'

The cellist became a favoured habitué of the grand court of the Czar, with the title of 'Soloist to His Majesty'. This was not some meaningless honorific. The position carried duties and expectations which in 1875 almost led to disaster, when the Russian court decided to entertain the visiting King and Queen of Sweden with a musical evening. The pianist and composer Anton Rubinstein was asked to make the arrangements. He drew up a programme, including Davidov both in a trio and as a soloist, which he presented to the Minister of the Imperial Household, Count Alderberg. Only then was it discovered that the cellist was not in St Petersburg, having left for a spontaneous tour of Finland. It was a serious matter; being absent without leave could have lost Davidov his position at court, with all the ramifications that disgrace implied. In vain did Rubinstein telegraph all the major cities of what was then a Russian Imperial possession. He could not find Davidov and went to Alderberg with a revised programme for the soirée. The Minister enquired as to the reason for the alteration, and upon being told, replied that if Davidov really was in Finland then there was no need to change the programme; he would be back in St Petersburg the following evening.

On the morning of the concert Davidov was surprised to be woken at five o'clock by the porter of his small hotel in Vibors, a Finnish fortress not far from the frontier. More alarming was the sight of the porter's companion: the chief of police, in full uniform, who told Davidov to dress immediately and go directly with his Stradivarius to the railway station. The cellist obeyed nervously but without demur; one did not cross Russian officialdom lightly. Once at the station, he was handed the piece of paper that explained his rude awakening:

> Telegraph order from the Minister of the Household
> to His Majesty the Czar:
> To all chiefs of police in Finland:
> Hunt up at once and find His Majesty's soloist
> Charles Davidov, and return him immediately per
> special train to Peterhof.

The train was there, waiting. As it sped through station after station on its way to the Imperial Palace Davidov was amused to see station-master and employees ranged in military fashion along each platform, saluting what they assumed must be a senior member of the Royal Family. He arrived in time for the concert.

One year later, in 1876, Davidov was appointed Director of the St Petersburg Conservatoire. The promotion meant that, like the Rubinstein brothers before him, Davidov was made a member of the Order of St Vladimir, of the Fourth Class. It was an important distinction, conferring noble status on him and his descendants, no small preferment in a feudal state where musicians otherwise had no rights and could be subject to passport problems at every frontier. Davidov's reign as Director would be remembered for its benevolence: the number of scholarships was greatly increased and free lodgings provided for the poorer students. Only as conductor of the St Petersburg Orchestra was he a relative failure. 'Gentle and timid by nature', in Aüer's words, Davidov 'lacked the energy, grasp and temperament to impose his authority and to inspire his players'. He lasted in the position for only one season.

THE YEAR THAT Davidov became Director of the St Petersburg Conservatoire was also the year of Joseph Böhm's death. He had no children and so his nephew Louis inherited the *Khevenhüller*. Himself a violinist, he had been his uncle's pupil and lodger at the same time as Joachim. By 1876 he was a Professor at the St Petersburg Conservatoire. Here he would have looked to Davidov for leadership. Surely some time over the next decade the Professor and his Director would have played together, each with his own Strad: probably the first time that two of our instruments met in the same piece of music.

Towards the end of his life Louis sold his violin to Viktor Popov, Professor at the Moscow Conservatoire, St Petersburg's great rival. This new owner finally saw that the *Khevenhüller* was provided with modern fittings, a full century after the first such transformations. The violin's original neck was probably close to wearing away, so it was not just tipped back by means of an insert, but replaced with an entirely new piece of maple, which was then grafted on to Stradivari's scroll.

In 1906 Popov's fellow Muscovite, Pierre de Ellisseiff, acquired another of our Strads, the 1680 *Paganini*. Monsieur Desaint, its purchaser from Vuillaume, had eventually sold it to a Monsieur Levers, of Poitiers; and he was the seller on this occasion. So *Khevenhüller* and *Paganini* were in the same city. It is seductive to imagine quartet evenings, the two Strads overcoming their fifty-year age difference in a sweet-toned combination.

BY THIS TIME Davidov was long dead. His downfall came when he took his concern for his pupils beyond the purely paternal. In 1887 he was found to be having an affair with a young piano student. Not only forced to resign all his appointments, he also, for a while, had to quit Russia altogether. He soon returned, but in January 1889, while still only fifty, became ill on stage during a performance of five Beethoven sonatas. He died two weeks later, leaving the *Davidov* Stradivarius to his family. An English dealer attempted to buy the instrument, 'but the price asked was what, in those days, was considered an exorbitant figure, namely 60,000 francs' [£165,000]. The same dealer would later remark: 'This fine example suffered considerably during Davidov's ownership, and it bears marks not only of wear but also of careless usage.' It would eventually be sold in Paris at the turn of the century. It was rare for a British purchaser to be outbid. The epicentre of the trade in Strads had by now shifted firmly to London.

Chapter Twelve

'AN IMMENSE RESERVE
OF STRENGTH'

Marie Hall, the Hills and the Edwardian era

IN JUNE 1890 a new monthly journal devoted to the violin and its sister instruments was launched upon the British public. Carrying news, reviews and advice for readers, it welcomed correspondence and declared that it would be totally independent, though of what is not clear. The journal's name – *The Strad* – had the imprimatur of quality about it. As the opening editorial itself put it, since its namesake's 'death, in 1736 [sic], violin-making has practically speaking come to a standstill'.

The subjects covered by *The Strad* – concerts, tips on playing, histories of the development of string playing – were of immense interest to the burgeoning middle classes. And Britain's wealth ensured that the inflow of Strads showed no sign of abating. So one of the first news items in the magazine, three months after its launch, was a report that the most famous of them all, the *Messiah* itself, had now arrived on British shores. Alard had died, and his prize violin had been bought from his son-in-law for £2,000 [£140,000], a record for any instrument. The purchaser was a Mr Robert Crawford of Edinburgh, whose agent in the transaction was W. E. Hill & Sons of London.

Few names in violin-making are as old as the Hills'. In 1660 Samuel Pepys had consulted a Mr Hill at his 'Musick Shop' in the Minories about 'ye altering of my Lute and my viall'. Sadly, it is hard to find a link between Pepys' Hill and the eighteenth-century Joseph Hill, based in the Haymarket, who made (according to his descendants) 'somewhat feeble copies' of Italian violins, violas and cellos. His grandson, William Ebsworth Hill, the leader of the family firm from the middle of the nineteenth century, had also started off by making violins. The profitability of this activity, however, was hit by free trade, which allowed in cheap continental imports. So he gradually came to concentrate on dealing in and repairing old violins. It proved to be an inspired decision.

As values rose and forgery or misattribution grew commonplace, the need to authenticate instruments became paramount. Labels had been unreliable since before Tarisio. Instead, a host of different clues went into determining the maker of a violin: the lustre of the varnish, the shape of the tool-marks, the slant of the soundholes, the quality of the wood, the swell of the curves. Expertise required a pictorial memory built from handling thousands of instruments. Only dealers were in this position, and W. E. Hill was the most authoritative of them all. In the words of one reminiscence, 'when a violin was shown him he gave one quick, comprehensive glance, and instantly declared the maker. Venture to doubt him, and quickly you were crushed under a perfect avalanche of proof, perhaps not unmixed with some biting, sarcastic expressions of astonishment at your failure to recognize what was so plainly obvious.'

A Hill & Sons certificate of authenticity appended to a

violin meant far more than any label inside it, and W. E Hill's expert testimony could decide a court case. Probably his most celebrated intervention was as a witness for the plaintiff, James Johnstone, against the Scottish dealer David Laurie. The latter had in 1883 reconstructed a Strad from disparate parts, cutting down the back to fit the front, and sold it to Johnstone with the following guarantee: 'Made by Antonius Stradivarius, of Cremona, date 1701, which I guarantee genuine in all its parts as being the production of this celebrated maker.' Upon discovering the violin's true provenance, Johnstone, a wholesale fish salesman, had, reasonably enough, asked for his money back. When Laurie refused, Johnstone sued and, with W. E. Hill on his side, won. The case turned not so much on the fact that the violin had been reassembled from three different predecessors, but more on Laurie's guarantee having claimed too much. One of the violin's ribs was not, in fact, genuine, and Laurie could not stand by the date of 1701. It seems amazing that he ever thought he could get away with it, except that he had the last laugh, finally selling the now-famous *Court* Strad for twice what Johnstone had originally paid.

Other dealers, meanwhile, felt aggrieved on Laurie's behalf: judges and fish salesmen should not get involved in matters they did not understand, but leave them to the true connoisseur. The truth is that Laurie was behaving as everyone in the trade always had. He was simply unfortunate enough to have been caught and challenged. A bit further down the pecking order, Edward Goodwin was trading in far less expensive violins, the kind that might still be found in continental market towns. In his reminiscences he happily admits to relabelling, setting up auction rings and (a particular favourite) buying instruments from French widows at a fraction of their true value. The overall attitude among most dealers seems to have been one of caveat both emptor and vendor. Since the days of Tarisio they had been the only people with the ability to identify both fakes and treasures; how they were to profit from this unique closed shop was surely their own concern?

ONE OF THE WAYS in which the Hills had started to distinguish themselves from their competitors was by producing elegant monographs on violins and luthiers. The *Tuscan* Stradivarius, one of the set made for the Medicis in 1690, had already been treated in this way, and books on Maggini and Stradivari himself were to follow. In 1891 they did the same for the *Messiah*.* It seems an odd choice. The book on the *Tuscan* can be interpreted as a discreet advertisement. The *Messiah* already belonged to Robert Crawford when the book was written. It had been only briefly in the care of the Hills and they had never even owned it. One way or another, however, they had started to feel the same attraction for the violin as Tarisio, Vuillaume and its other previous owners. Over the next fifty years the fortunes of the Hills and the *Messiah* were to become intimately entwined.

The book itself gave the Hills the chance to detail the *Messiah*'s history, and to wax lyrical over the craftsman-

---

* They called it the '*Salabue*', after its first famous owner, Count Cozio di Salabue.

ship that had gone into its construction. Many features were unique: the sharpness of the ridge between the purfling and the edge of the instrument, the squareness of the corners, the overall flatness of the violin and the wonderful state of preservation of its varnish. They could also give an opinion on the *Messiah*'s tone. In 1864 Fétis had asserted that 'in this new instrument, we find in combination all the qualities of power, mellowness, roundness, delicacy, freedom, with a noble and penetrating tone'. The Hills note this and then comment drily, 'Nevertheless it is our opinion after a careful trial that the instrument would be greatly improved in tone by further use.' It seems little had changed since Spohr encountered the violin seventy-five years before.

Over the period it was in Crawford's ownership, the *Messiah* was probably played more than at any other point in its life. Most famously, in 1891 Joseph Joachim was permitted to try it. His subsequent letter to Robert Crawford is still quoted whenever the question of the *Messiah*'s tone is discussed: 'Of course, the sound of the Strad, that unique "Messie", turns up again and again in my memory, with its combined sweetness and grandeur, that struck me so much in hearing it.'

The *Messiah* did not remain in Scotland for long. In 1904 Crawford sold it back to the Hills. William Ebsworth himself had died in 1895, but his business had continued to flourish under his three sons. In 1902 the brothers had brought out the first edition of their greatest work, *Antonio Stradivari: His Life and Work*. In the ten years since producing their monograph, the family's admiration for the *Messiah* had only deepened: '[It] stands alone for its unrivalled condition. Were it but eight days, instead of one hundred and eighty-six years old, it could not present a fresher appearance.' The Hills would not part with the violin again until 1913.

ANOTHER OF our Strads passed through the Hills' hands around this time. Karol Lipiński had died in 1861 and Dresden dealers had sold his violin to Professor Engelbert Röntgen at the Leipzig Conservatory. He was a fine violinist, owed a debt by later generations of music lovers for his scholarly editions of Beethoven's quartets, but he was no virtuoso. In his hands, the *Lipiński* conquered no more audiences. Then, in 1899, two years after Röntgen's death, Joseph Joachim heard the violin; it was probably one of the forty-four Strads played at his diamond jubilee concert in Berlin. Forty years before, a public embrace from Lipiński had been one of the milestone events in Joachim's ascendancy to worldwide acclaim. So an encounter with his old violin should have sparked happy memories. On this occasion, however, something was wrong with it and Joachim recommended that W. E. Hill & Sons would make the best repairs. From London the *Lipiński* went back to the continent, and a Dutch amateur who subsequently sold it back to the Hills. Turnover like this was all grist to the dealer's mill; together with the apparently inexorable rise in prices of old violins, it must have made the brothers bless their father's original decision to move away from manufacture.

SOME, HOWEVER, thought that prices must be plateau-ing. Surely they could not rise beyond £2,000 [£140,000]?

Debate already raged as to whether any violin could be worth the prices now being paid. Makers like Gemünder in New York were selling copies of Strads and del Gesù for something like $200 [£2,700]. Advertisements boasted of the violinists who played them, and carried what seemed like glowing testimonials. Attempts were made to compare instruments under more or less scientific conditions. One of the first experiments, in 1909, asked an audience to vote for their favourite violin, after each was played in a darkened concert hall by the same soloist. A relatively modern nineteenth-century French violin beat a Strad into second place, but the significance of the result was tainted when it turned out that the winning instrument belonged to the soloist. Similarly, it was hard to take seriously extravagant recommendations for a modern maker from virtuosi who continued to use Cremonese instruments in concert.

To most observers, therefore, violinists' continuing demand for Strads and other Cremonese instruments was proof enough of their superiority. Even Vuillaume's apparently perfect copies remained tonally deficient. There must be a secret to Stradivari's construction, as yet undiscovered. Whoever found it out could name their price. The chief focus, as ever, was the varnish. Where Vuillaume and Reade had blazed an investigative trail, hordes now followed. Intense discussions took place on the perfect methodology for melting amber; ever more elaborate recipes were devised; and the most exotic ingredients suggested. In all this, the Hill brothers were the voice of reason, pointing out that Stradivari's varnish was not confined to Cremona – even Stainer used it – and its recipe can hardly have been some great secret. Even they, however, succumbed to excitement when a descendant of Stradivari claimed to have found his ancestor's recipe for varnish in a family Bible. The story required the Hills to believe that the descendant had been the first to find the Bible for a century, and had then destroyed it. Clearly preposterous, it was soon proved to be a fabrication. The brothers' gullibility in the matter sits oddly with their overall scholarliness and is itself an indication of some kind of desperation.

If it was not the varnish, there must have been another answer. Some followed another of Vuillaume's lines of enquiry: the tonal difference between the belly and the back of the violin before the soundbox was put together. Vuillaume's work was extended, every component of the violin was weighed, books were written expounding ratios and the pseudo-science behind them. Yet another theory ascribed to Stradivari and his contemporaries nothing but luck. Quite by chance they were using wood that had first been soaked in water. The logs on sale in Cremona had been felled in the Alps and then floated down to market on the river Po. Nineteenth-century luthiers lost this benefit because of Napoleon; he built the roads that bypassed the river. Use wood that had been soaked in water and your violins would soon have a tone like Stradivari's. The advantage of every theory was that there was a perfect excuse for the resulting violins having a disappointing tone: they simply 'needed more time to mature'.

On 16 February 1903 the eighteen-year-old Marie Hall made her London debut at St James' Hall. Her story already had enough romance in it to satisfy any novelist.

Born in 1884 to a poor but musical family, Marie's memory of her Newcastle home was of the scampering and squeaking of rats that could be heard through the walls. Only by secretly learning Joachim Raff's *Cavatina* could she persuade her father, a harpist, to let her study the violin. Obvious talent led to a public concert when she was only nine; and that in its turn drew an offer from local businessmen to sponsor her education. Her father refused; Marie was needed in the home, and when the family moved to Malvern she was reduced to playing on street corners. One passer-by, however, was Edward Elgar. Although then far from famous, he could still recognize talent. Elgar collected money from friends, bought Marie her first Italian violin and sent her to be heard in London. Here, a performance of Mendelssohn's Violin Concerto was enough to convince August Wilhelmj, head of the violin department in the Guildhall School of Music. Marie was welcomed into his home.

Marie's future should have been secure, but, still only ten, she was unhappy and homesick. Within three months she was back with her family, by now in Birmingham. At least she was able to continue with the violin, so that, aged thirteen, she won a scholarship to the Royal Academy of Music. Once again, however, she had to turn it down; her father was too poor to spare her, and her help was needed with her three younger siblings. When the family moved to Bristol, Marie was back playing on the streets with her father. Occasionally they would be heard through a mansion's windows and be invited into the drawing-room.

Gradually, Marie built up a clientele. Showing admirable initiative – she was not yet fifteen – she decided to give a concert, selling tickets from house to house and hiring a venue. It became clear, however, that expenses were going to exceed sales; Marie had to cancel the concert and return the ticket money. That too must have taken courage, but the effort was not after all wasted. One member of the disappointed audience was a composer, Jane Jackson Roeckel. She arranged for the young violinist to meet Philip Napier Miles, not only another composer, but independently wealthy. The cycle of offers and refusals could finally be broken. Marie would go to London and her father would be paid £1 [£65] per week for the loss of his daughter and the earning-power she represented. It is a Dickensian tale, although Marie herself was more apt to compare herself to Cinderella and believed that her background of poverty and paternal dictatorship gave her a spiritual link with Paganini himself.

Marie spent three years in London, studying not only the violin but also French, German and English literature, under the tutelage of special governesses. Then, when she was seventeen, came a crucial encounter with Jan Kubelik, four years her senior and already dubbed a new Paganini by adoring audiences. Kubelik had been a pupil of Otokar Ševčík, whose 'method' would be responsible for a stream of young prodigies over the next few years. He advised Marie to follow in his footsteps; so off she went to Prague to spend eighteen months with the man she later called 'the greatest teacher living'. The compliment was repaid; declaring Marie the best pupil he had ever taught, Ševčík had her play for Bohemia's most famous composer, Antonin Dvořák, who agreed that she was now ready for her concert debut. The Prague audience was therefore the first to hear her; and it was on the back of her triumphant reception there that Marie was booked to play in the St James' Hall in London.

The sensation was huge and immediate. Marie's programme would have exhausted even an experienced soloist, but seems to have caused her no difficulties. Beginning with Paganini's Violin Concerto in E flat Major, she captivated the audience in the same way her spiritual ancestor had on his Viennese debut almost eighty years before. Her performance of the Tchaikovsky Violin Concerto brought six encores, a feat immediately bettered when Wieniawski's Faust Fantasia led to nine. Added to Marie's advantages of youth and gender was the fact that she was British; nobody could remember a predecessor creating so great a furore or arousing so much genuine interest on their first public appearance. She later admitted that, buoyed by the support of Henry Wood, and feeling as though Ševčík was present in the hall, she had never in all her career 'enjoyed a concert as much as that'.

The Strad was always quick to give its readers what they wanted; it featured Marie in its very next issue. A slight eighteen-year-old, dark and beautiful, with lips that might nowadays be called sensuous, stares out from its pages and it is all too easy to draw comparisons with modern players. Nevertheless, there is an air of determination about her – something of the level-headed woman later to lecture readers of *The Girls' Own Paper* on the importance of practice – that suggests she has worked hard to get this far and is not about to let all the adulation go to her head. Moreover, she will presumably have read the comments of *The Strad*'s own reviewer, 'Gamba', that

'She has got the most remarkable fluency of technique, a thin and rather poor tone, but a great deal of fire and "go", which will probably carry her far.'

It is hard to know whether the criticism of Marie's tone should be blamed on her immaturity, the reviewer's need to find fault (others called her tone pure and sweet) or the relatively poor carrying power of the Amati she had borrowed from Ševčík by comparison with the Strads and del Gesù that most other soloists were playing upon. Some answer may come from the fact that at her next concert she played a Stradivarius lent to her by the Hills. This time 'Gamba' admitted that Marie's playing showed 'manifest signs of the deeper and broader qualities', although he was still inclined to 'go slower' than some of her apparently less critical worshippers (in a later review he was positively catty: 'Something is missing. Is it charm?'). In this he was joined by the *Daily Telegraph*, which commented on one performance that her 'efforts were received with applause so demonstrative [that her audience] may become unpleasantly conscious that at first they rather overdid the thing'. In the end, all the attention was halted by something much more dangerous than public fickleness. In the summer of 1904, typhoid fever brought Marie Hall close to death. It took her eight months to recover. When she returned to performance it was with an added maturity that impressed all observers.

One other factor may have played a role in Marie Hall's progression from public adulation to critical acceptance. Whatever the rights or wrongs of the press frenzy of her early years, it achieved one thing for her: financial security. She was soon able to afford her own Cremona violin, which she first played in public at her comeback

Figure 17. Miss Marie Hall – 'fragile and attenuated' but with an 'immense reserve of strength' – holding her *Viotti* Strad, from a postcard c.1905.

concert in February 1905. Five years later Marie was to tell *The Strad* about it. 'You know, perhaps, that I have the *Viotti* Strad. It is a great treasure and it seems wonderful to think that it was two hundred years old last year, and is just as beautiful as ever.' Finally, Viotti's 1709 Stradivarius had emerged from the eighty years of obscurity that followed his death. *The Strad* reminded its readers of the importance of Viotti's performances on the violin at the Concert Spirituel. Of its history since his death, the magazine could only say that at one stage the *Viotti* had been in the possession of 'one of the royal houses of Europe', and that in 1860 it had been sold for £220 [£14,000].

Marie had bought the *Viotti* from the London dealer George Hart, paying him £1,600 [£100,000]. The price both gives an indication of the rise in the values of Strads over the previous forty years, and confirms the Hills' assessment of the 1709 *Viotti* as 'a grand example in every respect'. In the words of *The Strad*'s Blackpool correspondent, 'Lancastrian' (a pseudonym for Dr William Hardman, JP), the violin's tone was 'as perfect, all over, as I ever heard'. Moreover, its new owner got the best out of it. 'Lancastrian' could hardly believe the sound this 'fragile and attenuated' girl was able to produce. Was it an 'immense reserve of strength' or a mental attitude that meant she could work with her Strad, believing, in the words of another critic, 'in its extraordinary powers'? The marriage of musician and instrument would become one of the most successful pairings of the era.

The life of a concert violinist in the 1900s was very different from one in the 1780s. The *Viotti* soon accompanied Marie Hall on her first American tour, a total of sixty concerts. She found the New York public the most critical in the world, and very decided in their likes and dislikes, but conclusively won them over. In the words of one reviewer: 'In two minutes after the girl had begun to play everybody was sitting up straight and listening intently. Here was no mere pet of royalty, no injudiciously exploited bit of precocity.' The rewards of American fame were immense; in 1903 the Belgian virtuoso Eugène Ysaÿe had been guaranteed $75,000 [£1 million] for fifty concerts. More arduous, in the days before air travel, were the tours to South Africa, Australia, India and New Zealand. Marie was a bad sailor, which in her words 'spoils a great deal of the pleasure for me'. Australians, she found, were quick to show feelings, not tiring of something if they liked it. She was smothered with flowers there: harps and lyres, shepherds' crooks and bouquets after every concert. The need to make the most of the long journey, and to respond to audience demand, meant that the planned two concerts in Melbourne were extended to a run of seven in ten days, so that Marie had to play a staggering seventy different pieces. In Vancouver, on the other hand, the boat only stopped for a few hours and she was on the concert platform within ten minutes of landing.

One benefit of the slow journeys was presumably that the *Viotti* could adjust gradually to changes in temperature and humidity. On the other hand, the violin was certainly not given the two weeks that David Laurie was convinced Strads needed after every sea voyage to recover from *mal de mer*. The problem was at its most acute in the tropics, where the combined heat and humidity might even cause the glue to dissolve, reducing a violin to its constituent pieces. Marie Hall's solution involved special wrappings and a bespoke wooden case. The effect was such that on a tour to South Africa locals believed her to be carrying a coffin.

Both violin and performer must have found the conditions in Suva, capital of Fiji, a challenge. The concert was unscheduled, hastily arranged when the boat put in to take on cargo. All Marie's clothes were packed away, so she made a short visit to the only draper's shop in town to buy a cotton dress. Initially they could not let her have one, as everyone was going to a concert that evening, and expressed some astonishment that their customer was not doing the same. Suva had nothing like a concert hall, and the performance took place in a large tent, filled with about 1,000 people, every white person in town (what the indigenous Fijians thought of her, Marie does not recall). The piano had been tuned by an old, very deaf, sailor, who shortly before the performance expressed the view to Marie that – as she soon found to be the case – a piano always sounded more brilliant if the upper notes were a little sharp. The terrific heat meant that a man had to play an electric fan over the violinist's hands throughout the performance. Meanwhile, the Governor's presence required that proceedings include a rendition of 'God Save the King'. This was played by a local girl, who unfortunately elected to include about twenty variations, Marie and her audience standing throughout. Nevertheless, the whole evening was a great success, culminating in dinner at the Governor's house. That particular tour took eight months. The day after her return to Britain Marie gave a concert in New Brighton: an immense reserve of strength indeed.

There was one other obstacle that Marie Hall's career had to negotiate before she could achieve true longevity as a performer: marriage. The views of 'Lancastrian' are probably typical of the period. In a piece in 1908 he described how he had been taken to task by a married lady pianist for saying that Miss Annie Kirkman, for all her technical proficiency, had been lacking in warmth: 'How could he expect warmth in a young, *unmarried*, woman?' How indeed? But a 1909 review of Jan Kubelik showed that 'Lancastrian' did not apply the same rules to the well-established Marie Hall: 'In his style of playing Kubelik is completely altered. His countess* has taught him what Ševčík, with all his cunning, could not! Will anyone ever teach Marie Hall the same lesson? I tremble as I ask the question, for matrimony, which completes the man, always interrupts, and often writes FINIS to the artistic career of the woman.' He was soon to have an answer. On 27 January 1911 Marie married her manager Edward Baring, a choice that meant she could continue touring. Early in the following season 'Lancastrian' heard her again. While criticizing her choice of repertoire, he also thought he detected 'much greater intensity of feeling and also a much greater freedom of expression'. Her career would indeed continue, and the *Viotti* would continue to be heard, but few would have guessed the changes the next few years would bring for all violinists.

* Kubelik had married into the Hungarian aristocracy.

Chapter Thirteen

'NO MATTER WHAT THE PRICE'

Four Strads go to America

> He rises and begins to round,
> He drops the silver chain of sound,
> Of many links without a break,
> In chirrup, whistle, slur and shake . . .

GEORGE MEREDITH's lines from 'The Lark Ascending' could be read as a description of one of Paganini's more lyrical Caprices, or perhaps an attempt to evoke the versatility and clarity of tone that can be drawn from a Strad. The poem inspired the English composer, Ralph Vaughan Williams, to produce a Romance for Violin and Orchestra under the same name. The work received its orchestral premiere at the Queen's Hall in London on 14 June 1921. Marie Hall was the soloist and the piece is dedicated to her. She had helped the composer with his final revisions at a house party the year before; they were old friends and it is clear that *The Lark Ascending*, close to the top of polls whenever charts of twentieth-century classical music are compiled, was written with her and her Strad in mind. Viotti's old violin was continuing to inspire great music.

Both violinist and composer seemed to be in the ascendant. The First World War had, of course, put an end

to overseas tours, and many provincial festivals were cancelled for the duration, but the London concert season had
continued. A public desperate for entertainment would
not even be put off by the threat of airship raids; the
Proms were briefly moved to the afternoon before revert-
ing to the evening. The patriotic fury brought on by the
war could only benefit native composers like Vaughan
Williams. When hostilities began, concert-planners adopted
a measured response: Brahms and Beethoven were deemed
acceptable, while the more obviously Germanic Strauss
and Wagner were excluded. By 1917, however, they were
coping with newspapers demanding to know why 'German
music has still so many perverted advocates in our midst'.
The resurgence in English music that was already under
way met an eager audience; and Vaughan Williams was
one of the prime beneficiaries. Marie Hall, meanwhile,
saw her male contemporaries conscripted. Attitudes to
female musicians were forced to change. Her successors'
marriages might provoke occasional comment, but no one
would again imagine the ceremony spelling the end of a
career.

Even so, Marie must have realized at about the time
she gave *The Lark Ascending* its premiere that the cer-
tainties of her earlier existence had gone for ever. Violinists would come to look back on the Edwardian era as a
Golden Age. The economic ruin that the Great War
brought, and the technological progress that followed
in its wake, were to cause fundamental changes in the
structure of the music industry.

Music had been recorded since Thomas Edison's
invention of the phonograph in 1877 and Emile Berliner's
development of the gramophone ten years later. The first

pre-recorded cylinders for home use were produced as far back as 1892. Early discs captured the voice most success-fully, but among instruments it was the violin, with its *cantabile* tone and original affinity with the voice, that took best to the medium. Recordings exist of almost all the early twentieth-century violin virtuosi and Marie Hall is no exception. As early as 1907 her fans were able to keep in touch while she was on tour in Germany by attending a 'gramophone concert' at the Albert Hall. The recordings that survive, however, do not seem to do her justice. In the words of one modern critic, her style is 'anachronistic', her playing of a Paganini piece is 'facile', some shorter vignettes are 'dry-toned' and, worst of all, 'a horrendous 1916 recording of the Elgar Concerto (with the composer conducting) . . . can only serve to embarrass her memory'.

It is sad that Marie's association with the man who first discovered her almost thirty years before can now only be remembered through a substandard recording. The failure is even more difficult to understand in the context of *The Strad*'s view that Marie's rendition of the Elgar Concerto in 1912 had been the 'most striking' performance of the season by any violinist. 'It was the sheer beauty of her playing which held one's attention so strongly.' The reason probably lies in the problems posed by direct acoustic recording. This required the performer to play or sing by a trumpet that had to be perfectly positioned if tone was not to be lost, and even then some registers would be reproduced better than others. There must have been something in Marie's playing that the technology of the time simply could not capture. Her status as *The Lark Ascending*'s dedicatee is her single greatest claim to posterity, and George Meredith's poem probably captures her tone, playing her Strad, better than any of those unsatisfactory recordings.

RECORDED MUSIC would remain a sideline as long as it could only address a fraction of the potential repertoire. Its true breakthrough came with the development in the 1920s of electrical recording techniques. Now a performer or an orchestra could play under normal conditions and have the sound picked up by a microphone. Moreover, the electrical process whereby the signal from the microphone was converted to grooves on the disc produced less distortion than its acoustic equivalent. Home gramophones – first wind-up and then electrical – started to spread and an industry was born.

The effect of the gramophone on the violin is bound up with the advance of another ground-breaking invention, broadcast radio. Here too the basic technology dated back to the end of the nineteenth century and Marconi's pioneering experiments. Broadcast wireless, however, only became truly feasible with the invention of the vacuum tube during the First World War. By the early 1920s the Radio Corporation of America (RCA) and the British Broadcasting Corporation had made their first transmissions. Neither organization could devote much time to classical music. That first RCA broadcast was of a heavyweight boxing championship, while complaints about 'the rubbish put out by the BBC' started almost as soon as it began broadcasting. Nevertheless the new medium's influence was immense, especially when combined with the existence of reasonably faithful recordings.

For the first time players had the potential to reach audiences around the world without having to step on to a concert platform.

Musicians in England began to understand the potential influence of the gramophone in 1921. That was the year that the young violinist Jascha Heifetz came to Great Britain for the first time. The anticipation was immense, not because of reports of his playing, but because he already had a huge British audience: over the previous year he had sold 80,000 records. Russian-born, Heifetz trained at St Petersburg under Davidov's old quartet partner, Leopold Aüer, and had established his reputation in continental Europe when only eleven. Five years later, in 1917, he had arrived in New York by way of Siberia, Japan and California, fleeing the Russian Revolution. It was to become a well-trodden path. Aüer himself left Petrograd (as St Petersburg had become) the following year, and over the years so did almost all his other famous pupils, Mischa Elman and Efrem Zimbalist among them. All made their homes in America. It was natural to do so; Europe was poor and exhausted by the war, while the land of opportunity still had a history of welcoming refugees. America was also the centre of the new recording industry: it had invented the technology; it had the largest domestic market; and, increasingly, it was home to many of the greatest artists and orchestras. Before the war the pattern had been one of European soloists crossing the Atlantic to play in America; after it, the flow was increasingly in the opposite direction.

Similarly, it was starting to seem as if every Strad was destined for the New World. Not only did most of the top soloists now live there, but only American collectors could afford the prices the great instruments now commanded. Dealers would come over to Europe on scouting expeditions; one, Nathan Posner, even earned himself *The Strad*'s sobriquet of 'latter-day Tarisio'. Meanwhile, Europeans expostulated that their treasures were being ransacked to pay war debt and pressed for the levy of substantial export duties. Britons at least could hardly complain; American collectors were only following the example they had set over the previous century.

THE SIMPLEST WAY for European dealers to take advantage of America's new dominance was to move there, preferably with a few choice violins ready for sale. Emil Herrmann epitomizes the trend, although his route was even more convoluted than Heifetz's. The son of a Berlin violin dealer, Herrmann had spent his childhood in training, writing a one-page analysis of a new violin every day and always discussing instruments at the dinnertable. By the time he was eighteen, in 1906, he was ready to be sent on the road, almost immediately selling a fine Amati for 21,000 marks [£65,000]; he could not only identify great violins, he could sell them as well. All Herrmann's skills, however, were not enough to save him from war service eight years later. He went to fight on Germany's Eastern Front, only to be taken prisoner by the Russians. Fortunately for the young Emil, a local commander, the aristocratic General Yurkevitch, needed chamber music partners. Once again the violin was to be an agent of romance. Eyes met over the music stands; one thing must have led to another; Herrmann ended up marrying his gaoler's daughter. With the Revolution, the tables were turned. Yurkevitch found himself a fugitive; it was his new son-in-law who spirited the whole family out of the country, arriving in the USA via Vladivostok. Herrmann then returned to Berlin, having circumnavigated the globe.

To survive war and revolution, and then to flourish, Herrmann needed charm, initiative and nerve. It is no surprise that by the 1920s he was back in New York, established as one of America's premier violin dealers.

Herrmann's Russian experience brought him more than a wife. He seems to have built much of his initial success on rescuing instruments from the Bolsheviks, including two of our violins. Louis Böhm had taken the *Khevenhüller* to Russia, and it remained there when he sold it to Viktor Popov, Professor at the Moscow Conservatoire, who had finally seen it provided with modern fittings. At some point in the aftermath of 1917, however, the *Khevenhüller* ended up in the hands of Emil Herrmann. So did a Guadagnini cello that had also been owned by Professor Popov, who seems to have bought a 1752 Guadagnini violin from Herrmann around the same time. So by the end of it all, the Professor had exchanged the *Khevenhüller* and the cello for one rather cheaper violin. The difference in value may well represent Herrmann's reward for smuggling the instruments out of Russia. If he could take humans out through Vladivostok, violins would presumably have been a very simple proposition.

The route by which Herrmann acquired the *Paganini*, another of our violins, is only slightly less obscure. The Muscovite Pierre de Ellisseiff had bought it in 1906. Perhaps he was also forced to sell during the Revolution. If so, it was to another Russian, Boris Kitchin, from whom Emil Herrmann bought the *Paganini* in 1925, before selling it on to one of the great American collectors, David Walton.

The *Khevenhüller*, however, stayed in Herrmann's hands for longer: perhaps he always had greater plans for it; more likely he was waiting until the price was right. In the meantime, he found a way of advertising it when he published privately, in a limited edition of 200 English and 200 German copies, a small but elegant brochure: *Two Famous Stradivarius Violins: 'King Maximilian' and 'Prince Khevenhüller'*. Sumptuous colour plates illustrate both violins from every conceivable direction; reproductions of historical documents give evidence of their rich provenance; and portentous prose alerts the reader to Herrmann's altruism in publicizing these violins to the world. A short extract from the Introduction gives the flavour:

> Because these two violins of Stradivarius ... are among the foremost works of the master and, until recently, have not been known even to the musical profession, I feel called upon to describe them here in word and picture ...
>
> I hope that in publishing this little study I am rendering true service to all friends of music, lovers and connoisseurs of master-violins, who feel a living interest for Stradivarius and his creations.

THE HISTORICAL SECTION of Herrmann's brochure is discreetly silent over how he acquired the *Khevenhüller* from Professor Popov. When an instrument's provenance was unquestionably legitimate, dealers were only too happy to use the opportunity to promote themselves and their wares. So, on 29 November 1928, residents of New York could open their papers to read the following story:

'DAVIDOFF 'CELLO ARRIVES ON *PARIS*

Stradivarius Instrument of 1712 to Join the Wurlitzer String Collection

ITS VALUE PUT AT $85,000

Liner's Master in Charge of it on Trip . . .

The French liner *Paris* arrived yesterday morning with her most valuable bit of cargo not in one of her holds but in the cabin of Captain Yves Thomas, her commanding officer. It was the famous Davidoff 'cello, valued at approximately $85,000 and the work of Stradivarius of Cremona.

Made, it is said, in 1712 for the Grand Duke of Tuscany, and later owned by Davidoff, court musician to Russia. It was recently acquired for the Wurlitzer Collection which, as a result, now owns two of the ten Strad 'cellos in this country.

An art collection on the same liner received very much lower billing, and the last line of the article notes that Mr Jascha Heifetz was on the same boat. A famous story about Heifetz tells of an old lady coming up to him after a concert with the words, 'Your violin sounded wonderful this evening.' Holding the instrument up to his ear, Heifetz replies, 'I don't hear anything.' One can imagine that he was not terribly impressed at being upstaged by a cello.

The story of the *Davidov*'s arrival would be carried in

just about every major US newspaper (in Boston the value was quoted as $100,000). Its source must surely have been the cello's new owner, The Rudolph Wurlitzer Company, which over the last ten years had been building a name as America's leading dealer in string instruments.

Like Emil Herrmann, the Wurlitzers came originally from Germany. Rudolph had settled in Cincinnati in 1853, founding a firm that became the leading supplier of military wind instruments and drums in the Civil War. His first son took charge of the automatic instrument division with which we now associate the name; it produced 'The Mighty Wurlitzer' cinema organ and, later, the fabulous jukeboxes that help to define 1950s America. The second son, however, another Rudolph, set up the violin department with the help of another expert, Jay C. Freeman. By 1918 the Wurlitzer Collection, an ambitious name for what seems simply to have been the dealership's stock, already included over 200 instruments.

The *Davidov* may have arrived in America on 'The French liner *Paris*', but its last owners had been English. The Hills – who else? – had sold it to Wurlitzer's soon after they had themselves bought it from the brother of Monsieur Gabriel Goupillat, an amateur who had purchased it from Carl Davidov's heirs in 1900. The Hills had been the cello's frustrated buyers, put off by the 'exorbitant' price demanded of 60,000 francs [£165,000], when Davidov died in 1889. The value quoted by the newspapers in 1928, $85,000 [£600,000], put that in the shade, but the Roaring Twenties were, of course, reaching their peak. Booming stock markets had pulled up all asset values in their wake and Strads were one more potential investment. Certainly the *Davidov* itself was not destined for a player. Perhaps the publicity afforded to its arrival speeded the sale, but Wurlitzer's had soon sold the cello to a collector, Herbert N. Straus.

FOUR OF OUR instruments arrived in America in the years after the First World War. We have already traced the routes of three: the *Davidov*, the *Khevenhüller* and the *Paganini*. The fourth – and probably the first to arrive – was the massive *Lipiński*. We left this violin in the possession of the Hills in the early years of the last century. A few years later it may have passed through the hands of a Stuttgart dealership, Hamma & Co, or perhaps the firm had already handled the violin when it was in Germany after Lipiński's death. One way or another, Fridolin Hamma was able to include pictures of the *Lipiński* in his monumental book, one of the first attempts to bring together photographs of great Italian string instruments: *Meisterwerke Italienischer Geigenbaukunst*. The work added immeasurably to the prestige of the Hamma dealership. It was suggested by contemporaries that the best authentication for a Strad might consist of Hill's nineteenth-century guarantee, together with Hamma's from the twentieth, attached to a photograph to confirm identity.

By the time Hamma's book came out in 1930, however, the *Lipiński* had long since left Europe for America, having been bought by Wurlitzer's, again from the Hills, in 1922. Over the next decade and a half it would be sold by dealers in Chicago, Panama and New York, before eventually going to Cuba. Few of the violinists who played it have names that mean anything to modern ears.

The only one that commands any sort of recognition is Louis Persinger. He is remembered now not so much for his own playing as for his role as the first real teacher of one of the twentieth century's most influential violinists: Yehudi Menuhin.

'The ultimate wunderkind' (to use Itzhak Perlman's description of him) made his New York orchestral debut on 25 November 1927. He was eleven years old but pretending to be ten, a common subterfuge among child prodigies, and appeared on stage in velvet knickerbockers and white shirt. Chubby, needing help from the concert-master in tuning his Grancino violin, Menuhin's reward for a successful performance would be a tub of strawberry ice cream. It would have had to be a very large tub indeed. It was not just that he played Beethoven's Violin Concerto with flawless technique, he projected it with such maturity. Menuhin was already a celebrity when he was booked to play the solo; by the end of his perform-ance he had, in the words of the *New York Times* critic, Olin Downes, 'proved conclusively his right to be ranked with the outstanding interpreters of this music'.

Within three weeks Menuhin was back in Carnegie Hall for another recital. Again it was a triumph and this time, although he also expressed some reservations, Downes marvelled at the tone the violinist was able to extract from his 'rather poor instrument'.

Menuhin was not to suffer the handicap for long. Only about a year later, he was invited to call on Henry Goldman, a banker whose wealth can be judged by the fact that his name lives on in the world of finance, paired with Sachs. In his earlier days Goldman had been a door-to-door salesman of cheap violins, ones labelled as Strads but never in danger of being mistaken for the real thing. Now he was a patron of the arts and a music lover, and had been in the audience at another Menuhin concert where the prodigy seemed to struggle on a borrowed del Gesù. Some reviews had been damning, but the performance must still have had enough in it to impress the financier. Menuhin's visit to his New York apartment began with a tour of the art collection. Although now completely blind, Goldman still knew the details of every piece: the Cellini bronze inkstand, van Dyck portrait, Donatello sculpture and Holbein miniatures. Then the conversation turned to the purpose of Goldman's invitation, as the banker made a remarkable offer: 'Now, you must choose any violin you want, no matter what the price. Choose it; it's yours.'

Menuhin had the pick of all the instruments available for sale around the world. He took his time, visiting every New York dealer and asking older violinists for advice before he eventually decided – on Emil Herrmann's *Khevenhüller*. In his memoirs almost fifty years later Menuhin would describe the violin, which he still owned: 'Ample and round, varnished a deep glowing red, its grand proportions were matched by a sound at once powerful, mellow and sweet.' The violin would be described to the world as a twelfth-birthday present for the young violinist, who was in fact almost thirteen. The contrast between age and youth is hard to ignore. The violin itself was nearly 200 years old, made by a luthier in his ninetieth year. Menuhin, that most spiritual of violinists, was sensitive to the implications: 'A great violin is alive; its very shape embodies its maker's intention, and its wood stores the history, or the soul, of its successive owners. I never play without feeling that I have released or, alas, violated spirits.'

Herrmann threw in a Tourte bow with the violin. He could afford to be generous. The reported price of $60,000 [£400,000], when comparable Strads were going for half the price, is a tribute to his skills as a salesman. That brochure had done its job.

Among the violins that Menuhin had rejected in favour of the *Khevenhüller* was the *Betts*, the violin its namesake claimed to have bought in 1820 for £1. Made in 1704, towards the beginning of Stradivari's golden period, and described by the Hills as one of the great productions of his life, it was priced at $110,000 [£700,000]. The violinist, at least, had not abused his benefactor's generosity. It is not certain that the same can be said of Yehudi's father. There have always been rumours that he received a commission on the sale and it is curious that Herrmann's receipt – 'To Yehudi Menuhin – In Trust of his father, Moshe Menuhin . . . one violin . . . known as the "Prince Khevenhüller" ' – is for only $48,000 [£320,000]. The implication that Moshe pocketed $12,000 [£80,000] may be hard to swallow; perhaps he simply felt that $60,000 [£400,000] was a better figure for publicity purposes, or perhaps he felt that Mr Goldman would not notice the difference. If so, he was probably right. For the rest of his life the blind 'Uncle Henry', as he came to be known in the Menuhin household, would sit in the front row at his beneficiary's concerts. He must have derived considerable satisfaction from his purchase of a work of art that could be heard as well as seen.

Over the next decade the partnership of boy and violin

Figure 18. A publicity shot of Yehudi Menuhin – 'the ultimate
wunderkind' – from January 1929, showing him with
Mr and Mrs Henry Goldman, and the violin they
had just given him.

was to prove all-conquering. It was with the *Kheven-hüller* that Menuhin gave his famous Berlin concert in April 1929 of violin concertos by the three German masters: Bach, Beethoven and Brahms. In any venue this programme would require astonishing reserves of stamina and musicianship. Locating the concert in Berlin itself, the spiritual home of the three composers, indicates Menuhin's level of self-belief. The concert was to justify it. Albert Einstein, a member of the audience, would congratulate the young maestro after the performance with the celebrated phrase: 'Now I know there is a God in heaven.'

During the 1930s Menuhin's performance fees of $5,000 in the USA and 1,000 guineas [£40,000] in Britain were second to none. To many, this was the virtuoso's greatest period, before he started to analyse, and relearn, his technique. In contrast to Marie Hall and her *Viotti* Strad a generation before, recordings can do him and the *Khevenhüller* something like justice. The most famous of them all involves another juxtaposition of youth and age. Yehudi was only fifteen when, in 1932, he recorded the Elgar Concerto for His Master's Voice in their specially constructed electrical recording studios (the world's first) at Abbey Road in London. As with Marie Hall, and her own recording of the same concerto, the conductor was the composer himself, Sir Edward Elgar, then seventy-five. Unlike her version, however, Menuhin's is remembered as one of the century's greatest recordings. It has never been delisted since the day it was first released.

In 1936 Menuhin received an interesting presentation: an exact copy of the *Khevenhüller*, made by Parisian luthier Emile Français. To make the replica Français had, like a latter-day Vuillaume, taken the *Khevenhüller* apart to ensure every measurement was precise. His finishing touch was the varnish, applied in eighteen layers, each requiring two weeks to dry. Playing the copy for the first time on his nineteenth birthday, Menuhin declared that it possessed all the qualities of his Strad, 'save only the ripeness which time brings'. He would occasionally play it in concert. His audiences do not seem to have noticed any difference between it and the original.

HERRMANN HAD sold the *Khevenhüller* at the right time. The Wall Street Crash nine months later brought the stock-market boom to an abrupt halt. Strads held their value better than more speculative investments. Nevertheless the 1930s must have been lean times. The fortunes of the *Lipiński* are an illustration. In 1927 it had been sold for $21,500 [£150,000]; ten years later, Dr Martinez Cañas, a Cuban, paid only $16,000 [£120,000] for it. If nothing else, therefore, the bicentenary of Stradivari's death in 1937 represented a much-needed publicity opportunity. New York would vie with Cremona to put on the most magnificent celebration.

The interest in the anniversary shown by the town where Stradivari lived and died should not be surprising, except that Cremona had spent most of the preceding 200 years ignoring its most famous son. In 1868, claiming that the structure was unsafe, the town council had sold the Church of San Domenico to a local builder for 42,000 lire [£100,000] – its scrap value. The wreckers moved in. The Chapel of the Rosary, in which Stradivari's tomb lay, went the same way as the rest of the church; only the tombstone itself, and some human remains, were saved. Three skulls were taken to the builder's home, where they remained for some years until, tired of seeing them 'always in the way' the family took them down to the cemetery, where they were unceremoniously thrown into a common grave. The house where Stradivari and his family had lived from 1680 fared no better. In 1888 it was extensively remodelled to create a billiard room for the café next door. A British tourist who presumed to question the work was directed to the police. Forty years later the building, in the now renamed Piazza Roma, was pulled down entirely.

Similarly, the decline in Cremonese craftsmanship that set in after Stradivari's death continued through the nineteenth century. Lorenzo Storioni (1751–99) is usually known as the last of the classical Cremonese makers, already only a shadow of his predecessors. His pupil Giovanni Battista Ceruti founded a minor dynasty. David Laurie met its last member, Enrico, and was disappointed by his attempt to pass off a cheap German violin as his own work.

In 1893 came the first intimation that at least some residents were aware of their town's history, when Cremona accepted several Stradivarian 'relics' of doubtful provenance. However, it was the donation to the town of Stradivari's tools and moulds that really marked the beginning of Cremona's reawakening. Appropriately enough, they came from a luthier, Giuseppe Fiorini. He had bought them from the last descendant of Count Cozio, the Marquis dalla Valle, for 100,000 lire [£37,000] in 1920. Even before Cozio's death, his collection of the violins themselves had been scattered. It was a minor miracle that the Count's family preserved intact this, their ancestor's last purchase from Paolo Stradivari.

Cremona received the collection in 1930, and the Museo Stradivariano was opened in the same year. Scholars started to scour the town's archives to add to the meagre store of documentary knowledge on Stradivari's life. With 1937 approaching, it became clear that Cremona was at last acknowledging its greatest citizen. In fact, Italian interest in Stradivari went far beyond his native town, as Mussolini's Fascist government sensed the propaganda potential. A leading member of the regime was himself Cremonese and the resulting combination of civic and national pride was particularly potent. Two hundred years after the death of their most famous maker, Cremona's violins and cellos were as desirable as ever. What better way to show the world the continuing superiority of Italian culture and craftsmanship than through an exhibition of Cremonese instruments?

L'Esposizione di Liuteria Antica A Cremona opened on 15 May 1937. Seventy thousand lire [£25,000] was available in prizes for the best modern examples of violin-making, but the core attraction consisted of 134 antique instruments, insured for a total of 80 million francs [£23 million]. Thirty-nine Strads were among the exhibits: violins, cellos, viols and even that solitary harp, carved by Stradivari in 1681, but by now stringless and neglected. Among the del Gesùs was Paganini's Cannon itself, on a rare loan from Genoa. Over the month it was on, the exhibition and the concerts associated with it attracted 100,000 visitors, carried there on trains at a 50 per cent discount, courtesy of the Italian Ministry of Communications. It was a truly powerful demonstration of Cremona's ancient supremacy that Tarisio himself would have been hard-put to match, but not one of the instruments on display had a Cremonese owner. It is probably not surprising – given the political climate of the time – that none of them came from Britain, while thirty were lent by German owners. Perhaps more interesting is that twenty-five came from the USA, to which they duly returned with their certificates of participation.

It was Emil Herrmann who organized the American contribution to the Cremona exhibition, and it is in keeping with his talent for self-promotion that he was also behind the festivities in New York six months later. The Stradivarius Memorial Concert was held in Carnegie Hall on Monday, 20 December, 1937, one day after the actual bicentenary. The programme began with Bach's Violin Concerto in E Major and ended with his Double Violin Concerto in D Minor. Efrem Zimbalist was soloist for the former, and was joined by Sascha Jacobsen for the latter. In between came César Franck's D Major Quartet and Felix Mendelssohn's E flat Major Octet. Every violin, viola or cello played was a Stradivarius, twenty-three instruments in all. Whether the orchestra really needed half a dozen Strads in its second violin section alone is questionable, but it must have been remarkable both to hear and to see.

Herrmann had a much easier job of organization than his counterparts in Cremona. Almost every instrument was American owned, and this was still only a fraction of the Strads played by American musicians at the time: at least fifty, according to the concert's programme. Even that figure massively underestimates the number that were by then in America. Of the four instruments we have followed to its shores, for example, only one – Menuhin's *Khevenhüller* – is included in the list. The *Lipiński* had left the USA for Cuba and the ownership of Dr Martinez Cañas. The *Paganini* violin and the *Davidov* cello, on the other hand, were still in America, but owned by collectors rather than players. The implications of this were recognized by the concert organizers. The evening's proceeds were turned over to the newly incorporated Stradivarius Memorial Fund. Its object would be to make good violins available to 'the gifted students who are most seriously handicapped by the lack of the proper instrument'. It was a laudable objective, but the fund does not seem to have survived the Second World War.* Cremona's celebrations, on the other hand, led to a more permanent and significant foundation: the establishment of a violin-making school, intended to learn from and build on the achievements of the town's old masters. It seems ironic that Italy's bicentennial foundation was based on the belief that Stradivari could be bettered, and America's that he could not.

DESPITE THE vast numbers of violins that left Europe for America in the first half of the century, the most famous Strad of all, the *Messiah*, was not among them. That it was not – Henry Ford is said to have offered a blank cheque – is entirely due to the hold the violin exerted over the Hill Brothers. Like Tarisio and Vuillaume before them, William, Alfred and Arthur Hill seem to have been

* A more recent foundation (The Stradivari Society) has similar aims.

bewitched by the *Messiah*'s near-perfection. Having acquired the violin in 1904 from Robert Crawford, the brothers did not sell it again until 1913, to Richard Bennett. Owner of no fewer than seventeen Strads, all masterpieces, he could be trusted both not to play the violin and to keep it in Britain. In 1928, however, with his health failing, he sent the entire collection back to the Hills for the firm to sell on his behalf. William having died the year before, it was the two surviving brothers who decided to repurchase the *Messiah* for themselves.

By now, W. E. Hill & Sons was far more than a violin dealership. The Hill workshops were especially famous for their bows, which some held to be the best produced since the days of Tourte himself. The brothers had complementary skills: Arthur took care of the business, while Alfred managed the workshops and was the violin expert. In the former role he seems to have been paternalistic, a hangover from the Victorian era. Fifty years later, one bowmaker, Arthur Bultitude, could still remember the two questions asked at his employment interview: 'Was my father honest, sober and hardworking? Were we Church of England?' In the second role, too, Alfred stepped magnificently into W. E. Hill's shoes; he was the expert's expert, the man to whom others turned when they could not agree. Hills could claim to have handled and recorded about 700 Strads since the firm's foundation: a remarkable figure, greater than the number of Strads most other dealers knew to exist. Once, in court, a judge admonished Alfred for the disdain he displayed for dilettante connoisseurs: 'You don't think much of amateurs.' 'They are about as good as amateur lawyers,' came the justifiable reply. Fifty years of successful business had left the brothers rich. They did not need the money represented by the *Messiah*; they determined that it and other treasures from the Hill Collection would go on display in Oxford's Ashmolean Museum.

The donation had to wait for the construction of a dedicated room at the museum. So it was not until 1939 that the transfer finally took place. Fittingly, and in an echo of the *Messiah*'s previous history, that was the year of Arthur's death at the age of seventy-nine. Alfred, two years younger, lingered for only another year. The firm was sold to his brother-in-law, Albert Phillips, who obligingly changed his name to Albert Phillips Hill. In the meantime, however, another world war had begun. Air raids on Oxford were a distinct possibility. A private house in the country was rented for storage and the *Messiah*, together with other treasures from the Ashmolean, spent the war there.

Chapter Fourteen

'WHAT CAN WE SELL THIS AS?'

Violin dealers and the post-war world

ON 30 NOVEMBER 1942 the *Lipiński* made what seems to have been its last concert appearance. The occasion was a performance by the Havana Philharmonic Orchestra of the Glazunov Violin Concerto. According to the *Havana Post*, the young Cuban soloist Angel Reyes, who had borrowed the *Lipiński* from Dr Cañas, 'brought out tones of exquisite beauty from the $40,000 Stradivarius with which he appeared on Monday evening'. As an encore Reyes played Bach's Sixth Violin Sonata. How many times had the *Lipiński* played that piece before? One can imagine the ghosts of Tartini and, even more, Lipiński – his era's Bach player *par excellence* – approving Reyes's choice.

That same edition of the *Havana Post* is filled with news of war. Following the Allies' victory at El Alamein earlier in the month, fighting in North Africa had shifted to Tunisia, while the Russians were on the verge of encircling the Germans in Stalingrad. The destruction is apparent even in faraway Cuba, then a rich man's paradise. Yet it is hard to find an instance of a single Strad being lost in the whole course of the hostilities. There are rumours of violins stolen from continental Jews and plaintive accounts still circulate on the Internet of family heirlooms being confiscated at customs during post-war flights from Eastern Europe. Every story adds to Stradivari's mystique – to the possibility that a violin found bearing his label may, after all, be genuine. No account, however, is verifiable, and no famous Strad's history comes to an abrupt halt during the war. Some of the credit for this must go to the Stuttgart dealer Fridolin Hamma and how he behaved when ordered by Goering to search for master violins. Arriving in Paris, Hamma took the opportunity to look up all his old friends among the French dealers, and treated them to a meal that recalled pre-war munificence. At no stage did he even raise the subject of hidden violins, and after a reasonable period he returned to Berlin to report that nothing could be found.

In fact, the most catastrophic loss might well have been felt by Fridolin Hamma himself. In July 1944 his firm's offices were destroyed, along with much of Stuttgart, in an Allied bombing raid. The vault remained intact, but when opened was found to contain nothing but ash; only a few charred scrolls could be salvaged for souvenirs. Hamma's great instruments, however, including the Strads, had been safely hidden outside the city for the duration of the war.

None of the instruments we are following seems to have been in much danger. Yehudi Menuhin was the first musician to play in the Paris Opera House following the city's liberation, part of a European tour to bolster morale, but he left the *Khevenhüller* behind. It was too valuable to risk at concerts that in some places were still subject to German shelling. Menuhin took the Emile Français replica, but in Paris at least he borrowed the

Stradivarius of an old friend, the violinist Jacques
Thibaud.*

Soon enough, the *Khevenhüller* would no longer be
Menuhin's favoured violin. A successful Japanese tour in
1951 meant he was able to afford a Strad from the heart
of Stradivari's golden period, the 1714 *Soil*. Once again,
Emil Herrmann was the vendor. Twenty-five years later,
Menuhin would describe the *Khevenhüller* as 'a violin of
warm ample, strong and supple qualities . . . ideally suited
to my youthful romantic approach'; the *Soil*, on the other
hand 'has enormous power, great brilliance, a purity and
clarity of sound and a nobility of texture . . . It is
perfection, and must be played to perfection.' There was
no doubt as to which he preferred.

Moreover, Menuhin's devotion to Stradivari was not
total. Like many of his contemporaries, he was also
susceptible to the charms of del Gesù's instruments,
finding them more tolerant than the sensitive Strads. He
liked to claim that he was married to his Strads, while his
'illicit adventures' were with del Gesùs, which 'are wild
and earthy'. As if to prove it, Menuhin bought his second
Strad, the *Soil*, only a few years after he remarried: the
Khevenhüller belonged to an earlier phase of his life.
His devotion to his first del Gesù, a present from his
first wife, lasted rather longer. Intriguingly, this violin
has since been challenged as a nineteenth-century copy:
a rather different sort of 'illicit adventure' from the one
Menuhin had in mind.

*

* Tragically, this great French violinist died in an aeroplane crash in
1953; the accident also destroyed his Strad.

THE YEAR of the liberation of Paris, 1944, was also the tercentenary of Stradivari's putative year of birth. Europe was in no mood to celebrate, but things were very different across the Atlantic. Philadelphia led the festivities with what was fast becoming traditional, an exhibition and concert. Twenty instruments were featured, but the main attraction was the appearance of the Curtis Quartet on a set of Strads that, as their publicity eagerly emphasized, had once been owned by Paganini himself. The dream that he, his son Achillo and Vuillaume all shared had not died after all; it simply took another century to come to fruition.

The four instruments had been reassembled by Emil Herrmann. Thirty years earlier his father August had written in *Das Ideale Streichquartett* that no more than eleven all-Strad quartets could possibly be created, the limiting factor being the number of violas known to exist. Indeed, August wrote, to collect even one Stradivari quartet was a remarkable achievement. Emil Herrmann was by no means the first to bring together four Strads in this way; nevertheless, he must have exulted at the success with which he had met his father's challenge, and on instruments all owned by Paganini as well.

Herrmann had been accumulating the pieces since 1935, when he acquired the 1731 *Paganini* viola. The *Ladenburg/Paganini* 1736 cello soon followed. With its purchase, Herrmann's goal was in sight. Two Stradivarius *Paganini* violins had already passed through his hands in the 1920s; Herrmann knew where they were; all he had to do was watch and wait. And so, in 1944, he had reacquired first the 1727 *Paganini* and then, with the death of David Walton, the 1680 *Paganini*, the yellow violin that we saw being made in the year Stradivari moved to Piazza San Domenico.

The Philadelphia Exhibition provided the perfect opportunity for unveiling the new quartet to the world, even one that was still at war. Herrmann hoped, of course, that it would help him find a buyer, but he found this no easier than Vuillaume had a century before. Two years later he was reluctantly coming to accept the possibility that the quartet would have to be broken up once more.

Salvation came in the form of an ensemble that had just formed under the leadership of Henri Temianka. Although all its members were in place, the quartet still needed suitable instruments. The group's cellist, Robert Maas, who had been with the Pro Arte Quartet before the war, was the first to suggest they look at Herrmann's Paganini Quartet. The group must have found the trial convincing, but without funds they still needed a sponsor. Musicians were always likely to have more success in such an endeavour than a dealer; Maas and his colleagues soon found the necessary combination of wealth and artistic appreciation in Mrs Anna E. Clark, widow of the US senator and copper king, William Clark. She promptly sent Herrmann a cheque for $155,000 [£800,000]. Mrs Clark retained ownership of the instruments, but lent them to Temianka's ensemble. Not surprisingly, if a little confusingly, they immediately called themselves the 'Paganini Quartet'. And so our 1680 *Paganini* found its destiny. Its fate turns out to have been set from the moment Paganini acquired it.

*

EMIL HERRMANN had now been in the USA for almost thirty years. He left New York at the beginning of the 1950s, selling his business and semi-retiring to his country house, 'Fiddledale', in Connecticut. Here he persisted with his lifetime practice of walking every morning into his storage vault, picking out instruments and using them to remind himself of the characteristics of different makers, a routine he called 'playing a few scales'. He died in 1968. The various coups with which Hermann made his name as a dealer, spiriting instruments out of Russia, had little long-term significance; and in any case his public relations skills were always thought to run ahead of his knowledge of violins. Nevertheless, he had a lasting influence on the world of violin-making, for it was he who persuaded Simone Sacconi to come to America.

Sacconi was born in Rome in 1895. The son of a professional musician, he was soon obsessed with violins, so that when, aged eight, he spotted a hole in one of his father's instruments, he did not hesitate to find out more by prising it apart. Enlightened parenting meant that this resulted not in punishment, but in an arrangement for the young Sacconi to visit a luthier's shop every day after school. By the time he was twenty-one there was a ready market for his copies of Cremonese masterpieces. Then, in 1931, Emil Herrmann brought him to New York, where over the next twenty years he would build a reputation as the world's leading restorer of Cremonese masterpieces.

Towards the end of the 1950s, however, Sacconi began to return to his first love, imitation. To follow Stradivari's methods as closely as possible he went back to first principles in a way that few, if any, of his predecessors had attempted in the 200 years since Stradivari's death. Sacconi had two crucial sources of information: first, the Strads that had passed through his hands while he worked in New York; and second, the collection of Stradivari's tools and drawings, originally saved by Count Cozio and on display in Cremona since 1930. Together, these represented a massive body of knowledge; it seems remarkable that Sacconi was the first to realize its potential significance. He may not have been, but he was the first to share his insights. He is now remembered as a hugely generous teacher, keen to pass on his learning. Towards the end of his life he at least partially succeeded in doing so, when in 1972 he published the hugely influential book, *The 'Secrets' of Stradivari*.

The book is ghost-written and disordered. Large parts of it – notably the section on the mathematical thinking behind Stradivari's violin forms – have been discredited. The recipes that Sacconi suggests for varnish consist simply of what he was working on at the time. Nevertheless, some chapters are revelatory. Insights range from the methods Stradivari used to place his soundholes to the fact that he and del Gesù graduated the thickness of their violins' backs differently from other Cremonese makers.

Even in the questionable chapters Sacconi's common sense shines through: of course, the varnish consisted of ingredients easily obtainable in late-Renaissance Cremona, and it seems unarguable that the method of application was just as important as any 'secret' recipe. In fact, the book's title was probably meant to be ironic; Sacconi's whole thesis was that Stradivari had no secrets, at least from his contemporaries, and that those that had arisen since his death could, with a little effort, be rediscovered. It is a philosophy that can be mocked – 'How many luthiers does it take to change a light bulb? Three: one to do it and two to argue about how Stradivari would have done it' – but the lasting result would be a huge improvement in violin-making techniques.

FROM 1951, when Herrmann left New York, Sacconi had in fact been working for his main American rival, the Rudolph Wurlitzer Company. His transfer was part of a process whereby Rembert Wurlitzer, grandson of the original Rudolph, built a firm that was the main depository of violin expertise in the USA. Rembert had returned to America in 1930 from a period learning his trade in Europe. It had made him determined that Wurlitzer's should finally become a true rival and counterpart to Hill's in London, where he had spent six months. With that in mind, Rembert had in 1937 moved the violin department from Cincinnati to New York. In 1949, however, he took an even more radical step than a mere change of location, when he bought out the department from the rest of the firm. He was effectively starting again, if not from scratch, then with far reduced resources. As his expertise had developed, Rembert had come to understand quite how flawed many of the appraisals made by his predecessors at Wurlitzer's had been. That was embarrassing, to say the least, but it also meant that he faced an enormous problem from the outstanding guarantees on discredited instruments. He split off from the rest of the firm because, in his own words, he 'didn't want to spend the rest of his life buying back Jay C. Freeman's mistakes'.

At around the same time, Walter Hamma, son of Fridolin, was making a similar decision. From before the war the older Hamma's guarantees had become increasingly erratic. Perhaps remembering his wartime generosity in Paris, the charitable have attributed his more questionable appraisals to a desire to furnish Jewish friends with something of value as they fled the Nazis. If so, his philanthropy was misguided. Having paid 100 per cent export duty on their supposed Strads the refugees would arrive in New York or London only to find that their prized possession was something quite different and much less valuable. In any case Fridolin continued to issue suspect certificates after the war. Nowadays, he is remembered as a dealer who, on examining a violin would not ask himself, 'What is this?' but rather, 'What can we sell this as?'

It was only to be expected that the violin world would look for ways to supplant the need for a dealer's guarantee with more scientific, supposedly objective measures. Matters came to a head in Switzerland in the 1950s when it was realized that many of the Strads to have been exhibited at Cremona in 1937 were in fact nothing of the sort. What followed came to be known as the *liutomachia*, or violin war.

The opening shots came with the establishment of an 'advisory council' of two Swiss luthiers, a music historian and a violin teacher. It offered to appraise any instrument sent in and subsequently claimed that 90 per cent of them were falsely attributed to valuable makers: either straight copies or the work of another. As the scandal grew, the Zurich police became involved. Surely the techniques which had been so valuable in combating other counterfeiters could be applied to violins? Instruments were X-rayed, fluoresced with ultraviolet lamps, examined under microscopes and even subjected to chemical analysis.

It is not clear what any of this achieved. An ultraviolet lamp, for example, may show up new patches of retouched varnish, but it can offer nothing on whether the violin underneath is genuine. Nevertheless, the Zurich police's chief investigator was still able to announce that in some cases 'valuable violins turned out to be copies' and that they had found 'faked labels bearing the names of Stradivari, Amati and Guarneri del Gesù'. A well-known Swiss dealer was accused of fraud and falsifying labels, and found guilty on two counts out of twenty. Violin labels were given the status of legal documents. To contemporary observers the implications seemed enormous.

Time, however, has added perspective. For all the hullabaloo, nothing supplanted the established experts, the dealers. Nobody else had their knowledge, least of all the self-appointed 'advisory council'. Even today, dealers occupy the privileged position that they have since the days of W. E. Hill. Their certificates remain the most important component of a violin's value and the commission of up to 10 per cent that they charge for providing one could almost be regarded as cheap.

REMBERT WURLITZER'S attempt to create an American firm whose reputation matched the Hills' was entirely successful. Sadly, he did not enjoy the fruits for long, dying before he was even sixty, in 1963. His widow, Anna Lee, took over the firm, becoming one of the few women in a trade dominated by men. Perhaps that was why, when her fellow-widow Mrs Hermann Straus decided to seek offers for her late husband's Stradivarius cello, there was never any doubt that she would turn to the firm that had sold it to him.

For most of the thirty-five years since Straus had bought the *Davidov* from Wurlitzer's the cello had been part of his own private quartet of Strads. All four instruments had gone on display in New York in 1943, and there were occasional chamber music concerts in Mr Straus's home, but his enjoyment of the instrument had been largely private. The cello was lent for a time to Raya Garbousova, a Russian-born pupil of a pupil of Davidov himself, but by the early 1960s the *Davidov* was in storage at Wurlitzer's, where it was seen by Charles Beare. Then in his twenties, he was a trainee at Wurlitzer's, learning his trade with a friendly foreign rival of his family's firm, J. & A. Beare. A year or so later, in 1964, Beare heard through the violin-dealing grapevine that Mrs Straus had finally entrusted Wurlitzer's with the sale of the great cello.

Back in London, Beare had been making his name in the dealership founded by his stepfather's grandfather.* It was to him that Jacqueline du Pré turned when she needed a new cello. She already had a Strad, an early

---

* Whose first partner had been Edward Goodwin, that happy defrauder of French widows: the firm's reputation and clientele had certainly improved over the years.

model which had cost a little over £5,000 [£60,000] when it was purchased for her by the Courtauld Trust and her godmother, Isména Holland. That was just before Jacqueline's professional debut at London's Wigmore Hall when she was still only sixteen. The success of that concert sparked a now legendary career. Three years on, Jacqueline's talent was coming to maturity – she had already made Elgar's Cello Concerto her own – and she needed a spare instrument to take the strain off her Strad. Beare showed her several cellos in the £2–3,000 range, but nothing suited.

Meanwhile, the limitations of Jacqueline's early Strad were becoming more apparent. Cut down and with extensive internal patches, its tone could not project into the largest concert halls. Once again it was Isména Holland, the major purchaser of the first Strad, who provided the solution. In late 1964 Jacqueline was able to tell Beare that her godmother wanted to buy her a really fantastic cello, and asked if he knew of one that was available. The *Davidov* was destined to come to London.

That destiny could not be fulfilled, however, without the consent of Mrs Straus, the cello's owner. Unwilling to risk it on a transatlantic flight, she only agreed to the cello's journey if it was in the company of Mrs Wurlitzer. So cello and dealer travelled side-by-side in first class on the trip to London. Asked by fellow-passengers to play 'Auld Lang Syne' when drinks were served, its guardian could only plead that she had left her bow behind.

There was no guarantee that Jacqueline and the *Davidov* would be compatible. When it arrived she and her teacher, William Pleeth, tried it out at Mrs Holland's house. Pleeth's advice was clear: 'It's a wonderful cello, one of the truly great instruments of the world. The only thing is whether it suits you, and that you must decide for yourself.' As Beare remembers, 'Jacqueline played it for a few days, fell in love with it and agreed to take it.' Mrs Wurlitzer was able to telegraph Mrs Straus 'Returning without baggage', no doubt a cause of some relief to all concerned.

Mrs Holland's generosity cost her $90,000 [£430,000] and her gift came with some prophetic godmotherly advice: 'You know, dear child, this instrument is extremely valuable, very expensive. You must hang on to it as it's the only thing you've got. If anything should happen to you you've got this to sell.' For three years Jacqueline would play the *Davidov* almost exclusively. That would be a small fraction of most cellists' professional careers. In Jacqueline du Pré's case it represents almost a third. Moreover it is the central third, when her playing matured and peaked. The recordings that Jacqueline made on the *Davidov* are probably her most successful. The most famous of them all – of the Elgar Concerto with Sir John Barbirolli as conductor – was made only a few months after instrument and player came together. In the words of Jacqueline's biographer, Elizabeth Wilson, 'we can hear an extra luminous sheen in the cello sound, a result of the combination of an outstanding player and an incomparable instrument'.

THE *Davidov* had been valued in 1928 at $85,000 [£600,000], and almost forty years later it sold for very little more. Mr Straus's investment had not even kept pace with inflation. Those predictions at the beginning of the twentieth century that violin prices had peaked seemed to have been not far off the truth.

If a Strad suffered damage along the way then its price was quite likely to have declined. The *Lipiński* provides an example. In 1927 it was sold for $21,500 [£150,000]; ten years later, Martinez Cañas paid only $16,000 [£120,000] for it. That reduction in value can probably be put down to the Wall Street Crash and the recession that followed. Nevertheless the price on its final recorded sale in 1962, $18,000 [£77,000], is striking. The violin's deterioration probably provides some reason for the decline in value. In 1945 it could be described as 'in good physical condition ... well covered with varnish of rich reddish colour'. Yet the notes accompanying its sale in 1962 state that the top 80 per cent of the interior had been lined (presumably for strengthening), and the lower half revarnished. Perhaps Jose Cañas, who inherited the violin from his father around 1950, was not a very careful owner. More likely, the violin had at some point fallen into the hands of unscrupulous restorers. Liberal revarnishing and thinning out of the *Lipiński*'s plates would have had an immediate beneficial impact on its looks and tone, but with long-term effects that are all too easy to predict.

The *Lipiński*'s loss of value and condition in the twentieth century is all part of what – in retrospect – seems like one long decline. Its first owner was also its greatest: few subsequent players could have matched Tartini, one of the true innovators in violin playing and teaching. Lipiński was a great violinist, even if little remembered now, but each subsequent change of ownership seems to bring further obscurity. That final sale in 1962 was to Richard Anschutz, who purchased the

Lipiński for his wife, Ely Livak. Perhaps she was, or still is, a fine player, but I can find no record of any performances, and with its sale to her husband, the *Lipiński* slips out of sight. It may achieve some sort of fame again, but for the time being its story is over.

THAT VIOLINS could re-emerge from semi-obscurity is demonstrated by the 1709 *Viotti*. Marie Hall's career had never regained the heights of her heyday before the Great War. Like so many of her peers, she was unable to shine in the new era ushered in by the brilliance of Jascha Heifetz. An audience remained for her, but it had shrunk, and was no longer international. In the 1930s she toured England as half of 'The Sonata Players' together with Miss Mary Ramsay. The very name conjures up genteel, unambitious images that are probably all too close to the truth. The post-war edition of *Grove's Dictionary of Music* visited the ultimate indignity on her of falsely reporting her death in October 1947. Her former champion, *The Strad*, compounded the error, publishing a letter in July 1955 from a reader pointing out the *Grove* entry and, very reasonably, wondering why there had been no obituaries. It was only in the following issue that the magazine carried the rather sheepish announcement: 'We are happy to be able to report that Miss Marie Hall . . . is alive and well, and is actively pursuing her career. She makes a limited number of public appearances, and has, of recent years, specialized in recitals of sonatas and ensemble works for violin and piano with her daughter, Miss Pauline Baring.' A little over a year later, however, the notices were correct. Marie Hall died, aged seventy-two, on 11 December 1956.

Pauline Baring, an only child, inherited her mother's violin. She waited for thirteen years before eventually deciding to sell it. Even then, she chose an unusual method to do so. Rather than leave the violin on consignment at Hill's or Beare's, the traditional way of disposing of the best violins, she elected to sell it at Sotheby's. Her choice of auction house was also strange: Sotheby's did not have an independent instrument division at the time; Puttick and Simpson, by then part of Phillips, had been the dominant violin auctioneer for the past 120 years. Nevertheless, the Sotheby's catalogue for 7 November 1968 was proud to carry notice of lot 21, 'An ex-Viotti Stradivari', a 'highly-important Italian violin bearing the original label Antonius Stradivarius Cremonensis Faciebat Anno 1709'. Bidding started at £5,000 and went up in £1,000 jumps. By the time it reached the hammer price of £22,000 [£214,000], paid by an English industrialist, Mr Jack Morrison, the previous world record for a violin at auction – £13,000 – had long since been smashed. Some observers were unsurprised; in the words of one, 'those who can look back on Marie Hall's concert days will remember her lovely tone'. The true lesson, however, was that Stradivari's prices were on the rise again. This violin, which had been famous for 150 years, was the harbinger of that fact.

Chapter Fifteen

'THE SOUND KEPT ON COMING AND COMING'

The *Davidov*, the *Paganini*, the *Khevenhüller*, the *Viotti* . . . and the *Marie Hall*

On 11 December 1971 Jacqueline du Pré came to the end of a two-day recording session at EMI's studios in Abbey Road. It had been arranged at short notice. Jacqueline had been unwell for some months, so when she suddenly felt better the session was quickly set up. She and her husband since 1967, the pianist and conductor Daniel Barenboim, used the two days to record sonatas by Chopin and César Franck, but some time remained. As Suvi Grubb, EMI's producer, later recalled, 'When we had finished she said that she would like to start on the Beethoven sonatas. Barenboim and I were concerned, for she looked tired, but we recorded the first movement of Op. 5 No.1. At the end of it she placed her cello back in its case with 'That is that' and did not even want to listen to what we had taped.'

That was Jacqueline's final appearance in the recording studio. She gave a few recitals the following year, and began an intended comeback at full pace in 1973. Concerts in Washington and New York were followed by two performances of the Elgar Cello Concerto back in London. Sir Neville Cardus's review in the *Guardian* has entered folklore as a premonitory epitaph to du Pré's career: 'Jacqueline went to the heart of the matter with a devotion remarkable in so young an artist . . . telling of Elgar's acceptance of the end. The bright day is done and he is for the dark.' Immediately after the second concert Jacqueline flew back to New York, first to be conducted by her husband in the Lalo Concerto and then for a scheduled four performances of the Brahms Double Concerto with Pinchas Zukerman on the violin. By the third concert she could no longer feel the strings under her fingers. The last had to be cancelled. Jacqueline was never heard in public again. Multiple sclerosis was finally diagnosed nine months later.

The prophetic nature of Isména Holland's advice to her goddaughter is all too apparent: the young virtuosa would have to lay aside the *Davidov* sooner than anyone might have suspected. But there is more to the story than that. Jacqueline fell out of love with the great cello long before her multiple sclerosis was diagnosed, or even had a discernible effect on her playing. In June 1968, five years before she retired from the concert stage, Jacqueline called Charles Beare to tell him that the *Davidov* was unplayable. The immediate cause was probably the humidity change as the cello returned to England from one trip too many abroad. The arrangements that Marie Hall used to make for her Strad may have worked in the days of sea voyages but air travel is another matter. String players nowadays are familiar with the problem; it is not unusual for a violin on a foreign tour to be kept in a hotel bathroom with the shower running. In the late sixties, however, jets (and perhaps hotel bathrooms) were still a novelty; such expediencies had yet to be discovered. As Charles Beare now remembers, the *Davidov*'s strings were 'lying flat upon the fingerboard' and an alternative had to be found for a concert at La Scala the following day.

Beare's had a Venetian cello by Francesco Gofriller in stock; Jacqueline borrowed and then bought it. The Gofriller turned out not to be just a temporary stopgap, but became her preferred instrument – at home and abroad – for the next year and a half. She had a greater problem with the *Davidov* than simply its poor reaction to travel. The romantics would say that there was only room for one love in her life. Daniel Barenboim had occupied that position and would brook no opposition. He, however, has always denied this, explaining that any dislike he had for the instrument was motivated only by his wife's clear discomfort while playing it. So what was the cause of this discomfort? The answer, it seems, lies in Jacqueline's playing style. 'The thing about a Strad,' Beare says, 'is that you have to draw out the sound.' The warm and sensitive sound of the *Davidov* is ideal for a player who is happy to coax the instrument into life. 'In retrospect, it was the wrong cello for her.' With emotion and expressivity the great hallmarks of du Pré's playing, the last thing she needed was a cello which prevented her from letting go. Beare now thinks that one made by Gofriller's contemporary Domenico Montagnana would have been perfect for her; with his cellos, 'the more you put in the more you get out'.

In the last two, interrupted, years she played in public,

Jacqueline's main cello was that true rarity among professional string soloists, a modern instrument. Its maker, Philadelphian luthier Sergio Peresson, gave it to her just as she was to go into rehearsals for yet another performance of the Elgar Concerto in his home city. Finding that the cello generated exactly the sound she was looking for, and was easier to play than its Italian forerunners, Jacqueline impulsively decided to use it at that night's concert. The new instrument reawakened her enthusiasm at a time when her still undiagnosed MS was beginning to take a real toll. The Gofriller was almost entirely set aside, and the *Davidov* remained silent apart from a period when Jacqueline lent it to a friend, Anna Shuttleworth. Soon after Jacqueline's MS was finally diagnosed the instrument was sent to Paris. A Labour government had just taken power in Britain, and it was prudent for a valuable asset like a Strad to be taken offshore, away from socialists considering a wealth tax.

For a little under a decade the *Davidov* sat unplayed in the storeroom of Parisian luthier Etienne Vatelot. Then, in the early 1980s, Jacqueline's husband Daniel Barenboim met Yo-Yo Ma. Only ten years younger than Jacqueline, he was just beginning a professional career, long after hers had ended. Ma had received his first cello lesson, aged four, in Etienne Vatelot's shop, sitting on three telephone directories. It seems appropriate that he should have fallen in love with the *Davidov* under the Frenchman's aegis. That occasion consisted of only 'fifteen glorious minutes', but in 1983 Jacqueline and her husband decided to lend the great instrument to Ma. He would later compare the process of reawakening the sleeping cello to the opening up of a really great wine.

It took about two months' playing, but thereafter 'the sound kept on coming and coming'.

In the vast majority of MS patients, the disease goes through periods of remission, when the sufferer can enjoy something closer to a normal life. Part of Jacqueline's tragedy is that her MS was especially virulent. She died in 1987 aged only forty-two. The *Davidov* was once more put up for sale. Yo-Yo Ma was naturally the first to be offered the instrument, at a relatively undemanding price. Even so, and however reluctantly, he had to turn down the opportunity. With two young children, Ma was not prepared to accept the considerable burden of extra concerts over perhaps ten years that paying for the *Davidov* would require. The Strad could not compete with his family; the instrument was returned to Vatelot. Ma reconciled himself to playing on his other masterpiece, a 1733 Montagnana, which he had kept in tandem with the *Davidov*.

Then, for the third time in its career, private philanthropy ensured that the cello would, after all, be played by a great cellist. An anonymous enthusiast, interested in the *Davidov*'s future, heard of Ma's decision from Vatelot. The purchase was made, and the instrument returned to Ma; he has its use for life. Even so, he says, he has never been able to play the Elgar Concerto on the *Davidov* without sensing Jacqueline's presence on the instrument. There is even a hint of a link between Ma and his Strad's other famous owner, Carl Davidov, the unwilling rehearser who had no time for his cello. As Ma says, 'Since I don't like to work hard, I've had to become efficient in my practising.'

In the late 1990s Ma used the *Davidov* to help him

explore the possibilities of seventeenth-century music, recording arrangements of Bach and Boccherini with the Amsterdam Baroque Orchestra. To do so, he took his Stradivarius back as far as possible to its original set-up: gut strings over a baroque bridge, played with a baroque bow. Most significantly, removing the end-pin forced Ma to grip the *Davidov* between his legs: 'As I walked away from rehearsal I could imagine someone asking, "Excuse me, are you a cowboy or a baroque cellist?"' The experience was a revelation: 'playing on my altered instrument . . . gives a much more intimate sound. By removing the innovations that over time have been made for the cello, you actually arrive at a different kind of expressivity.' Ma now seems convinced of the *Davidov*'s greater suitability for period music. Recently he has been concentrating on modern composers, and for this he pre-fers his Montagnana. For the last few years the *Davidov* has been largely silent.

SOON AFTER MA was lent the *Davidov* he and the Cleveland Quartet played together on a recording of Schubert's Quintet for Strings in C Major, D956. It would be an unremarkable event – such collaborations are the bread and butter of the virtuoso's existence – except that this is the only recording I can trace on which two of our Strads can be heard together. For the Cleveland Quartet were by now the proud players of the Paganini Quartet, including the 1680 *Paganini* violin.

The Quartet has never been split since Anna Clark bought it from Emil Herrmann in 1946. When she died in 1965 ownership passed to the Corcoran Gallery of Art in Washington, DC, whose eclectic collection had already been swelled by bequests from her copper-king husband. Meanwhile, the four instruments in the Quartet were played by, successively, the National Symphony Quartet, the Iowa String Quartet and, in 1982, the Cleveland Quartet. At this last group's instigation all four instruments were comprehensively restored. Following the work, Peter Salaff, second violin in the Quartet, had this to say apropos of his new Strad, our 1680 *Paganini*:

> the sound of a Guadagnini [his previous instrument] matched the Quartet exceptionally well; for the second violin part it gave tremendous support. I find the Strad is a wonderful instrument but it has different qualities. It has a wonderful sheen in the sound and has a tremendous edge too. It will work well as the second violin and this edge will give an inner balance to the Quartet.

The Cleveland Quartet would play on the Paganini Quartet for almost fifteen years, in a bond that survived several changes of personnel.

When the Cleveland Quartet finally disbanded in the mid-1990s the Corcoran decided to sell its instruments, which sat oddly with the rest of the Gallery's collection. The Paganini Quartet was eventually purchased, for $15 million, by the Nippon Music Foundation, which immediately lent the instruments to the Tokyo Quartet. How should that $15 million be divided? Probably more than half applies to the viola. There are so few good violas made by Stradivari that the rare examples have a value which perhaps ignores the fact that he never totally mastered the form. Certainly the smallest proportion would apply to the 1680 *Paganini*. It is the least distinguished of the four instruments. More than that, there are rumours in the violin world that the Tokyo Quartet is not entirely happy with it. As Peter Biddulph says: 'What do you expect? It's an early Strad.'

Coping with a second violin that does not match its counterparts must make for difficulties. What is most important, according to Siegmund Nissel of the Amadeus Quartet, is for the second violin to have power in its lower strings so that it can be a bridge between the viola and the first violin. This is much more characteristic of Stradivari's later violins, including Nissel's own, made in 1731. Early Strads like the 1680 *Paganini* may well have a sweet tone, but that is something quite different. It is hard to escape the conclusion that the violin's current position is more the result of its background and fame than its suitability for the role.

YEHUDI MENUHIN finally parted with the *Khevenhüller* in the early 1980s. The reason was prosaic: he needed the money. Menuhin and his second wife, Diana, had decided to move from the house they had owned since 1959 in Highgate, North London, to the city's centre. They had bought a grand classical house in Chester Square, Belgravia, reported to have cost £425,000 [£850,000].* Finding a buyer for the old house turned out to take longer than

---

* Following Diana Menuhin's death, the house came on to the market in 2003 with a guide price of £5 million. Over the last twenty years, London houses have probably proved even better investments than violins.

expected:* the *Khevenhüller* would have to fill the gap; it was sent on consignment to Charles Beare. It too, however, proved to be a difficult sale; a year later the violin was still at Beare's. Then Michael Scheinin walked into the shop. An Egyptian based in Milan, Scheinin was for a brief period in the 1980s one of the violin world's most influential collectors. He had just bought two violins at Sotheby's and needed a double case for them. 'Do you have any Strads?' was an afterthought; and Charles Beare's reply – 'Only the *Khevenhüller*' – cannot have anticipated the response it received. Scheinin was not just a devotee of Yehudi Menuhin, he also regarded those early recordings as something close to the peak of violinistic achievement. Among all Strads, it was the *Khevenhüller* that he coveted the most. The deal was soon agreed and after more than fifty years, Menuhin and his first Stradivarius were finally parted. Scheinin kept the *Khevenhüller* for a number of years, but it had started the wanderings that were to bring it – via Japan and America – back to London and the dealer Peter Biddulph in 2000. Its current owner, who 'had change from $3 million', is a Swiss private collector. His daughter plays the violin, but it seems unlikely that the *Khevenhüller*'s 'powerful, mellow and sweet sound' will be heard in public any time soon.

JACK MORRISON sold Marie Hall's 'ex-Viotti' 1709 Strad through Hill's in 1974. It reappeared at Sotheby's in 1988, sent there from the Middle East as a late entry

* It would eventually be sold to the pop star Sting.

to the March sale. Once again, it set an auction record: £473,000 [£720,000]. As *The Strad* commented at the time, 'there are more renowned Strads in the world, but this lovely example has been described as the finest toned violin to be offered within living memory'. The purchaser was Geraldo Modern, an enthusiastic member of amateur string quartets in Brazil. He kept the violin for a few years before selling it on once more to Taiwan. The great Strad is now a museum piece, a star exhibit in the Chi-Mei Collection, lent occasionally to local players, but it will never belong to a violinist again.

Before he sold the violin, however, Modern lent it for six weeks to Thomas Bowes, who used it in various broadcasts and one public recital, on 6 May 1990, in London's Purcell Room. The programme notes for that concert, quoted in Chapter One, naturally described the distinguished provenance of the *'Viotti-Marie Hall'*, especially its role in Viotti's ground-breaking appearances at the Concert Spirituel in the 1780s. The notes were simply repeating what Marie Hall herself said about her violin, and what many of the standard reference works on Stradivari also believed.

Yet all these authorities were wrong. That Purcell Room concert was not only the last London outing of the *'Viotti-Marie Hall'*, it was also the last time it was called by that name. Viotti probably never even played the violin. As is now clear, he only had it for a short time, and soon sold it to the Duke of Cambridge.* Successive owners then included the Duke's aide-de-camp and a

* On the basis of this provenance, it may well be the violin that the Duke of Cambridge acquired from Viotti for 50 guineas in 1817.

pupil of Wilhelmj, before George Hart sold the violin to Marie Hall in 1905. She is really the only famous player in its provenance. The Chi Mei Collection calls its 1709 Strad the '*Marie Hall*'.

This book was meant to be following five violins but it turns out to have followed six. In tracing the history of the *Viotti*, the *Marie Hall* was a false trail, one that lasted for almost a century. I was brought up short when I first learnt its true history. It was enough to make me doubt everything. Is there even a 'real' 1709 *Viotti*?

There is; and its history explains how it came to be confused with the *Marie Hall*. For nearly two centuries, ever since it was sold to pay back Mrs Chinnery, the *Viotti* has been hidden from the public eye. In 1855 François Fétis named it, with striking precision, the 'third best' Strad in existence; five years later it changed hands for 5,500 francs [£14,000]. In May 1897 it came over from Paris to W. E. Hill & Co, who sold it on to Baron Knoop, a collector whose name crops up in the histories of many instruments. He sold the violin back to the Hills in the early 1900s and they did not sell it on again until 1906, to another collector, Richard Baker.

So the real *Viotti* was in London in 1905 when Marie Hall bought her Strad from George Hart there. In fact, both violins were to a certain extent under the Hills' control, since their firm not only owned the *Viotti* but had a half-share in the *Marie Hall* as well. With two 1709 Strads around, each with a link to Viotti, and each with a single-piece back made from the same log of strongly figured maple, it seems less surprising that Marie should have assumed that hers was the violin with which Viotti amazed audiences across Europe. She may have been encouraged to make the mistake by George Hart, who might have over-stressed one part of the violin's provenance when he sold it to her. Or perhaps Marie Hall simply wanted to believe that she had Viotti's violin. There are inescapable parallels between their careers: the early poverty, the discovery and education by wealthy patrons, and the overwhelming success sparked by a single concert. Marie may have found the idea that she had the *Viotti* too irresistible for scepticism.

It is harder, perhaps, to understand why the Hills did not act to clear up the confusion, which they must have observed;* they always had the true histories of both instruments in their archives. It was probably the firm's brief encounter with the *Marie Hall* in 1974 that first gave that violin its correct provenance, although this still took some time to become widely known; such was the attractiveness of its false history. The very existence of the *Viotti*, meanwhile, remained practically unknown. In 1992, however, W. E. Hill & Sons ceased to trade. Its bank of histories and instrument information was initially said to be destined for a well-stocked bonfire. In the event, the firm's diaries at least were saved. Originally bought by Peter Biddulph, it seems fitting that they have ended up in the possession of Charles Beare, the man who assumed the Hills' crown.

Biddulph paid £67,000 for the diaries. It sounds like a bargain. Knowledge was at the core of what set the Hills

---

* In fact, they exacerbated the situation by extolling the virtues of yet another *Viotti* Strad, made in 1712, in their book on Stradivari; there is no other evidence for the existence of this violin and the reference seems to be a misprint.

apart from the competition. That is probably why they guarded the history of the true *Viotti* so closely: they had no desire to advertise its existence to their rivals. Certainly Richard Baker, its purchaser in 1906, does not seem to have looked elsewhere when he decided to sell it in 1924. So the Hills once again became the violin's owners, selling it in 1928 for £8,000 [£270,000]. Even then, the Hills noted in their diaries that they could have got much more for the *Viotti* in America but wanted it to stay in Britain.

And so it has. The last owner of the *Viotti*, son of that purchaser in 1928, died in late 2002. He hoped to leave his Strad to the Ashmolean, to be displayed alongside the *Messiah*. It was not something I expected when I began this book, but I find it strangely satisfying that two of our violins may end up together for their foreseeable futures.

Chapter Sixteen

'A RUN-OF-THE-MILL STRAD'

Interpreting the *Messiah*

THE *Messiah*'s story seemed to come to an end soon after the Second World War, when it took up residence in Oxford's Ashmolean Museum. For fifty years it hung there in semi-splendour, its varnish pristine, its corners unworn, its purfling exact, the most perfectly preserved example of Stradivari's workmanship from the very peak of his golden period. It was certainly not forgotten; its condition alone made it the starting-point for any discussion along the lines of 'What makes Stradivari so special?' There was, however, little drama to a life in a museum gallery.

But at the end of the twentieth century, the *Messiah* came into the news once more. Was the world's most famous violin a fake?

The violin always had its detractors. Part of the problem was the *Messiah*'s 'newness', the very characteristic that made it unique. The patina of age is an inherent part of an instrument's beauty. The process of 'antiquing' violins is as prevalent today as it was with Vuillaume: there is no intent to defraud, it simply makes a violin easier on the eye and easier to sell. With all the appearance of a brand-new violin, the *Messiah* looks well made, to be sure, but incongruous. As soon as it went on display, there were mutterings that it simply could not be an eighteenth-century antique; it must be younger, a product of one of the great nineteenth-century Stradivari copyists. Proponents of this theory did not have to look far for the culprit: Vuillaume had made the *Messiah*; his story about finding it in Tarisio's Fontaneto farmhouse was just that – a story.

But the *Messiah*'s defence was strong. Supporters pointed to the fact that while every detail – the curve of the soundholes, the bee-stings of the purfling in the corners, the confidence of the scroll – shouted 'Stradivari, 1716', the *Messiah*'s overall pattern was a one-off; it had no twin. Surely Vuillaume would have copied another Stradivarius rather than make up his own design. In any case the *Messiah* had the best sort of provenance prior to Vuillaume; Giuseppe Rocca's copies of it, made in Turin from 1843 onwards, pre-date the *Messiah*'s appearance in Vuillaume's workshop in 1855. Clearly Rocca came into contact with the violin while Tarisio owned it, and, like Vuillaume, recognized it for the superb template that it is. 'Ah,' said the doubters, 'but what if Rocca's violins are the originals, copied by Vuillaume?'

There the debate might have rested, with the balance of the arguments always with the *Messiah*'s supporters – it was simply too good to be Vuillaume's work – but for the emergence of fresh research. First, the translation and decipherment of Cozio's notebooks revealed a number of discrepancies between his 'most beautiful and large violin of 1716' and what we call the *Messiah*. He made three references to it, between 1803 and 1816. Of the two later entries, one was rather vague and the other used a measuring system that has still not been deciphered.

Only the earliest carried any real details of the instrument. Crucially, it referred to two separate patches in the belly of the violin, one placed there by Stradivari himself, the other by Guadagnini, presumably on Cozio's own instructions. The *Messiah* had only one such patch and it seemed to be in a different location from either of those mentioned by Cozio.

An even more serious problem arose when researchers started to consider what the 'G' inked on the base of the *Messiah*'s pegbox might indicate. Only a few Strads carry initials like this. They are clearly ancient and are rare because the substitution of a violin's neck when it wears out also removes the relevant portion of the pegbox. Most of the initials to have survived apparently read as 'PS', so that the Hills and others assumed that Paolo Stradivari had discreetly identified his own violins. Towards the end of the twentieth century, however, it was realized that all these 'PS' violins shared the measurements of the Stradivari workshop's 'PG' mould. The markings had probably been made before the violins were varnished, to enable easy identification of the mould around which they were constructed. The Hills, however, had misread the second letter 'G' as an 'S'.

The *Messiah*, however, remained an anomaly. It had once, of course, been in Paolo's ownership and its original pegbox was still intact. The Hills had therefore looked for the initials 'PS', but were interested to note, in their book on Stradivari, that it 'does not appear to have been so marked'. That much is already odd: why did the Hills not mention the 'G' that was there? Nevertheless, the implication that the *Messiah* was made on the 'G' mould seems clear. The real bombshell came when Stewart

Pollens, Associate Conservator at New York's Metropolitan Museum of Art and author of the most authoritative book on Stradivari's internal moulds, made measurements which convinced him that the *Messiah* followed the lines of the 'PG' mould.

Pollens deduced that in the years after the Hills wrote their book, someone had become aware of the meaning behind the lettering in the pegboxes of other Strads. Realizing that the *Messiah* should have had similar markings, that person had decided to boost the credentials of what could only be a post-Stradivari copy by adding them. The use of the wrong letter – 'G' – simply added

Figure 19. The base of one of the crucial pegboxes: it is easy to see how the Hills might have read 'PG' as 'PS'.

confusion to the attempt at deception. It was time to expose the world's most famous Stradivarius as a fraud.

Pollens turned to a tool whose origins lie in archaeology but which is also applicable to violins. Dendrochronology is based on the fact that the width of a tree's growth ring in any given year is dependent on climatic conditions for that year. Measuring a sequence of these rings when they appear as grain in a piece of wood gives a timeline of different widths. If this correlates with an established 'reference chronology', based on trees from the same region whose age is known, then a researcher can assign dates to the wood. In particular, the youngest tree ring gives the earliest possible date at which the originating tree can have been felled. Applying the technique to the spruce in a violin's belly may therefore disprove its attribution to a specific date, if the wood turns out to be younger than the supposed age of the instrument.

Pollens had got the chance to examine the *Messiah* in 1997 when he received authorization to take high-quality photographs of the violin. The pictures seemed good enough to be used as the basis for a dendrochronological investigation, and Pollens sent one of the violin's belly to Dr Peter Klein at the University of Hamburg, one of the most highly regarded dendrochronologists in the world. One can imagine Pollens's excitement at Klein's initial report: the last datable ring on the *Messiah* grew in 1738, one year after Stradivari's death; Stradivari's 'masterpiece' could not have been made by him at all.

Rumours of the results started to spread, causing consternation among violin experts. If the *Messiah* was a fake, how could any attribution to Stradivari be accepted?

The entire basis of the trade in old violins would be called into question. The only hope was that Klein's results must somehow be wrong. Convinced of it, a powerful alliance of Charles Beare, the present generation of the Hills (still the *Messiah*'s gatekeepers) and the Ashmolean Museum decided to counter science with science. They commissioned a further dendrochronological study of the *Messiah* from a British pair who had been building their own reputation in the field: luthier John Topham and scientist Derek McCormick. Accepting the commission, the two men insisted on full access to the violin, and the right to publish their results in a peer-reviewed journal.

Topham and McCormick had already developed the apparatus necessary to undertake the study. It consisted of a microscope on a travelling carriage that accurately measured its movements. By sliding the microscope so that the cross-hairs in its eyepiece moved across the grain of the *Messiah*'s belly, they could record the distance between each growth ring. They soon had a sequence of widths that covered almost 100 years' growth of alpine spruce. In fact they had two such sequences, one from each side of the *Messiah*'s belly. Moreover, both showed a strong match with similar sequences measured from two other Strads made in 1717. All three violins used wood from a similar source.

That was the easy part. The match with two other Strads should have been enough to convince most doubters of the *Messiah*'s origin in Stradivari's workshop, but it did not assign a date to its wood. Unlike Klein, the British pair could not find a reference chronology that matched the *Messiah*. They needed more certainty.

The answer came from the ease with which Topham

and McCormick had matched the *Messiah* with the two other Strads. It led them to bring in measurements from other Cremonese instruments: violins, violas and cellos, twenty-one in total, a mammoth undertaking. Each timeline could be matched with others in the group so that the resulting graph combined all their separate measurements into one chronology specific to Cremonese instruments. It also averaged out variations among the growth patterns of individual trees, and could be matched with an established reference chronology.* Now, finally, Topham and McCormick could date the wood in the *Messiah*. The spruce on its treble side has growth rings corresponding to 1581–1675, and on its bass side to 1590–1682 – dates entirely feasible for a violin constructed in 1716.

Even before this final dating, Topham had taken his measurements from the *Messiah* and the two 1717 Strads to Klein in Hamburg, who started to doubt the accuracy of his own curve. Perhaps Pollens's photographs were not after all good enough for dendrochronology? Exasperated by this apparent backtracking, Pollens recruited a third dendrochronologist, Dr Peter Ian Kuniholm at America's Cornell University. He supported Klein's dating to 1738, again on the basis of photographs alone. Six months later, in November 1998, Klein and Topham met at the Ashmolean to cooperate on yet another set of measurements. Klein was forced to use Topham's equipment, as the jeweller's loupe that he was planning to slide across the surface of the *Messiah* might have damaged its

* Wood from a barn close to Innsbruck provided a particularly good match.

varnish. The apparent collaboration did not produce any agreement on what to do next, and Klein had to leave the museum without his measurements.

Pollens and his partisans began to suspect a cover-up. More dendrochronologists demanded access to the *Messiah*; Topham and McCormick's methodology was questioned; insults started to fly. Even when an account of their investigations was finally published in the *Journal of Archaeological Science* in March 2000, having gone through the full review process, the pair's critics were not silenced. Scenting a story, the journalists moved in. The *Wall Street Journal* took an interest. An article in the London *Times* in October 2000 told enough of the story to reawaken my schoolboy interest in Stradivarius, eventually leading to this book.

Transatlantic consensus was only achieved when a trio of American dendrochronologists effectively confirmed Topham and McCormick's conclusions. The wood used to build the belly of the *Messiah* grew until 1682; there is a good cross-match between it and that in other Strads. Everything about the *Messiah*'s wood is consistent with its label, 'Antonius Stradivarius Cremonensis Faciebat Anno 1716'.

SO WITH POLLENS and his supporters seen off, the *Messiah* can settle comfortably back into its role as the most famous Stradivarius in the world and the violin trade carry on much as before? Well, up to a point. Dendrochronology can never give an instrument absolute authentication, but who would now pay millions for a Strad on the basis of stylistic assertions alone? The

Messiah's dating to 1716 has been reinforced, but for a few other instruments the reverse is true. Violins have been withdrawn from sale when their wood has been dated to decades after their original attribution. Even the expertise of the trade's gods – men such as Alfred Hill – has been challenged. These days, an accompanying dendrochronological report from John Topham is almost a prerequisite when the most valuable instruments reach the sale rooms.

And what of the *Messiah*? It must surely be a Strad; we would be stretching our belief in Vuillaume's powers too far to suggest that he found perfect wood with which to make his perfect copy. Nevertheless, the anomalies that first led Pollens to challenge it with dendrochronology have not gone away. Naturally they can be explained. Perhaps the 'G' in the pegbox is just a workshop error? Perhaps one of the patches mentioned by Count Cozio has since been removed? Perhaps Cozio simply made a mistake when describing his 'most beautiful and large violin of 1716'? Few, however, would stake their lives on the unassailability of the *Messiah*'s entire provenance. Charles Beare, for example, is certain that it is a Strad, certain that it was made in 1716 'or perhaps 1715', and certain that it was bought by Vuillaume from Tarisio's heirs; but he acknowledges that its earlier history rests on much less solid foundations.

All this uncertainty highlights another concern. Is the *Messiah* any good as an instrument? The Hills liked to believe that Stradivari himself felt so strongly about his greatest creation that he could never bring himself to sell it. Few would now claim that status for it. In the words of luthier John Dilworth, 'It is simply a run-of-the mill

Strad that has survived better than any other, but a run-of-the-mill Strad would still be anyone else's masterpiece. We go into ecstasy about it because of the varnish. It's the only one that tells us what Strad's varnish looked like new, and it's fabulous.'

Some might go further. What if, in fact, Stradivari kept the *Messiah* simply because nobody wanted to buy it? There is little evidence that it has ever produced a great tone. The *Messiah*'s supporters point to the letter that Joseph Joachim wrote to Robert Crawford, the violin's owner, in 1891 and its reference to the 'combined sweetness and grandeur' of the *Messiah*'s sound. Joachim's credentials as a judge are impeccable, but his letter could be no more than politeness. At about the same time both Crawford and the Hills were admitting that in fact the *Messiah* needed some playing to reach its full potential. The curious fact remains that the single most influential of all Stradivari's violins, the one that has been most imitated and has done most to affect the development of violin-making in the nineteenth and twentieth centuries, is, tonally at least, an unknown quantity.

One other possibility is suggested by small anomalies in the *Messiah*'s construction. Many could be shared by other Strads, but hidden on them by wear and dirt. Others are less easily explained. A recent article by John Dilworth notes the thinness of the *Messiah*'s back plate around the edge on its lower bout, 'a rare lapse of gouge control on Stradivari's part', he suggests. Then there is the asymmetry of the *Messiah*'s scroll, something 'that appears on other Stradivari instruments but not to such an extreme extent'. That patch on the belly is probably filling a resin pocket. It is not particularly unusual, but it is an imperfection. More intriguing still is the joint in the centre of the *Messiah*'s lower rib. In almost every other Strad this would originally have been a single strip of maple from corner to corner. On its own none of these incongruities would be surprising, but taken together they present a sort of case. Might some of the work in the *Messiah* be that of an apprentice?

The notion that the *Messiah* is – wholly or partly – apprentice work probably raises even more hackles than its ascription to Vuillaume, but it is too attractive an idea to suppress. In 1716 Giovanni Battista, the eldest son from Stradivari's second marriage to survive infancy, was thirteen, just the sort of age when, after maybe two years in the workshop, a fast learner might have expected to have a hand in his own instruments. If the *Messiah* was one of them, then never mind the implications for the violin; consider what it says about Giovanni Battista. Generations have hailed the *Messiah* as a masterpiece and its maker as a genius. Perhaps, if Giovanni Battista had not died in 1727, aged only twenty-four, Antonio Stradivari would have had a worthy successor after all.

Afterword

It turns out to be Culture Week, whether in the whole of Italy, Lombardy, or just Cremona, I cannot tell. My Italian can do little more than distinguish *Andante* from *Presto*, and the helpfulness of the girl in the tourist office extends only to booking me a last-minute room before she is submerged under a wave of new arrivals. Whichever is the case, there is no charge for entry to any of the museums in the city; I can save my euros. So, clutching my free ticket, I climb the long flight of stone steps leading up from the Piazza del Comune into the Palazzo Comunale, Cremona's Town Hall.

Discovering Cremona, freely available at the tourist office, tells me that the Palazzo is a typical Lombard *broletto* with a closed quadrangle shape around a courtyard. That does not do justice to the imposing magnificence of the red-brick structure I am entering. It is across a medieval piazza from the Duomo, Baptistry and Torazzo, a grouping that took my breath away when I first came across it last night at the end of a narrow alleyway. Even then I found it hard to understand the *Rough Guide*'s analysis of the town as quiet and relatively unexciting, 'not an obvious place to spend a night'.

I have not, however, come for the buildings. The Town Hall is also a museum. Not the Museo Stradivariano: I will visit that and its collection of the great luthier's tools and moulds later in the day. The Palazzo Comunale contains Cremona's collection of great violins: only seven exhibits, and only one Strad, but together they span the entire period of Cremona's golden age.

At the top of the stairs all is activity; a photographic exhibition is being set up on the landing. Ignoring it, I follow everyone else into some kind of anteroom, already full of coach-loads of Italians of a certain age: Culture Week clearly brings its disadvantages. Across the room is my objective, the Hall of Violins, apparently open, but my way is blocked by a tanned and handsome guard who gestures me to take a seat like everyone else. I resign myself to a long wait.

This is clearly more than just an anteroom. The Salone dei Quadri must still be used as Cremona's council chamber. The coach-loads are waiting on mahogany benches – half desk, half pew – that face a more imposing set of throne-like chairs, at the roped-off end of the room. The arrangement casts the waiting tourists as an audience and the guide to one party seizes the opportunity, lecturing his group on what they are about to see; the few words I can recognize – 'Stradivari', 'harmonica' – at least tell me that we are all waiting for the same reason. In the meantime I have ample opportunity to ponder the massive paintings on each of the long side walls. One shows Christ and the 'Multiplication of the Bread' and the other the Israelites finding manna in the desert, although I would never have guessed either without the benefit of its caption. As far as artistic merit goes, it is clear that Cremona's true masterpieces lie on the other side of that door.

It is a door that is now shut. One final party has

emerged through it, the room locked behind them, provoking angry shushes from the party listening to the voluble guide, who now has the attention of the whole room. Surely we are waiting for something more than this? At the far end of the chamber, a side door opens to reveal a grey-haired man in a tweed jacket and tie. He is carrying a violin. Someone tries to shut the guide up; at first he shrugs off the interruption, but then realization dawns; he turns round, admits to himself that here is something his party would rather listen to, and gracelessly quits the floor. The grey-haired man begins to play.

I have no idea what we hear: something simple if soulful, something baroque, something lively, pieces which seem designed to test and demonstrate the full range of the violin's notes and moods, without overtaxing its player. Even my inexpert ears can tell that he is not the reason we are here; there's the occasional wrong note, the faintly plodding way in which he puts the violin through its paces. No, we are here for the instrument alone. There really is something about its tone. Warm and vibrant, it seems to inhabit the room. Quite by chance – I could hug myself – I have arrived to witness the weekly exercise outing of one of the town's treasures; the only question is: which one?

The recital ends. The player retreats to applause. The violin room is unlocked and I manage to inveigle myself into the first small group to be allowed in. Seven violins are on display, each hung in its own glass case for viewing in the round. Unsurprisingly, perhaps, my fellow-tourists turn out to be in the charge of the loquacious guide. He immediately leads them to the case at the far end of the room, and continues his exposition as if he had never been interrupted. I am left free to look at the two violins nearest the door. The first is one of the set made by Andrea Amati for Catherine de Medici in the 1560s. Two years younger than its sister in the Ashmolean, this violin could be played tomorrow. For all practical purposes, it is in perfect condition, even if the gold leaf on its back has flaked off so that the original design of the French royal coast of arms is no longer discernible. It is breathtakingly beautiful, but my eyes are drawn to the case next door.

By comparison with the Amati, its neighbour is brand-new. Its varnish gleams brash and red. The ebony fingerboard's mother-of-pearl inlay and the dark swirling tracery within the maple sides testify to the hours of work spent perfecting the instrument. And yet the violin has nothing like the charm of its plainer companion. The curves and symmetry of a violin give it a simple grace that is only marred by this sort of ornamentation. More than that, this violin seems to have no soul. Most violinists would find it unplayable. By a curious irony, this, by far the newest violin in the room, is the only one still to be set up in the old style that all the other instruments have long since cast off. Its stubby neck and wedged fingerboard make it a throwback, two centuries out of date. There is reason to all this, of course: Simone Sacconi made it in Cremona in the 1960s as an exact copy of Stradivari's *Hellier* violin. The violin is a work of artifice, not of art.

The coach party is leaving the room and the tanned guard beckons me to do the same. The queue outside is getting restless; the next batch of visitors is due to enter

– no time for me to look at the other violins, those made
by successive generations of Amatis and Guarneris. I can
contain my frustration. That afternoon I will return to
the Town Hall to find it empty and look at instruments
uninterrupted. Now, however, I must pose one final
question to the guard. We share no common language;
even so, we can understand each other. Yes, the violin I
heard only ten minutes before was the one at the far end
of the room, the one the coach party clustered round, the
one made by Antonio Stradivari.

Was that the first time I heard a Strad close up?
Probably: my mother and I once queued for three hours
so we could be in the front row of a Yehudi Menuhin
concert, but by then he would have been playing his
del Gesù. Cremona's Town Hall was certainly a suitable
venue for the experience. Moreover, this Strad, now
called the *Cremonese*, was made in the peak year of 1715,
and has a provenance that includes Joachim. The combination of history and location has undeniable resonance,
but what really interests me about the *Cremonese* is what
has happened to it in the last thirty years. In particular,
there was the announcement when Cremona bought it in
1962 that it would be put through every test imaginable.
The *Cremonese* stands as a symbol of science's failure to
come to grips with the secrets of Stradivari.

VIOLINS AND violin-making have been subjected to scientific methods since the days of Vuillaume, but with
little success. Varnish has been analysed by X-ray diffrac-
tion, the tool used to decipher the structure of DNA.
Spectrometers have studied its composition, identifying

the individual elements and compounds that block specific wavelengths in the spectrum of light. Acoustic tests approached the problem from a different direction. One compared instruments' loudness at different frequencies and appeared to show Cremonese violins at a slight disadvantage. Another, looking at how loudness fades over time, showed Strads and the like holding their tone for longer. A further set of investigations used three-dimensional X-rays, giving every possible physical measurement and variations in the density of the wood. Most recently, dendrochronological analysis of Stradivari's wood has shown how its density was affected by the mini-Ice Age that reached its peak in Europe between 1645 and 1715.

Little has been achieved. In most cases it has been too difficult to separate Stradivari's intentions from what time has subsequently wrought. Were the molecules identified by spectrometers part of Stradivari's original recipe, or contaminants from tools or crucibles, or created by later oxidation as the varnish aged? What effect has maturation of the wood had on its measurements and density? What can we read into the Ice Age theory, when we know that every maker in Europe used wood from the same source as Stradivari? In fact there have been only two possible 'Eureka' moments, and even their results are disputed.

The first revelation came with the use of electron microscopes. They showed a particulate layer – some kind of powder – between the wood and the varnish on Cremonese instruments. In the last few years it has been analysed using EDAX technology (Electron Dispersal Analysis by X-ray) and tentatively identified as Pozzolana earth, a volcanic ash. There are many potential reasons why Stradivari and his contemporaries might have used it: the ash is waterproof; it hardens and homogenizes the wood, and enables it to take a polish; its red colour may in some way impart a stain to the overlying varnish. Whether it also has an acoustic effect remains unknown. Some luthiers regard this as the 'answer', the counter-intuitive Holy Grail, the goal of researchers since the days of Reade and Vuillaume. Others are equally dismissive: 'Pozzolana earth is only one possible interpretation of the EDAX results, which actually give quite different results for different instruments . . . [It] is a bit of a red herring, I think.'

The other putative discovery has a longer pedigree. Something very like it was first mooted over 100 years ago, when it was suggested that Napoleon's roads had superseded the river Po as a medium of transportation for alpine spruce. The modern version of the theory has at least two forms. One is that Stradivari's logs may have been accidentally soaked in seawater because he was using the Venetian navy's rejects. It is an appealing notion, but hard to support on the evidence from dendrochronology that violin-makers around Europe were using the same wood. The other is that Cremonese luthiers deliberately impregnated their wood in some form of salt solution in an attempt to preserve it. It is based on the observation that Cremonese instruments do not seem to have suffered from as much woodworm infestation as their equally aged counterparts. The theory's proponents have been convinced by the results of acoustic tests on samples of wood soaked in various solutions. There are, however, few luthiers among them. Most would say that

Cremonese instruments show little woodworm damage simply because, being valuable, they have always been well looked after.

In short, there has been no definitive breakthrough. If Cremonese craftsmen had a secret, then science has yet to find it with any certainty. Instead, most modern luthiers still seek guidance from the work of one of their own: Simone Sacconi. For all its soullessness, his copy of the *Hellier* is a worthy exhibit for Cremona's Town Hall. His philosophy sparked off a resurgence in violin-making that continues to this day. Schools have sprung up around the world. Their output is tested in any number of international concourses. Dealers who once concentrated on French nineteenth-century instruments now do better with the works of modern makers (although it still helps if they have an Italian name, or work in Cremona). Twenty-five years ago, Charles Beare saw luthiers struggling to match Vuillaume, let alone the great Cremonese craftsmen. Now he thinks that standards are finally approaching what Stradivari and his contemporaries achieved. It seems that so much energy was devoted for so long to discovering the 'lost' formula of Stradivari's varnish that huge advances have come from simply trying to make the best instruments.

THERE ARE successors to Sacconi who believe that all Stradivari's techniques have now been discovered – that their modern copies simply need a maturation period and at last we will have violins whose tone matches Cremona's great classical creations. We have, however, been here before. Vuillaume's best violins are worth perhaps one hundredth as much as the best Strads, Gemünder's, one thousandth. They and countless others have not lived up to their makers' claims. Cremona's Golden Age came to an end more than 250 years ago. For at least half that time successors have been trying to discover its secrets. Is the current generation any different from its predecessors?

The players who find that new instruments work for them continue to be in a tiny minority. Anthony Marwood of the Florestan Trio was once a member of this select band: 'I remember when I was so thrilled with myself when I played a modern violin for a couple of years because I thought, great, I'll show them. I'll play on a modern instrument. I don't need to get involved in this rat race, fantastic. And then after a while I realized that unfortunately I probably did need to and there wasn't really any way beyond that.' At the very least it seems clear that no modern instrument has yet matured for long enough to compete with a Strad.

Ultimately, attempts to copy Stradivari seem doomed to failure. There are too many variables. If we take just two controversies – the usefulness or not of Pozzolana earth and whether or not to impregnate the wood with salt solutions – then we already have four different options, and that is before we even start to think about the method of application of the earth or the precise concentrations of the salt solutions, let alone their ingredients. Testing each option would mean building the violins, letting them age, perhaps for fifty or 100 years, and then ensuring that they are played for long enough by a good enough player to bring out their best tone. It is absurd. Stradivari can never be matched through imitation.

All we can copy is Stradivari's approach: single-minded devotion to the aim of producing instruments better than any predecessor's. Many factors have contributed to Stradivari's supremacy: an uninterrupted tradition already over a century old when he began; a methodical and disciplined mind; a certainty about carving that meant he could easily translate his ideas into practice; a life long enough both to experiment and to reap the benefits of that experimentation; at least two dutiful helpers. He may also have been a genius; no one expects to match Bach or Shakespeare. But the violins he made are not perfect: they can be moody, have off-days. Modern luthiers benefit from a whole set of other advantages, the knowledge brought by history and science. Perhaps it will need another genius, but surely we can imagine that one day someone will produce instruments that not only match Stradivari's but supersede them.

We must hope so. For there is a lesson to be drawn from the lives of the instruments this book has followed. Four of the five violins with which we started are now in private collections or museums. So is our false trail, the *Marie Hall*. The two remaining instruments – the *Davidov* cello and the *Paganini* violin – are still played, but neither sustains the full career of a virtuoso soloist. Perhaps it is the gradual decline in the prestige of the *Lipiński* that is the most telling: even Strads can wear out.

Over the last twenty years David Fulton has parlayed a fortune from software into the greatest collection of string instruments in private hands. He defends himself robustly against the charge that he is locking up great violins: an instrument which has been played in concert for most of its life is never likely to compare favourably with one that has been relatively untouched. It ends up 'worn and damaged . . . I think the twentieth century was very hard on Strads.' It is hard not to agree with him. The Strads that nowadays grace the concert stage tend to be recent discoveries, little played. We may already be hearing instruments from the lower leagues of the Master's output.

Talk for a time to people who operate in the violin market and you will eventually be told, darkly, 'You know, there are many bad Strads,' instruments that may once have been great but no longer have a following. They gather dust in storerooms in New York, London or Tokyo, ostensibly for sale, waiting for the player who will fall in love with them, whose technique happens to be exactly what is required to coax them back to their best, when in fact they are just not good enough, instruments destroyed by time. One day, supplies of the great classical violins will run out. We need a new Stradivari.

Chronology of classical luthiers

1500–05   Birth of Andrea Amati

1530–35   Gaudenzio Ferrari paints representations of
          three-string violins/violas and cello

1540   20 May, birth of Gasparo Bertolotti ('da Salo')
       Birth of Antonio Amati

1555   Balthasar de Beaujoyeux's dance band arrives at
       French court

1561   Birth of Girolamo Amati

1564   Date on earliest surviving violin, made by
       Andrea Amati in Cremona and part of set ordered
       for Charles IX

1572   Date on earliest surviving cello, also made by
       Andrea Amati in Cremona and also ordered
       for Charles IX

1577   26 December, death of Andrea Amati

c.1580   Birth of Giovanni Maggini

1581   Balthasar de Beaujoyeux composes first music
       specifically for the violin

1596   3 December, birth of Nicolò Amati

1608   Death of Antonio Amati

1617   Birth of Jacob Stainer

1620s   Nicolò Amati's hand visible in 'Brothers Amati' instruments

1628   Death of Girolamo Amati

c.1632   Death of Giovanni Maggini

c.1644   Birth of Antonio Stradivari

1666   Earliest known violin by Antonio Stradivari

1666–90   Stradivari's Amatisé period

1667   4 July, Antonio Stradivari marries Francesca Feraboschi

1671   1 February, birth of Francesco Stradivari

1679   14 November, birth of Omobono Stradivari

c.1680   Earliest known cello by Antonio Stradivari

   Stradivari makes the *Paganini* violin

   Stradivari moves to Piazza San Domenico

1683   Death of Jacob Stainer

1684   Death of Nicolò Amati

1690–98   Stradivari making long-pattern violins

1698   20 May, death of Francesca Stradivari (née Feraboschi)

   21 August, birth of Giuseppe Guarneri 'del Gesù'

1699   24 August, Antonio Stradivari marries Antonia Zambelli

1700   Traditional date for beginning of Stradivari's 'golden period'

1703   11 November, birth of Giovanni Battista Stradivari

1709   Stradivari workshop makes the *Viotti* violin

1712 Stradivari workshop makes the *Davidov* cello

1715 Stradivari workshop makes the *Lipiński* violin

1716 Stradivari workshop makes the *Messiah* violin

c.1720 End of Stradivari's golden period

1727 1 November, death of Giovanni Battista Stradivari

1733 Stradivari workshop makes the *Khevenhüller*

1737 3 March, death of Antonia Stradivari (née Zambelli)

18 December, death of Antonio Stradivari

1742 9 June, death of Omobono Stradivari

1743 15 January, death of Francesco Stradivari

1744 17 October, death of Giuseppe Guarneri 'del Gesù'

1746 Carlo Bergonzi becomes Paolo Stradivari's tenant in Piazza San Domenico

1747 Death of Carlo Bergonzi

Appendix Two

Glossary

Andante – Italian for 'walking', hence 'at a moderate pace'.

Archings – The outward swell of the *back* and *belly* of the violin.

Arquebus – A portable long-barrelled gun dating from the fifteenth century.

Back – The arched lower surface of the *soundbox*, made from hardwood.

Bass-bar – A softwood rod glued along the inner surface of the *belly*, almost from top to bottom and passing directly under the left-hand foot of the *bridge*.

Bee-sting – The sharp point of the *purfling* seen in some instruments as it comes into the four *corners* of the *belly* and *back*.

Belly – The arched upper surface of the *soundbox*, made from softwood and containing the *soundholes*.

Blocks – The six internal shaped wooden pieces at top, bottom and *corners* glued inside the *ribs* to hold their shape and help support the *belly*; the top *block* also strengthens the join with the *neck* and the bottom *block* the join with the *tailpiece*.

Body – The *soundbox*, made up of *back*, *belly* and *ribs*.

Bouts – The four curves making up the outline of the *soundbox*: convex top and bottom and the two concave C-bouts.

Bridge – The thin piece of carved wood that holds the strings up over the *belly*, and is itself kept in place by the strings' tension.

Cantabile – With a singing style.

Caprice – A piece of music, generally for one instrument, composed without any rules as to its form.

Chin-rest – A piece of wood or hard plastic clamped to the bottom and generally left-hand side of a violin or viola that is shaped to the chin and enables the player to grip the instrument between chin and shoulder.

Col legno – Italian for 'with the wood', where the bow is used to strike the strings with its wood, rather than its hair.

Concerto – A composition, generally in three movements, and generally for a soloist with orchestral accompaniment.

Corner – The four points in the outline of the *body* where the concave C-bouts meet the convex top and bottom *bouts*.

Curls – Alternating light and dark shading of wood, across the *grain*, seen in *maple* because of pressure as the tree grows.

Dendrochronology – The science of dating wood back to the point at which it was cut down by measurement of growth rings as they occur in the *grain*.

Ebony – A hard black wood, from a number of tropical and sub-tropical trees.

F-holes – The *soundholes*, in the shape of cursive fs, that are placed on either side of the bridge in members of the violin family.

Ferrule – On the bow, the metal band that, with the wedge, grips and spreads the horse-hairs where they are attached to the *nut*.

Figure – Another name for *curls*.

Fingerboard – The long piece of *ebony*, flat but with a gentle curve on its top, that is glued along the top of the *neck* between it and the strings and runs from the *pegbox* down beyond the end of the *neck*, to a point roughly between the tops of the *soundholes*; the player's fingers press the strings against it to change the *pitch* of the string.

Frequency – The rate of oscillation of a string or the sound-wave it creates, normally expressed as beats per second, or Hertz (Hz); the higher the *frequency*, the higher the note.

Fretted – Describes the placing of frets, or small metal bars, across the *fingerboard* at various points along its length so that the strings are pressed against them; only applies to instruments of the lute, guitar or viol families.

Grain – The arrangement or direction of fibres of the wood, running longitudinally up the tree and visible in many woods as a result of growth rings in the originating tree.

Harmonic – A *frequency* which is a whole multiple of a string's fundamental *frequency*; natural *harmonics* – curiously pure notes – are created by gently resting the finger on the string at a point that will be a point of zero vibration for a *harmonic* – halfway along, two thirds of the way along, and so on.

Head – The carved structure at the end of the *neck*, that includes the *scroll* and *pegbox*.

Legato – The smooth playing of a sequence of notes so that each runs seamlessly into its successor.

Linings – Thin strips of softwood running along the top and bottom of the interior of the *ribs*, reinforcing the join between them and the *plates*.

Luthier – Literally a maker of lutes, hence a maker of any string instrument.

Maple – A European hardwood, encompassing a number of subspecies.

Meno vivace – Italian for 'less quick', hence an instruction from the composer to slow down.

Mitres – The joints at the *corners*, where all joins occur along the diagonal rather than by squaring off one piece against another.

Neck – The piece of carved *maple* that runs up from the *body* towards the *head*.

Nut – The heel of the bow, close to where it is held, to which the horse-hairs are attached and by which their tension is adjusted.

Peg – A tapered wooden pin inserted through two holes, one on either side of the *pegbox*, around which the strings are wound; by twisting the peg the tension, and therefore *pitch*, of the string can be adjusted.

Pegbox – The open-topped box at the top of the *neck* which holds the *pegs*.

Pernambuco – A Brazilian hardwood favoured in the shafts of bows for its elasticity, density and strength.

Pitch – A synonym for *frequency*; the higher the *pitch*, the higher the note.

Pizzicato – Plucking the strings with the fingers, usually of the bow-hand.

Plates – The *back* and *belly* of the *soundbox*.

Presto – Italian for 'very quick'.

Purfling – A narrow inlay of wood set into a channel carved just within the border of the *back* and *belly*; it usually comprises three narrow strips of wood: two dark on either side of a central pale band.

Quarter-cut – Wood cut like a wedge or cake-slice out of the trunk of the tree.

Reference chronology – In *dendrochronology*, a sequence of tree-ring widths to which dates are attached, available for matching against undated sequences.

Resonance – The enlarged sympathetic vibration that occurs when a system is excited at its natural *frequency*.

Ribs – The four (or five, or six) strips of *maple* that make up the curved edges of the *soundbox*, separating the back and belly.

Scordatura – The tuning of the strings of an instrument to anything other than their usual notes.

Scroll – The ornamental spiral at the top of the *head*.

Sforzando – A sudden and emphatic increase in volume.

Shoulder-rest – An attachment to the *back* of the *soundbox*, removed when not playing, that sits opposite the *chin-rest* and forms part of the same system for gripping the violin between chin and shoulder; not in universal use.

Slab-cut – Wood cut as a section across the trunk of the tree.

Sonata – A composition usually in several movements (most commonly three or four); violin and cello sonatas are usually for the single instrument accompanied by the piano or its forerunners, occasionally for the single instrument alone, and occasionally (especially in seventeenth-century music) for multiple string instruments with and without keyboard.

Soundbox – The part of a string instrument that takes the vibrations of the strings and amplifies them to generate notes.

Soundholes – The holes in the *belly* of the *soundbox*, f-shaped in members of the violin family, that allow sound to escape.

Soundpost – An interior softwood rod that appears as a strut between *belly* and *back*; it is placed a little below the right-hand foot of the *bridge* and is held there by the tension of the strings.

Spruce – A light softwood encompassing several subspecies.

Symphony – A composition for full orchestra of between three and six movements.

Staccato – The playing of a run of notes so that each is detached, clearly separate from its successor.

Tailpiece – A piece of *ebony* fastened by a loop to the bottom of a string instrument and to which the strings are fixed after going over the *bridge*.

Volute – The spiral-shaped sections of the *scroll*.

Appendix Three

Price conversions

Any conversion to modern purchasing power is bound to be an imprecise process. Retail price indices are based on baskets of goods, whose contents naturally change significantly over the course of 300 years.

To convert sterling amounts into their present-day equivalents my main source was *Inflation: the Value of the Pound 1750–1998*, House of Commons Research paper 99/20, 23 February, 1999.

For prices before 1750, there are at least two possible sources, both to be found in *British Historical Statistics* by B. R. Mitchell, 1988, Cambridge University Press, Cambridge.

'The Schumpeter-Gilboy Price Indices 1661–1823' show fluctuations but no general trend from 1661 to 1750.

'Indices of Prices and Real Wages of Building Craftsmen – Southern England, 1264–1954' (Henry Phelps Brown and Sheila V. Hopkins) show an approximate doubling in wage rates from 1630 to 1750, but with an implication that this shows an increase in living standards rather than more general inflation.

For the sake of simplicity, I have therefore assumed that there was no general price inflation between 1630 and 1750.

To convert non-sterling amounts into the then sterling equivalent, before multiplying up to give a current sterling equivalent, as above, I used the following approximate exchange rates and sources.

	£1 equivalent	*Date*	*Source*
ITALY	4.4 ducats	1637	Snelling

Assumes correspondence refers to accounting term/silver ducats rather than gold ducats

	23 lire imperiale	1680	Snelling

Stradivari's house purchase specifies this form of the lire

	30 'current' lire	1688–1738	Snelling

Assumed for all other transactions

	2 gigliati	1776	Snelling
	4.0 scudi	1828	*GQ*
	75 lire	1920	Officer
	100 lire	1937	Officer
RUSSIA	5.6 roubles	c.1780	Snelling
FRANCE	22 livres	c.1785	Snelling
	25 francs	1800–1900	Mitchell
	125 francs	1937	Mitchell
AUSTRIA	6.7 gulden	1828	*GQ*
GERMANY	20.7 marks	1906	Mitchell
UNITED STATES	$4.9	Pre-1931	Mitchell

Not 1915–24

	$4.0	1946	Mitchell
	$2.8	1949–67	Mitchell

Sources

Mitchell, B. R, *British Historical Statistics*, 1988, Cambridge University Press, Cambridge

Officer, Lawrence H., *Exchange Rates between the United States Dollar and Forty Other Countries, 1913–1999*, Economic History Services, EH.Net, 2002 URL: http//www.eh.net/hmit/exchangerates/

Snelling, Thomas, *A view of the coins at this time current throughout Europe*, 1766, London

The Gentleman's Quarterly, 1740, London

Bibliography and sources

The nature of this book means I have not burdened the text with endnotes. Nevertheless I hope that what follows will help interested readers follow up publications, and indicate my other sources. Where appropriate I have added commentary to indicate a title's usefulness, or the stories drawn from it.

BOOKS

Alburger, Mary Anne (ed.), *The Violin Makers, Portrait of a Living Craft*, Gollancz, London, 1978. Charles Beare quote on where violin-making had got to in the 1970s

Alexander, John, *Catherine the Great, Life and Legend*, Oxford University Press, Oxford, 1989

Aüer, Leopold, *Violin Playing as I Teach It*, Duckworth & Co., London, 1921

Aüer, Leopold, *My Long Life in Music*, Duckworth & Co., London, 1924. Reminiscences of Davidov, including the 'special train' story

Bachman, Alberto, *An Encyclopaedia of the Violin*, Da Capo, New York, 1966

Baillot, Pierre Marie François de Sales, *The Art of the Violin*, edited and translated by Louise Goldberg, Northwestern University Press, Evanston, Illinois, 1991

Baines, Anthony, *Musical Instruments Through the Ages*,
        Penguin, London, 1969

Balfoort, Dirk, *Antonius Stradivarius*, translated by W. A. G.
        Doyle-Davidson, Sidgwick & Jackson, London, 1949

Baruzzi, Arnaldo, *La Casa Nuziale, The Home of Antonio
        Stradivari 1667–1680*, translated by Desmond Hill,
        William E. Hill & Sons, London, 1962

Beare, Charles, with the collaboration of Bruce Carlson,
        Antonio Stradivari – The Cremona Exhibition of 1987,
        J. & A. Beare, London, 1993. Foreword by Yo-Yo Ma
        describes the *Davidov*; the Introduction gives an
        excellent summary of Stradivari's life

Belford, Ros, Dunford, Martin and Woolfrey, Celia, *Italy: The
        Rough Guide*, Rough Guides, London, 1996

Blom, Eric (ed.), *Grove Dictionary of Music and Musicians*,
        5th edition, Macmillan, London, 1954

Bonetti, Carlo, Cavalcabò, Agostino and Gualazzini, Ugo,
        Antonio Stradivari, Reports and Documents,
        Cremonabooks, Cremona, 1999

Bouvet, Charles, *Une Leçon de Giuseppe Tartini et une
        femme violoniste du XVIIIe siècle*, Paris, 1910

Boyden, David, *History of violin playing from its origins to
        1761 and its relationship to the violin and violin music*,
        Oxford University Press, London, 1965

Boyden, David, *Catalogue of the Hill Collection of Musical
        Instruments in the Ashmolean Museum*, Oxford
        University Press, London, 1969

Burton, Humphrey, *Menuhin, A Life*, Faber and Faber,
        London, 2000

Cairns, David (trans. and ed.), *The Memoirs of Hector
        Berlioz*, Victor Gollancz, London, 1969

Campbell, Margaret, *The Great Violinists*, Elek: Granada, London, 1980

Campbell, Margaret, *The Great Cellists*, Gollancz, London, 1988

Charlton, Jennifer A., *Viols, Violins and Virginals, the Hill Collection of Stringed Instruments at the Ashmolean Museum, Oxford*, the Ashmolean Museum, Oxford, 1985

Chi-Mei Culture Foundation, *The Chi-Mei Collection*, Taiwan, 1997

Chiesa, Carlo and Rosengard, Duane, *The Stradivari Legacy*, Peter Biddulph, London, 1998. A very important source on the second half of Stradivari's career

Choron, Alexandre Etienne and Fayolle, François Joseph, *Dictionnaire historique des Musiciens*, Paris, 1811, reissued Georg Olms Verlag, Hildesheim, 1971

Codignola, Arturo (ed.), *Paganini Intimo*, Genova, 1935. Letters, including that to Merighi

Comitato Stradivariano, *L'Esposizione di Liuteria Antica A Cremona nel 1937*, Cremona, 1938

Delbanco, Nicholas, *The Countess of Stanlein Restored*, Verso, London, 2001

de Courcy, G. I. C., *Paganini The Genoese*, University of Oklahoma Press, Norman, 1957. By far the most authoritative account of Paganini's life

d'Eymar, A. M., *Anecdotes sur Viotti*, Geneva, an VIII [1799–1800]

Dipper, Andrew and Woodrow, David, *Count Ignazio Alessandro Cozio di Salabue*, Taynton Press, Taynton, 1987

Dissmore, George A. *The Violin Gallery*, Des Moines, 1890

Doring, Ernest N., *How Many Strads? Our heritage from the Master*, Bein & Fushi, Chicago, 1999. An enlarged and expanded edition of a book first published in 1944, which gives the basic story of every Stradivarius the author could identify; indispensable

Doring, Ernest N., *The Guadagnini Family of Violin Makers*, William Lewis & Son, Chicago, 1949

Draper, Muriel, *Music at Midnight*, William Heinemann, London, 1929

Falkner, John Meade, *The Lost Stradivarius*, Oxford University Press, Oxford, 1991

Fanzago, Francesco Luigi, *Elogi di Giuseppe Tartini*, Padua, 1792

Farga, Franz, *Violins and Violinists*, translated by Egon Larsen, Rockliff, London, 1950

Fétis, François Joseph, *Notice of Anthony Stradivari*, translated by John Bishop, William Reeves, London, 1964

Forbes, Elliot, *Thayer's Life of Beethoven*, Princeton University Press, Princeton, 1964. Quotes from Joseph Böhm

Fry, George, *Italian Varnishes*, Stevens & Sons, London, 1904

Gillett, Paula, *Musical Women in England, 1870–1914: Encroaching on All Man's Privileges*, Palgrave Macmillan, London, 2000. Early life of Marie Hall

Goodkind, Herbert K., *The Violin Iconography of Antonio Stradivari 1644–1737*, published by the author in Larchmont, New York, 1972. An immense and generally accurate collection of photographs, rare articles and valuable indices

Hamma, Walter, *Meister Italienischer Geigenbaukunst*,

Schuler Verlagsgesellschaft, Stuttgart, 1964. History of Hamma & Co

Hart, George, *The Violin and Its Music*, Dulau & Co., London, 1861

Hart, George, *The Emperor Stradivari*, Schott & Co., London, 1893

Hart, George, *The Violin: Its Famous Makers and Their Imitators*, with additions and emendations by the author's son and Towry Piper, Schott & Co, London, 1909. Correspondence between Paolo Stradivari and Count Cozio and best source on Tarisio

Harvey, Brian W. and Shapneau, Carla J., *Violin Fraud*, 2nd edition, Oxford University Press, Oxford, 1997

Henley, William, *Antonio Stradivari*, revised and edited by C. Woodcock, Amati Publishing, London, 1961

Heron-Allen, Edward, *Violin-making as it was and is*, Ward, Lock & Co., London, 1884

Herrmann, Emil, *Two Famous Stradivarius Violins: 'King Maximilian' and 'Prince Khevenhüller'*, Emil Herrmann, New York, c.1928

Hill, W. E. & Sons, *The Tuscan and Le Messie*, W. E. Hill & Sons, London, 1976

Hill, William Henry, Arthur F. and Alfred Ebsworth, *Antonio Stradivari – His Life and Work (1644–1737)*, Dover Publications, New York, 1963. A reissue of a book first published in 1902, written by the greatest experts on Stradivari then alive; it has been superseded in parts, but remains the best single source on Antonio Stradivari

Hill, William Henry, Arthur F. and Alfred Ebsworth, *The Violin-makers of the Guarneri Family (1626–1762)*, Dover Publications Inc., New York, 1989

Holman, Peter, *Four and Twenty Fiddlers, The Violin at the English Court 1540–1690*, Oxford University Press, Oxford, 1993

Kennedy, Michael, *The Works of Ralph Vaughan Williams*, Oxford University Press, London, 1964

Kennedy, Nigel, *Always Playing*, Weidenfeld & Nicolson, London, 1991

Knecht, R. J., *Catherine de Medici*, Longman, London, 1998

Lahee, Henry C., *Famous Violinists of To-day and Yesterday*, G.P. Putnam's Sons, London, 1902

Lalande, Hubert, *Voyage d'un François en Italie*, Venice, 1769

Lang, Paul Henry (ed.), *One Hundred Years of Music in America*, G. Schirmer, New York, 1961

Laurie, David, *The Reminiscences of a Fiddle Dealer*, T. Werner Laurie Ltd., London, c.1924

Lebet, Claude, *Le Quatuor Stradivarius 'Nicolò Paganini'*, Les Amis de la Musique, Spa, 1994. Includes Vuillaume's letters to Achillo Paganini

Leonard, Richard Anthony, *A History of Russian Music*, Jarrolds, London, 1956

Mace, Thomas, *Musick's Monument; or, a Remembrancer of the Best Practical Musick*, John Carr, London, 1676. Statement that old instruments are valued before new

Menuhin, Yehudi and Primrose, William, *Violin and Viola*, Macdonald and Jane's, London, 1976. Comparison between the *Soil* and the *Khevenhüller*

Menuhin, Yehudi, *Unfinished Journey*, Methuen, London, 1996

Moreau, Annette, *Emanuel Feuermann*, Yale University Press, London, 2002

Moser, Andreas, *Joseph Joachim, A Biography 1831–1899*, translated by Lilla Durham, P. Wellby, London, 1901

Mozart, Leopold, *A Treatise on the Fundamental Principles of Violin Playing*, translated by Editha Knocker, Oxford University Press, Oxford, 1951

Niederheitmann, Friedrich and Quarrell, W. H. (trans.), *Cremona: an Account of the Italian Violin-makers and their Instruments*, R. Cocks & Co, London, 1894

Nissel, Muriel, *Married to the Amadeus*, Giles de la Mare, London, 1998

Norwich, John Julius, *A History of Venice*, Allen Lane, London, 1982

O'Shea, John, *Music and Medicine, Medical Profiles of the Great Composers*, Dent, London, 1990

Palmer, Tony, *Menuhin, A Family Portrait*, Faber and Faber, London, 1991

Phipson, Thomas Lamb, *Biographical Sketches and Anecdotes of Celebrated Violinists*, London, 1877

Phipson, Thomas Lamb, *Famous Violinists and Fine Violins*, Chatto & Windus, London, 1896

Pick, Robert, *Empress Maria Theresa: the Earlier Years, 1717–1757*, Weidenfeld & Nicolson, London, 1966

Pierre, Constant, *Histoire du Concert Spirituel 1725–1790*, Société Française de Musicologie, Paris, 1975

Pollens, Stewart, *The Violin Forms of Antonio Stradivari*, Peter Biddulph, London, 1992

Pougin, Arthur, *Viotti Et L'Ecole Moderne de Violon*, Paris, 1888

Pougin, Arthur, *A Short History of Russian Music*, translated by Lawrence Haward, Chatto & Windus, London, 1915

Powrozniak, Józef, *Lipiński: His Life and Times*, translated by Maria Lewicka, Paganiniana Publications, Neptune City, N.J., c.1982

Professional Violin-makers' Association of Cremona, The,

Classical Violin-making: a Method, The Association, Cremona, 1984

Rattray, David, *Masterpieces of Italian Violin Making*, Balafon Books, London, 2000

Reade, Charles, *Readiana. Comments on Current Events*, Chatto & Windus, London, 1883. Includes letters to *Pall Mall Gazette*

Reid, Joseph V., *You Can Make a Stradivarius Violin*, William Lewis & Son, Lincolnwood, 1967

Reston, James Jr, *Galileo, A Life*, Cassell, London, 1994. Note that the correspondence quoted is to be found in the Hills' book on Stradivari

Roth, Henry, *Master Violinists in Performance*, Paganiniana Publications, Neptune City, 1983. Critique of Marie Hall recordings

Sacchi, Federico, *Count Cozio di Salabue*, edited by A. T. Piper, Dulau & Co, London, 1898

Sacconi, Simone F., *The Secrets of Stradivari*, Libreria del Convegno, Cremona, 1972

Sadie, Stanley (ed.), *The New Grove Dictionary of Music and Musicians*, 2nd edition, Macmillan, London, 2001. A monumental work but one that does not entirely replace its predecessor

Sadler, Richard, *W. E. Hill & Sons, 1880–1992, a Tribute*, Ealing Strings, London, 1997

Sandys, William and Forster, Simon Andrew, *The History of the Violin*, William Reeves, London, 1864

Santoro, Elia, *After Stradivari*, translated by Lyn Hungerford, Editrice Turris, Cremona, 1991

Scholes, Percy A., *The Oxford Companion to Music*, 9th edition, Oxford University Press, London, 1955

Seaman, Gerald R., *History of Russian Music*, Basil Blackwell, London, 1967

Spohr, Louis, *Autobiography*, translated from the German, Longman, London, 1865

Stasov, Vladimir Vasilevich, *Selected Essays on Music*, translated by Florence Jones, The Cresset Press, London, 1968

Stowell, Robin (ed.), *The Cambridge Companion to the Violin*, Cambridge University Press, Cambridge, 1992

Stowell, Robin (ed), *The Cambridge Companion to the Cello*, Cambridge University Press, Cambridge, 1999

Stradivarius Memorial Association, The, *Stradivarius Memorial Concert in commemoration of the bicentenary of the death of Antonius Stradivarius 1644–1737*, New York, 1937

Veinus, Abraham, *The Concerto*, Cassell & Co, London, 1948

Vidal, Antoine, *Les Instruments à Archet*, (facsimile edition), The Holland Press, London, 1961

Wechsberg, Joseph, *The Violin*, Calder and Boyars, London, 1973. Emil Herrmann's childhood and retirement; and the *liutomachia*

Wilson, Elizabeth, *Jacqueline du Pré*, Weidenfeld & Nicolson, London, 1998

Woodrow, David, *The Shape of Stradivari Violins*, Taynton, Oxford, 1991

Wurzbach, Dr Constant von, *Biographisches Lexikon des Kaiserthums Oesterreich*, Vienna, 1856–91. Brief details of life of Prince Khevenhüller

Zaslaw, Neal (ed.), *The Classical Era: From the 1740s to the end of the eighteenth century*, Macmillan, London, 1989

Other publications

The Art of Violin: The Devil's Instrument; Transcending the Violin, film written and directed by Bruno Monsaingeon, 2000

The Boston Post, Boston, 29 November 1928

The Connoisseur, A Magazine for Collectors, London, November 1911, 'Viottiana', Heron-Allen, Edward

The Guardian Weekend, London and Manchester, 31 August 2002, 'Fiddles', Kirsta, Alix. The Segelman affair

Conoscere Cremona – Discovering Cremona, Comune di Cremona, Assessorato al turismo

The Havana Post, Havana, 30 November 1942

Journal of Archaeological Science (2000), 'A Dendrochronological Investigation of Stringed Instruments of the Cremonese School (1666–1757) including "The Messiah" violin attributed to Antonio Stradivari', Topham, John and McCormick, Derek

The Musical World, Volume 12, London, 1839. Viotti and Betts

The New York Times, New York, 29 November 1928

Purcell Room programme, 3.15 p.m., Sunday, 6 May 1990, McGee, Andrew. Tom Bowes's concert on the *Viotti-Marie Hall*

Scientific American, 10 June 2002, 'Secrets of the Stradivarius: An Interview with Joseph Nagyvary', Choi, Charles

Sotheby's catalogue, London, 7 November 1968, Lot 21

Sotheby's catalogue, London, 31 March, 1988, Lot 38

The Spectator, London, 21 August 1999, 'On the Trail of a Master Violin Maker', Todes, Rafael

The Strad, Orpheus, London. Specific issues are listed below,

but from 1890 onwards the magazine gives a terrific feel
for the issues then current in the violin world
November 1891 et seq. Report on 1888 paper by E. J.
Payne, President of the Cremona Society
June 1895. Obituary of W. E. Hill
September 1898. Vuillaume reminiscence
August 1900. Story about Lolli at Court of Catherine the
Great
March 1903, April 1903, May 1903, May 1906, May 1910,
August 1910, September 1911, September 1912, January
1913, March 1926, July 1955, August 1955. Marie Hall
February 1925. Reader's letter with story about Vuillaume
and Alard
May 1927 et seq. Reminiscences of Edward Goodwin
May 1937. Cremona Exhibition
June 1940. Obituary of Alfred Hill
January 1952. Davidov
December 1968. Sale of Marie Hall's violin
August 1971. Interview with Anna Lee Wurlitzer
October 1982. Paganini special issue
January, February and May 1988. Yo-Yo Ma on the *Davidov*
June 1988. Sale of the *Marie Hall*
April 1989. EDAX
April 1991. Menuhin quote on 'illicit adventures' with del
Gesù
July 1991. Response curves
December 1991, March 1992. The Amatis
April 1992. Hills cease to trade
November 1994. Kikuei Ikeda on his 1719 Strad
July 1996. Peter Salaff on role of second violin
May 1997. CT scans
August 1998. Vuillaume history

December 1998. Scanning electron microscope

August 2001. History relating to the *Messiah*

December 2001, 'A varnished triumph', by Roger
　　Hargrave. Description of *Davidov*

November 2002. Interview with David Fulton

The Times, London, 27 October, 2000, 'A Stradivarius riddle',
　　Giles Whittell. The *Messiah* controversy

The Violin Times, London, a temporary competitor to *The Strad*
　　December 1895, January 1896. Lipiński's account of how
　　he acquired his Stradivarius

　　March 1905. Marie Hall

Yo-Yo Ma, Simply Baroque, sleeve notes by Steven
　　Ledbetter, Sony Music, 1999

Yo-Yo Ma, Simply Baroque II, sleeve notes by Jackson
　　Braider, Sony Music, 2000

UNPUBLISHED SOURCES

Heron–Allen archive, Royal College of Music, London.
　　Personal papers of Viotti, including his will, varied
　　correspondence, and the statement he made when sent
　　into exile from Britain

Letter from Alfred Hill to the Rudolph Wurlitzer Company,
　　giving details of the *Lipiński*'s history, 26 October 1922

Letter from Alfred Hill to the Rudolph Wurlitzer Company,
　　giving details of the *Davidov*'s history, 15 November,
　　1928

Many quotations and other information in the book come
from interviews; for a list of the people I spoke to please see
the Acknowledgements.

Index

Acknowledgements

One of the joys of writing a book like this is the people you get to meet and how generous they turn out to be with both time and information.

Christina Beale, Thomas Bowes, Howard Davis, Steven Isserlis, Anthony Marwood, Siegmund Nissel and Raffy Todes helped me to understand the relationship between a player and his or her instrument, and told me what it was like to play a violin or cello by one of the great classical luthiers. I hope I have captured something of their enthusiasm.

Charles Beare and Peter Biddulph provided the perspective of two of the world's top violin experts, and filled in many of the gaps in my instruments' histories. Tim Ingles and Graham Wells from Sotheby's did the same and were supportive at an early stage in my research. John Topham was my first interviewee; he told me about his work with dendrochronology and suggested several valuable lines of enquiry. David Rattray both answered my questions and took me round the superb collection of string instruments at London's Royal Academy of Music, for which he is responsible. As I finished the book Professor Curtis Price, Principal at the Academy, was both informative and encouraging.

I owe a special debt to Carlo Chiesa and John Dilworth. Both gave me a lot of time not just when we met, but also when they subsequently corrected and commented on a draft of this book. It was Carlo who with Duane Rosengard discovered Stradivari's will; and their research provides an important new source for the second half of Stradivari's life. John gave me a luthier's view on numerous aspects of my research; his involvement has been invaluable.

My written sources are listed in the bibliography. Almost all of them could be found in the British Library – a great institution. Several individuals helped me track down or identify specific publications. Dr B. J. Cook, Curator of Medieval and Early Modern Coinage at the British Museum, told me how to translate Italian currencies into sterling. Robert Bein and Jennifer Jeffries at Bein & Fushi in Chicago gave me remote access to their excellent library. Likewise, in London, Peter Biddulph and his assistants, Jamie Buchanan and Jennifer Laredo, let me borrow books I couldn't find anywhere else. Richard T. Rephann at the Yale Library and Oliver Davies at the Royal College of Music Portraits Department both consulted their archives on my behalf. Yo-Yo Ma and his assistant Betsy Gill answered an important question. Alan Cromartie and Christian Hess helped me with some translation; Roger Davis kept me up to speed on the Festival Hall's concert schedule. Ashwin Adarkar was a fund of ideas for titles; and Joe Way gave me the source on the Beethoven/Böhm story.

Many people have been involved in the gestation of this book. It was my agent, Caroline Dawnay at PFD, who first persuaded me to turn an idea into a proposal. She and her assistants, first Will Francis and now Alex Elam, have been always supportive. In the US Michael Carlisle and his former partner Christy Fletcher have done the same. Other readers – and improvers – of early drafts include my father, Dr Thomas Faber, my stepmother, Dr Liesbeth van Houts, and a friend, Joanna Wagstaffe.

Katie Hall at Random House (US) and Anya Serota at

Macmillan originally commissioned the book, to be succeeded by, respectively, Susanna Porter and Jason Cooper. To lose one editor might be thought a misfortune; to lose two could have been disastrous. Jason and Susanna's continuing enthusiasm promises that this will not be the case. Both have helped me make this a better book; and I am particularly grateful that, as lead editor, Jason took so much trouble over a book he inherited.

Above all, however, I want to thank my wife, Amanda. She has encouraged me at every stage, and her thorough reading of successive drafts provided a vital mix of enthusiasm and criticism. Goodness knows how the book would have turned out without her.

PICTURE ACKNOWLEDGEMENTS

The sources for pictures used are listed below. The author and publishers have made every effort to contact copyright holders. The author would also like to express his gratitude to Mr Andrew McGee for making available items from his own collection of violin memorabilia.

Figures 1, 2, 4, 8, 9, 11 – from Herbert Goodkind, *The Violin of Antonio Stradivari 1644–1737*, 1972. *Figure 1* reproduced by kind permission of the Ashmolean Museum, Oxford.

Figures 5, 6, 19 – from W. H. Hill et al, *Antonio Stradivari – His Life and Work (1644–1737)*, 1963.

Figure 10 – by L. Boilly, 1824. Private Collection. Reproduced with kind permission of Mr Andrew McGee.

Figure 12 – from Franz Farga, *Violins & Violinists*, 1950.

Figure 13 – from Emil Herrman, *Two Famous Stradivarius Violins: 'King Maximillian' and 'Prince Khevenhüller'*, c.1928.

Figure 14 – from *Musical Instruments Through the Ages*, by Anthony Baines. Copyright © Penguin Books, 1961. Reproduced by permission of Penguin Books.

Figure 15 – One of several sketches of Paganini by Sir Edward Henry Landseer.

Figure 16 – Karol Lipiński painted in 1822 by Walenty Wankowicz, from Polskie Wydawnictwo Muzyczne, *Tematy Muzycze W Plastyce Polskiej*, 1956. Reproduced by permission of Warsaw National Museum.

Figure 17 – From a postcard c.1905. Private collection. Reproduced with kind permission of Mr Andrew McGee.

Figure 18 – Copyright © Bettmann/Corbis.